# Gender Violence

*Introductions to Engaged Anthropology* is a series of thematic books by individual authors that demonstrate how an anthropological perspective contributes to reframing the public discourse on important and timely social issues. Volumes are thoughtful nuanced treatments on subjects that are publicly, ethically, and politically relevant in a changing world, and are of intellectual importance not only within anthropology, but in other fields such as law, gender, human sexuality, and health and social welfare. An important objective of this new series is not just social critique, but active engagement in the problems of broader global communities. *Introductions to Engaged Anthropology* books are written primarily for students, educators, and intellectuals to provide a deeper analysis of the social, political, and ethical debates in which anthropological and cross-cultural analyses are vital contributions to the public discourse, and help to redefine public policy.

**Published volumes**
*Gender Violence: A Cultural Perspective*
Sally Engle Merry

# Gender Violence:
# A Cultural Perspective

Sally Engle Merry

**WILEY-BLACKWELL**

A John Wiley & Sons, Ltd., Publication

This edition first published 2009
© 2009 Sally Engle Merry

Blackwell Publishing was acquired by John Wiley & Sons in February 2007. Blackwell's publishing program has been merged with Wiley's global Scientific, Technical, and Medical business to form Wiley-Blackwell.

*Registered Office*
John Wiley & Sons Ltd, The Atrium, Southern Gate, Chichester, West Sussex, PO19 8SQ, United Kingdom

*Editorial Offices*
350 Main Street, Malden, MA 02148-5020, USA
9600 Garsington Road, Oxford, OX4 2DQ, UK
The Atrium, Southern Gate, Chichester, West Sussex, PO19 8SQ, UK

For details of our global editorial offices, for customer services, and for information about how to apply for permission to reuse the copyright material in this book please see our website at www. wiley.com/wiley-blackwell.

The right of Sally Engle Merry to be identified as the author of this work has been asserted in accordance with the Copyright, Designs and Patents Act 1988.

All rights reserved. No part of this publication may be reproduced, stored in a retrieval system, or transmitted, in any form or by any means, electronic, mechanical, photocopying, recording or otherwise, except as permitted by the UK Copyright, Designs and Patents Act 1988, without the prior permission of the publisher.

Wiley also publishes its books in a variety of electronic formats. Some content that appears in print may not be available in electronic books.

Designations used by companies to distinguish their products are often claimed as trademarks. All brand names and product names used in this book are trade names, service marks, trademarks or registered trademarks of their respective owners. The publisher is not associated with any product or vendor mentioned in this book. This publication is designed to provide accurate and authoritative information in regard to the subject matter covered. It is sold on the understanding that the publisher is not engaged in rendering professional services. If professional advice or other expert assistance is required, the services of a competent professional should be sought.

Library of Congress Cataloging-in-Publication Data

Merry, Sally Engle, 1944-
    Gender violence : a cultural perspective / Sally Engle Merry.
        p. cm.
    Includes bibliographical references and index.
        ISBN 978-0-631-22358-0 (hardcover : alk. paper) – ISBN 978-0-631-22359-7 (pbk. : alk. paper)
    1. Women–Violence against. I. Title.
        HV6250.4.W65.W477 2009
        362.88–dc22

                                                        2008014693

A catalogue record for this book is available from the British Library.

Set in 10.5/13pt Minion by SPi Publisher Services, Pondicherry, India
Printed in Singapore by Utopia Press Pte Ltd

1    2009

# Contents

# Preface

A book is always a collaborative project, building on the work and insights of others and benefiting from their research, activism, and personal experiences. This book has been especially collaborative, since its goal is to bring together the ideas, insights, and experiences of a social movement, of those who have survived violence, and of those who have studied and tried to understand gender violence. For the last 17 years, I have talked to leaders of the movement against gender violence, people working on the problem in local courts and programs, and people who have experienced or perpetrated violence in their families and communities. While my work in the 1990s was based in the USA, since 2000 I have been studying the international movement, looking in particular at efforts in the Asia Pacific region and the work of international organizations such as the United Nations. I have met and talked to inspirational activists and survivors in all these settings, and hope that this book reflects something of their wisdom and commitment. To all who gave their time and insights to me, I am most thankful. I hope that this book will be a contribution to the public's general understanding of the issue, as it pulls together much of their knowledge, experience, and wisdom.

The scope of the book is very broad, endeavoring to discuss many forms of gender violence. I have drawn on a growing body of published literature, particularly recent work in anthropology that offers an ethnographic portrait of gender violence. An anthropological perspective has been adopted, differing from much of the current literature which takes a more psychological approach. Many wonderful research assistants have contributed in significant ways. My undergraduates at Wellesley College worked on specific sections, providing me with invaluable information and insights: Clare McBee-Wise on transgendered people and violence, Dante Costa on refugee women, Hao Nguyen on immigration laws and practices, and Rebecca Goldberg on female genital cutting as well as her experiences with anorexia and the insight this gave her about genital surgeries. These students took a course I offered at Wellesley with Nan Stein called "Gendered Violations." Collaborating with Nan in teaching this course and sharing our interests in gender violence and sexual harassment have been of great benefit to my intellectual life and to the shaping of this book. The work in Hawai'i benefited from the research work of Marilyn Brown and Madelaine Adelman. My graduate students at New York University also contributed: Nur Amali Ibrahim worked on the section on rape and genocide in Rwanda and Jennifer Telesca worked on the discussion of Ciudad Juárez. Jennifer Telesca also prepared the discussion questions and video resources. My undergraduates at NYU did a test drive of the book in the spring of 2007 and learned something from it, which seems a good omen.

The book includes some of my own research on approaches to gender violence in Hawai'i, India, China, and the United Nations. I have been generously supported by the National Science Foundation Law and Social Sciences and Cultural Anthropology programs, grants SES-9023397, SBR-9320009, SBR-9807208, BCS-9904441, SES-0417730, the National Endowment for the Humanities, the Canadian Institute for Advanced Research, the Mellon New Directions Fellowship at Wellesley College, and the Wenner-Gren Foundation for a related conference. Peggy Levitt, my collaborator in my current research project on the localization of women's human rights in China, India, Peru, and the USA, has also contributed significantly to this project. My research was supported by my time as a Fellow at the Carr Center for Human Rights Policy at the Kennedy School at Harvard University and at the Bunting Institute at Radcliffe College. Wellesley College and New York University have both provided a supportive working environment for my research and writing.

Finally, I would like to thank Jane Huber of Blackwell for proposing that I write such a book, one that is far broader and more ambitious in scope than others I have written. Her enthusiasm has kept me at a project that seemed daunting at first, and in some ways still does. I have tried to use stories and ethnographic case studies as much as possible, while weaving these together with analytic anthropological arguments. I am particularly indebted to two anonymous reviewers who provided detailed and insightful advice. Any errors, of course, remain mine.

I would like to dedicate this book to my daughter, Sarah, who has provided me with support and encouragement in many of my endeavors, and my sister Patricia, whose work on international child development and nutrition has been an inspiration. My husband and son have also been, as always, steadfast supporters of my penchant for writing books.

Sally Engle Merry
Wellesley, MA
January 2008

# 1

# Introduction

Gender violence is not a new problem. It takes place in virtually all societies around the world, but only in the last thirty years has it become visible as a major social issue. Historically, forms of violence taking place within the family were treated as less serious than those occurring in the public sphere. Much of recent feminist activity has been directed toward reformulating the legal and cultural notion of the private sphere of the family, in part to foster societal and legal intervention into families. In the 1990s, gender violence was defined as an important human rights violation for the first time. Now it is considered the centerpiece of women's human rights.

Despite its near universality around the globe, local manifestations of gender violence are highly variable. They depend on particular kinship structures, gender inequalities, and levels of violence in the wider society. They vary depending on how gender is defined and what resources are available to those who are battered. Violence against women in the home is shaped by patterns of marriage and the availability of divorce, by conceptions of male authority and female submission, and by the family's vulnerability to racism, poverty, or marginalization. The prevalence of sexual violence against women during armed conflict depends on ideas of militarized masculinity and the use of rape to dishonor enemies. Some legal systems are far more effective in punishing gender violence than others, and communities vary a great deal in the kinds of informal and formal social support they offer victims of violence.

Although women are disproportionately the victims of gender violence, in many situations men are also victimized. Male rape in prison, torture of men in wartime, patterns of hazing and harassment in male organizations, and homophobic assaults on gay men are only a few of the kinds of violence directed against men. Both men and women are targeted by the cultural practice of genital surgeries, although those performed on women are generally more severe. Violence between intimate partners includes women's attacks on men as well as men's on women, although women are more likely to be injured. Individuals in same-sex relationships use violence against their partners at about the same rate as those in opposite-sex relationships.

Although gender violence is often an assault by a male on a female, this is hardly a universal feature of male behavior. The large majority of men do not practice gender violence against women, and many seek to intervene to protect women as well as other men from gender violence. While gender violence is a widespread pattern, it is far from a universal one.

Gender violence is embedded in enduring patterns of kinship and marriage, but it can be exacerbated by very contemporary political and economic tensions. In recent years, increasing economic inequalities, warfare, nationalism, and insecurity have increased rates of gender violence. For example, in China, where domestic violence was traditionally legitimated by a family system based on male authority, female obedience, and filial piety, with the tumultuous changes of the last half century such as the Cultural Revolution, the one-child policy, the turn to a capitalist economy that has eliminated much of the socialist welfare system and forced many women to lose their jobs or retire early and to share a husband with a concubine, the incidence of domestic violence is on the upswing (Liu and Chan 2000: 74–84; Human Rights in China 1995). In many parts of the world, the kinship-based systems that long served to control violence within families are weakening in response to urbanization, wage labor, mobility, and the economic and cultural effects of globalization. Neoliberal economic policies which reduce state and community support for the poor affect women disproportionately, making them more vulnerable to violence. Poor men are also more likely to experience violence from other men and from their female partners than wealthy men.

Many forms of gender violence are part of wider conflicts such as ethnic attacks, military occupation, warfare, and movements of refugees. Migration of peoples across borders increases their vulnerability to violence, particularly when migrants are illegal or unprotected in the country of arrival. Warfare and local armed conflict between religious, ethnic, or regional groups often rely on rape and violence against women, while it is primarily women and children who flee these situations and become refugees. In wartime, men are often the victims of sexualized forms of torture as well as brutality in the course of combat.

Violence in intimate relationships is inseparable from societal conflict, violence, and injustice. As this book shows, interpersonal gendered violence and structural violence – the violence of poverty, hunger, social exclusion, and humiliation – are deeply connected. It is impossible to diminish violence against women without reducing these other forms of violence and injustice. The conditions which breed gender violence include racism and inequality, conquest, occupation, colonialism, warfare and civil conflict, economic disruptions and poverty. Impunity for violators contributes in important ways, whether they are violent spouses, so-called "honor" killers, or political leaders. Patterns of kinship and sexuality provide the justifications for gender violence and determine the possibilities of escaping it. Given this context, it is not surprising that three decades of activism around the world have increased awareness of the problem but not slackened its incidence. Only the achievement of a more just and peaceful world will improve the safety of both women and men.

## Defining Gender Violence

In this book, I define gender violence as violence whose meaning depends on the gendered identities of the parties. It is an interpretation of violence through gender. For example, when a blow is understood as a man's right to discipline his wife, it is gender violence. When a mob lynches an African American man for allegedly raping a white woman, the violence is defined through gender and race. Thus, the meaning of the violence depends on the gendered relationship in which it is embedded. These relationships are used to explain and even justify the violence. For example, a man may justify hitting his wife because she was disobedient. A prisoner might explain his anal rape of a fellow prisoner by saying that the victim is less than a man because he was a sexual predator against children. A soldier can explain raping an enemy woman as a way to dishonor his enemy. Not everyone who commits gender violence tries to justify it, of course, but when individuals do offer explanations of the incidents, they typically draw on ideas of gender and its responsibilities and entitlements.

Understanding gender violence requires a situated analysis that recognizes the effects of the larger social context on gender performances. When men abuse women in intimate relationships, they use the violence to define their own gendered identities. A batterer often wants to show the woman that he is in control or to prove to other men that he controls her. He may view the violence as discipline that the woman deserves or has provoked. Perhaps she failed to take care of the house or has dressed provocatively and awakened his suspicions and jealousy. Men often use violence to establish power hierarchies, both against other men and through raping other men's wives. This form of gender violence is a fundamental strategy of war as well.

Gender violence is now an umbrella term for a wide range of violations from rape during wartime to sexual abuse in prisons to insults and name-calling within marriages. Although the early movement against gender violence in the USA centered on rape and battering in intimate relationships, the movement now uses a far broader definition both in the USA and internationally. International activists continue to expand the scope of violence against women, to include cultural practices such as female genital cutting, illegal acts such as dowry deaths, the trafficking of women as sex workers, the effects of internal wars such as displaced people, and the vulnerability to violence experienced by migrants in the context of contemporary globalization. The scope of gender violence is continually changing.

Gender violence occurs throughout the world, but it takes quite different forms in different social contexts. It is located in particular sets of social relationships, structures of power, and meanings of gender. It does not fall into any simple pattern, such as being more prevalent in traditional societies than in modern ones. There are no universal explanations for gender violence. It is best understood in terms of the wide variety of particular contexts that shape its frequency and nature. Although enhancing gender equality is commonly thought to diminish gender violence, more egalitarian societies are still plagued by widespread violence. Traditional or rural societies are not systematically more violent than modern or urban ones. In fact, the transition to a modern, capitalist society can exacerbate gender violence, as it has done in China. Violence does not diminish with the shift to more modern or urban forms of social life, but it may change its form and meaning.

## Defining Violence

An introduction to gender violence must begin by exploring its key terms: "violence" and "gender." Violence, like gender, is a deceivingly simple concept. Although it seems to be a straightforward category of injury, pain, and death, it is very much shaped by cultural meanings. Some forms of pain are erotic, some heroic, and some abusive, depending on the social and cultural context of the event. Cultural meanings and context differentiate consensual or playful eroticized forms of pain from those of a manhood ritual and those from a cigarette burn on a disobedient wife. Gender violence is both physical and sexual. Although historically there has been a division between activists working on domestic violence and those focused on rape, in practice the two usually happen together. Domestic violence frequently takes sexualized forms, while rape is typically violent. Gender violence is often the result of a jealous desire to control another's sexual life. Violence can be erotic. In recent years, the terms "sexual assault" and "sexual violence" have been used to indicate the interrelatedness of sexual and physical forms of violence.

Activists in the battered women's movement have expanded the meaning of gender violence from hitting and wounding, including rape and murder, to a far more varied set of injuries and degradations. Leaders in the field emphasize the emotional and psychological dimensions of gender violence, recognizing that it includes insult, humiliation, name-calling, driving by a person's house and calling out insulting words, telling a woman that she is fat and useless and will never be attractive to other men, and myriad other insults. Some battered women told me that these assaults on their self-esteem hurt more than blows. Gender violence includes threats, harassment, and stalking – actions that evoke fear even when there is no physical harm. Injuries to those one cares about, including children, pets, or personal possessions, or threats to injure them, are also forms of violence. The plate thrown against the wall subtly says, "It could have been you." A lack of care such as withholding money or food from a partner or child can also be considered violence. Threats of sorcery or supernatural injury are forms of gender violence that evoke fear and the threat of harm. Violations that a person experiences as a result of racism, class humiliation, and poverty often have gendered dimensions.

In their overview of anthropological work on violence, Nancy Scheper-Hughes and Philippe Bourgois emphasize that violence is a slippery concept that cannot be understood only in physical terms. It also includes assaults on personhood, dignity, and the sense of worth and value of a person (2004: 1). Violence is fundamentally a cultural construct. "The social and cultural dimensions of violence are what give violence its power and meaning" (Scheper-Hughes and Bourgois 2004: 1). They argue that there is no simple "brute" force, but that violence has a human face and is rarely "senseless." Instead, it often has meanings that render it heroic, justified, reasonable, or at least acceptable. From an anthropological perspective, violence as an act of injury cannot be understood outside of the social and cultural systems which give it meaning.

Nor are the meanings of violence stable, since they depend on the social position of the observer and the social context of the event. Some violence is interpreted as legitimate, such as the actions of state police controlling unruly mobs, while other violence is defined as illegitimate, such as that of the protesting mobs themselves. Police violence against criminals is to some extent authorized while the violence of criminals is not. One person's heroic revolutionary is another's terrorist. These distinctions are often murky. When a community lynches an offender because the police fail to act, as has occurred in parts of Bolivia, it can be defined either as legitimate community policing or as illegitimate vigilante justice (see Goldstein 2004; 2007).

## Structural violence

An important dimension of violence is structural violence, violence that impacts the everyday lives of people yet remains invisible and normalized. It includes poverty, racism, pollution, displacement, and hunger. Structural violence is usually concealed within the hegemony of ordinariness, hidden in the mundane details of everyday life. Violence is sometimes highly visible, as revolutionary violence or state repression, but it is often hidden in the everyday violence of infant mortality, slow starvation, disease, destitution, and humiliation (Scheper-Hughes and Bourgois 2004: 2). Structural violence is intimately connected to more interpersonal forms of violence. For example, upper-caste men in parts of India use the rape of lower-caste women to maintain their dominance (e.g. Srivastava 2002: 272–275). Bourgois's work on crack dealers in East Harlem, New York reveals links between self-destructive substance abuse, the gendered violence of family life and adolescent gang rape, and the structural violence of US urban apartheid (Scheper-Hughes and Bourgois 2004: 3). Scheper-Hughes argues that the family is a violent institution, but sees its violence as responsive to larger socio-economic conditions which make violence the only option (2004: 3). In postcolonial societies, such as Papua New Guinea, violence is embedded in systems of power such as colonialism, family institutions such as bride price, development projects and their large-scale environmental degradation, and the poverty and social exclusion experienced by poor rural migrants to the city who face unemployment and residence in squatter settlements without adequate drainage and sewage systems or clean water. They confront high levels of violent crime as well as disease (see Dinnen and Ley 2000: 2–3). Violence here includes the violence of police and security forces as well as the fear of sorcery.

## Domestic violence: a case study

Dora's story (a pseudonym) illustrates the complex blending of threats, fear, and physical violence in domestic violence situations. Her story comes from a small town in Hawai'i during the early 1990s, the beginning of the battered women's movement. Dora is in her early twenties, a mainland white woman from a middle-class family with two years of college and an adequate family income. When I interviewed her she said, "I had the stereotype that it doesn't happen to people like me with a house and education. I thought it just happened to welfare people." Like many other battered women, Dora turned to the courts only after years of violence from her husband. She wrote this account of the violence in 1992 as a request for compensation as a crime victim:

> Sam and I have been together for almost five years. There has been abuse on and off for the first few years. This past year has been the worst, it got to the point where he would beat me at least once a day and for about four weeks he beat me two or three times a day. It was so hard living with him. I have no family out here, only myself and our son. I lived in constant fear of Sam, never knowing of his coming here, afraid of what he was going to be like. Sam has threatened me with guns, spear guns, knife on one occasion. He would drag me down the hill by my hair, rip my clothes off of me, smash pans over my head. We had to replace or fix all but two doors in our house because he threw me through the other doors.
>
> There was so much constant abuse it seemed like it would never end. Many times I thought that when I died it would be because my husband killed me. I was afraid to have him arrested because I knew he wouldn't stay in that long and I thought that he would kill me when he got out. Finally, on May 31, 1992, I couldn't deal with it. We were driving home from Hilo, my husband was sitting in the back of our truck. I was driving because Sam was too drunk. We were driving down the road and he reached through the back window and grabbed my face, scratching my face, then he tried to choke me and I felt that if he got open the door he would kill me. I looked over at my son in his car seat. He was frightened, screaming, crying and I knew I couldn't put up with this terror any more. I managed to drive away when he got out of the back to open my door. I just wanted the hell that my life had become to end. Since that time Sam has started ATV classes [a violence control program] and is making much improvement. He knows that he needs to change to keep his family, and that abusing me is wrong. I feel that calling the police was the hardest, and best thing I ever did.

They had been married for three years, and he had abused her most of the time. Dora explained his violence in terms of his cultural background, saying that in Samoa it is the man's responsibility to keep the woman in line. After this incident, Dora called the police to help her get her things and go to the shelter, but the police let him follow her alone into the bedroom, which frightened her. Then the police started "talking story" with him, discussing where to go fishing. They took him away, but only to his sister's house which was four houses away. Ten minutes later he was back. The next day he was still there and she called the police, discovering that he had a 24-hour restraining order against him. This meant that he got arrested for violating the order of the court. Dora said that she always thought that if he were arrested, he would kill her, so his sister went down and posted bail. Using the law clearly represented a powerful challenge to him.

Dora got a restraining order against Sam that prohibited him from seeing her, but he came to visit her at the house anyway. Two weeks after the incident they went together to family court, which required both of them to attend Alternatives to Violence (ATV), the feminist batterer intervention program. "It was scary going to court. I didn't know if they would send him to jail. But I was also glad because he had to go to classes now." Both attended meetings at the ATV program. She was pleased that the court required him to attend ATV because otherwise he would not have gone. Three months later, Dora told me that things had gotten a lot better. He had not been violent for three months and she had learned a lot about his controlling actions toward her. Before it felt like she was in prison, forced to go places with his family who didn't like her because she was white, but now she was better able to gauge what was happening to him. Although Dora thought that the police were overly lenient, telling her that there was hardly a scratch on her and that they couldn't arrest him, the family court judge firmly said this was wrong and was concerned about her safety. Dora was reluctant to see the violence she experienced as a crime worthy of court intervention. This was the first time she had been to court, and she did not know anyone else who had tried. Although the police treated the problem as relatively unimportant, the stern family court judge and the feminist ATV program convinced her that what she had endured was a serious form of violence. Clearly, she learned a new way of defining the everyday threats and attacks she had long experienced in her marriage.

## Gender policing: violence against transgendered people

People who fail to conform to normative expectations of male or female appearance or behavior face high levels of violence and murder. The term "transgender" refers to people whose gender identity or expression does not conform to the social expectations for their assigned sex at birth (Currah et al. 2006). People who fail to conform to heterosexual male and female identities face gender policing in the form of harassment and violence. This violence, often delivered randomly by strangers, is a mechanism for enforcing what has been called a heteronormative binary system. This refers to the requirement that all humans fit into a binary – that is, male and female – heterosexual arrangement of gender identities. Those who fail to conform face a variety of forms of violence. For example, in 2003 Gwen Araujo, a transgender teenager from a small town in California was killed by a group of young men who beat her to death with a shovel after discovering that she had male genitalia. Their attorneys argued that she was guilty of "deception" for not disclosing her identity to them. As Currah et al. (2006: xiv) point out, this incident is only one of thousands of hate crimes against transgender people. A study by a Boston activist group, Gender

Public Advocacy Coalition or GenderPAC, reported that over the past ten years, more than 50 young people under 30 were violently murdered for their failure to conform to gender stereotypes (Gender Public Advocacy Coalition 2006). Most of the murder victims were biologically male but presented themselves as more or less feminine. Many were black and Latina. They were killed by young males in acts of unusual violence. Research suggests that violence against transgender people is related to their gender variance, with those who regularly pass as either gender reporting a lower frequency of violence (reported by Dr. Scout, Director of National LBGT Tobacco Control Network, speaking at Baruch College, New York 2007; see also Namaste 2006). David Valentine's study (2003) of transgendered sex workers in New York City shows how those who are poor are less able to protect themselves from violence and murder. They have more dangerous jobs, such as street prostitution, and are less able to afford surgery in order to pass more effectively. Those without the funds to biologically reshape their bodies to conform to their gender identities are less successful at passing as the other gender and therefore face a greater risk of violence. Even when a person does not experience violence directly, these narratives create an environment of danger and threat. Thus, violence ranges from physical injury and death to threats and forms of humiliation and degradation that injure a sense of self even when the body is spared.

## Defining Gender

In the social sciences, the concept of gender has changed dramatically over the last 30 years. The new conceptions redefined the movement in very significant ways. Before the 1970s, most social scientists failed to pay attention to what women thought or did. In anthropology, for example, with some notable exceptions such as Margaret Mead, women were portrayed in the background or were neglected altogether. The first anthropologists to think about gender simply tried to add a focus on women. They began to write studies of kinship in which women were agents rather than pawns and of politics that included women's struggles for power in the extended family.

Anthropologists who began to focus on women in the 1970s were primarily concerned with explaining women's universal subordination to men (see Rosaldo and Lamphere 1974a). This was a political as well as an analytic problem, raised by feminism and the contemporary interest in Marxist theories of class and power (see di Leonardo 1991b). Sherry Ortner (1974) attributed women's inequality to a cultural linkage between women and nature and between men and culture, while Michelle Rosaldo saw women's subordination as the result of their embeddedness in the private sphere while power resided in the public sphere (Rosaldo 1974). While these dichotomies were analytically useful, they did not help us to understand the myriad ways gender shapes social relationships (see Sanday 1981). Micaela di Leonardo (1991b) points out that the nature/culture dichotomy is not universal and was formed in the Enlightenment, while the private/public sphere was developed in nineteenth-century Europe. Neither describes universal features of women's and men's lives.

However, challenging the distinction between the public sphere and the private sphere was politically important to feminists. Seeing women as embedded in the private sphere excluded them from politics, power, and authority. It situated them in the protected sphere of the home and family where they were governed by men. It justified the state's reluctance to intervene in the family, even in cases of violence. By locating men in the public sphere and women in the private sphere, this ideology legitimated gender inequalities. Under the claim that "the personal is political," advocates for battered women battled to tear down the walls between the public and the private to enable social and legal intervention into violence in families.

Studies of other societies suggested that women's subordination was less intense in small-scale hunter-gatherer societies (Shostak 1981). Some anthropologists searched for matriarchies – societies in which women exercised power – but found only myths that women in power abused it and destroyed the society (Bamberger 1974). Feminist social scientists began to focus on violence as a major explanation for the universal subordination of women.

Out of this intellectual ferment and political activism came several significant developments in the sociological theory of gender (see e.g. Rosaldo and Lamphere 1974b; di Leonardo 1991a; Ginsburg and Tsing 1990; Lamphere, Ragone, and Zavella 1997). Here I focus on the contributions of anthropology, but this was a very inter-disciplinary intellectual movement. Three developments are particularly important: the shift from sex to gender, from roles to performances, and from essentialized gender identities to intersectional ones. Each of these theoretical changes had a major impact on the gender violence movement, particularly in the USA.

## Sex to gender

Anthropologists initially discussed women through the framework of sex roles and sex differences. Sex differences were understood to be rooted in biological fea-tures. Sex roles were sets of expectations of behavior rooted in particular sociocul-tural systems based on sex differences. As anthropologists looked more carefully at sex roles, however, it became clear that they were highly variable and that they were produced through social processes of learning and training that instilled ideas about what it means to be a man or a woman into each person's consciousness. Instead of referring to sex roles, anthropologists adopted the concept of gender to talk about the social dimensions of sex differences. This term expresses the idea that differences between men and women are the product primarily of cultural processes of learning and socialization rather than of innate biological differences. "Sex" refers to genitalia while "gender" describes the social aspects of how men and women are expected to act. This term has now become international. For example, when the Chinese word for gender is translated back into English, it becomes "social gender."

However, even the concept of sex is less certain than this analysis suggests. A person's sex is also a product of cultural definition. For example, a study in Brazil of men who dress as women but work as male prostitutes suggests a very different division by sex than the conventional male/female divide on the basis of genitalia (Kulick 1999). These men, referred to as *travesti*, enjoy anal penetration as a sexual experience. They seek to transform their bodies into a more feminine shape through hormones and silicone injections. When they have sex through anal penetration of other men, they are socially defined as men, and when they are penetrated by other men, they are defined as not-men, as sharing gender with women. Similarly, effeminate gay men who enjoy anal penetration also acquire the identity of not-men, or women. Thus, Kulick argues, the distinction between men and women, or more accurately men and not-men, depends on the role a person plays in the sexual act, with the penetrator retaining a male identity and the penetrated taking on the not-man identity, or the gender of a woman. It is because they desire to be appealing as women that the *travesti* devote substantial energy to producing buttocks and female curves in their bodies, but they are clear that they are men, not women. Thus, not only is gender a culturally created and defined social position, but so also is sex. It cannot be seen as a clear biological category any more than gender.

## Role to performance

In a second development, anthropological theory has shifted from role to performance. In the 1970s and earlier, anthropological research focused on exploring the discrete roles of women and men in every society. Roles were sets of expectations of behavior that evoked sanctions when individuals failed to conform. They were shared, expressed as norms, and relatively stable, although they were not necessarily always followed. Although societies differed in their gender roles, they shared an emphasis on the centrality of gender as the basis for the division of labor – of the tasks each person was expected to do based on their identity. One study, for example, showed that every society had a distinct set of male and female tasks (Parker and Parker 1979). As the authors listed the tasks allocated to women and to men in societies around the world, they described them as differences in sex roles.

However, the concept of role proved too simple and static to describe the way gender operates in social situations. Since the 1980s, anthropologists have increasingly theorized gender as a performance directed at an audience (see Butler 1990). As a performance carried out in a particular situation, gender is expressed in different ways depending on the context. The same person can enact gender differently for different audiences. Such an analysis sees gender as created through the performance of tasks and activities. For example, in Segura's study of Chicana women in white-collar jobs in California, she argues that gender and race-ethnicity are not simply categorical statuses but accomplishments: identities produced through dynamic interaction and performance (Segura 1997: 293). As women do work, particularly in female-dominated jobs, they also "do gender," enacting what they see as the essential nature of women. Women in service jobs, for example, affirm themselves both as workers and as women. Employment in supportive service tasks enables them to do work and do gender at the same time. They reaffirm themselves as members in good standing of gender and race-ethnic categories. They establish themselves as Chicanas through work, family activities, child care, and a host of other activities. For these Chicana women, doing housework or child care allows them to accomplish both gender and race-ethnicity. In contrast, those who challenge these traditional patterns undermine their culture-ethnic maintenance (Segura 1997: 295). Thus, occupational segregation on the basis of gender and race is maintained as women seek jobs that reinforce the way they think about themselves and their membership in groups (Segura 1997: 305).

The connection between the performance of an identity and maintaining membership in a gender/race group is a serious obstacle for those who wish to act differently. For example, Kath Weston (1992) demonstrates how certain kinds of work, such as automobile repair, incorporate expectations of risk-taking and physical strength which are not inherently necessary to the work but reinforce the gendered performance of the work. Men carry heavy toolboxes not because it is necessary but because it shows that they are enacting male strength.

During the 1980s and 1990s, as anthropology moved to a more performative understanding of gender, it saw gender less as a fixed role than as an identity produced through action. Gender is closely linked to other social practices and identities and is a fundamental dimension of power relationships. The analysis was contextual and comparative. Some explored the role of gender, sexuality, and violence in larger processes such as colonialism. For example, Ann Stoler (1997a: 375) pioneered the examination of colonialism from the perspective of race and sexuality, noting that there is a close relationship between the sexual control of European women and racial tensions and anxieties. The conversion of colonized women into concubines and "keeps" represented an important part of the colonial theft of resources and reinforced racial hierarchies, while anxieties about sexual attacks on European women by allegedly "primitive" men of color fueled mechanisms of policing and control over both (Stoler 1997a: 377, 381). Both in the American South and in many colonial contexts, violence and the practice of lynching African American or colonial men was justified by the need to protect white women from them.

From a performative perspective, doing violence is a way of doing gender. In some situations and contexts, the performance of gender identities means acquiescing to violence or being violent. By putting up with violent assaults without complaint, minimizing the violence, calling it deserved, or treating it as inevitable, women "do" gender. Just as some women steer away from less "feminine" jobs, they may resist labeling their experiences as crimes. The woman who refuses to put up with male violence and takes her batterer to court risks defaulting on her gender performance. She faces exclusions and pressures from both his kin and her own. When a man uses violence against a partner whom he suspects of flirting with another man, he also accomplishes gender. His actions demonstrate that he is a man who cannot be cuckolded, who is in control of his woman, and who is a person of power and authority. When men batter women, they are performing masculinity not only for the woman but also for other men, who assess their masculinity by the performance (Connell 1995). Men in batterer treatment groups also perform gender as they discuss their own violent actions (Anderson and Umberson 2001). As in Segura's example, however, gender performances are refracted through race and class, so that notions of how to do masculinity in the face of a woman's apparent disobedience are shaped by specific cultural expectations. Performing masculinity among young white street youth in the USA, for example, is quite different from the way it is enacted among older middle-class African American professionals.

As theoretical work on gender developed in anthropology, it became clear that a dichotomous model of men and women was too simple. Research showed that male and female gender identities fall along a continuum from masculine to feminine. Some individuals are at either end, while many are closer to the middle. In some social situations, those in the middle face considerable pressure to conform to the ends, while those who refuse the terms of the continuum altogether face sanctions and even violence, as happens with some transpeople. Work on gay/lesbian identities played a critical role in moving anthropological analysis toward a notion of gender performance that was not organized into binaries but that recognized wider variability and multiple sexualities (e.g. Rubin 1975: Lewin and Leap 2002). As anthropologists moved toward a more performative model of gender, they criticized earlier models of gender that assumed universal characteristics of men and women.

## Essentialism to intersectionality

The third shift in anthropological theory was from essentialism to intersectionality. This move was similarly reflected in new ways of thinking about race and class in the American battered women's movement. Anthropologists labeled modes of analysis that assumed that male and female identities were more or less fixed as essentialism. They critiqued this idea, arguing instead that gender is always defined and redefined in interactions as it is performed for different audiences. For example, Matthew Gutmann's (1997) study of male identities in a lower-class neighborhood of Mexico City revealed a wide diversity of ways of performing masculinity in this context. He challenged assumptions that masculinity is defined only by concepts of machismo. Instead, he found increasing engagement of men in housework and child care. Younger men are particularly likely to play with and care for their children and to say that they are not macho since they help out at home and do not beat their wives, an important attribute of machismo. Theoretical work on gay/lesbian identities has also contributed in significant ways to challenging essentialist theories of gender and recognizing the variability of gender performances (Lewin 1996).

Essentialism argued that men and women are basically the same because of their gender. However, feminists pointed out that people are defined by a host of other identities based on race, class, ethnicity, nationality, disability, sexual orientation, and many other characteristics as well as gender (Crenshaw 1994). Any notion that there is a single, stable identity of "woman" or "man" fails to recognize this diversity. Gender is therefore intersectional, shaped by the way it interacts with other identities such as race and class. Thus, "woman" means something different for an upper-class, urban, educated, secular, wealthy white woman than it does for a poor, rural, evangelical Christian white woman living on welfare.

Although this argument makes sense analytically since it recognizes the complexity and variability of women's life situations, it inhibits political organizing along gender lines. A strength of the 1970s and 1980s women's movement in the USA was its insistence that all women share common problems of subordination to men. While this made good political sense, it ignored the diverse situations of women, particularly the differences between wealthy and poor women or white women and women of color. For example, a major issue in the women's movement of the 1960s was women's inability to work outside the home. But this was a middle-class women's problem. Poor women, single women, and many poor minority women had always worked; it was largely educated, middle-class white wives who were excluded. Thus, the demand to participate in the labor force was not a universal problem but one specific to women of a particular social class and marital status. Making claims in the name of "women" obscured these differences, and emphasized the demands of some women while ignoring those of others, such as the improved working conditions and better pay wanted by poor women.

The early feminist movement against violence was largely white and middle class, although some women of color played critical roles in the anti-rape movement (see Schechter 1982). In the last two decades, the battered women's movement has developed a far more varied and nuanced understanding of the intersections among gender, race, and class. Thinking about gender intersectionally, which means looking at race, class, and other identities as well as gender, reshapes the analysis of gender violence. For example, the situation of a poor woman being beaten by her husband is very different from that of an affluent woman who has far more resources to escape the relationship. But a woman with no income living with a rich man is also imprisoned. For example, in a letter to the school newspaper a college graduate expressed her frustration and vulnerability to violence.

### Speaking against violence

To the Editor:

Seven years ago, I graduated from Wellesley College with sky-high confidence and a belief that I could take on the world – and win.

The atmosphere at Wellesley, along with wonderful professors, had taught me to expect success and not to settle for anything less. But, life is not always filled with success – there are usually mixes of ups and downs. Unfortunately, during the last seven years, my life has been filled with more downs than ups.

For six years, I was trapped in a violently abusive marriage – a relationship where I often woke up in the morning not sure that I would survive until that night.

Even though I eventually escaped – only two months ago – those last six years have exacted a terrible toll on my family and loved ones. And I am left with physical and emotional scars. My youngest child – a baby boy – was murdered by my husband. And my daughter remains trapped in Russia with my husband.

But, these terrible years have taught me two important lessons; lessons that unfortunately I had to learn the hard way.

First, I learned that the skills that Wellesley had equipped me with – skills that were designed to help me take on the world – were also skills that kept me strong even during the darkest periods and always kept me from giving up.

And second, and perhaps most importantly, I learned that some issues – like domestic violence – cut across all income, education, racial and social lines.

Simply being a confident, intelligent Wellesley woman does not protect one from the ravages of domestic violence. In fact, these very facts sometimes make it more difficult to cope with the problem if it occurs.

I remember so many times my pride battling with my fear.

And too often, my pride would win out; I would remain silent, and I would be battered and tortured on a daily basis. But, when I finally did speak out, I found out that it was not so scary – that there were people out there who were willing to listen and support; people who were not going to judge and criticize.

I will never know if I would have done things differently, if my son would still be alive today or if I would have saved myself hundreds of trips to doctors, hospitals and emergency rooms and police stations in America and Russia. In fact, given the pervasive attitudes and misconceptions about domestic violence in Russia, and the unwillingness of authorities inside of the country to address and combat the violence, I have doubts that anything that I would have done or said would have changed my horrific situation. But still, I have doubts and I wonder. I do not know for sure.

But what I do know for certain is that silence never solves the problem of domestic violence. It didn't for me and it won't for anyone else who is in an abusive controlling relationship.

Speak up. And remember the voice that you are developing here – a voice that may someday lead a Fortune 500 company, teach future generations astrophysics or write a bestselling novel – is also the best tool to keep yourself safe.

The statistics are startling. The personal stories of abuse survivors are horrifying. Make sure that you do not become yet another statistic. Wellesley Alum '97 (*Wellesley News* (May 5, 2004))

Racism shapes gender violence in many ways. A poor woman of color is doubly disadvantaged in finding paths to escape violence and in seeking alternative housing and forms of support (Crenshaw 1994; hooks 1997; Smith 2005). Women of color experiencing violence face particular dilemmas in their use of the police. While calling the police is typically the first line of protection for women experiencing violence, this means turning the men of their community into the hands of a system often seen as oppressive and racially biased. As the number of incarcerated and supervised African American and Native American men mushrooms, women find themselves reluctant to summon the police against them (Davis 2001; Incite! 2006). Immigrant women who are battered face difficulties if their residence in the country depends on their spouse. Their partners may resist filing the papers to make them legal residents (Mendelson 2004). In the USA, immigration officers often challenge women's marriages, asking if they have married only in order to immigrate (Bhattacharjee 1997). Despite some legal protections for immigrant women who are victims of domestic violence, such women are especially vulnerable (Coutin 2000). They may be more socially isolated, lack the dominant language, and feel that their presence in the country is completely dependent on their partner's acceptance.

One of the enduring challenges of the violence against women movement is the tension between the political value of gender as an essentialized category versus the analytical value of the intersectional analysis of gender identities. Since essentialism is the claim that all women are, in significant ways, the same, it facilitates the argument that all women are subordinated by gender violence. This position was enormously effective in promoting the battered women's movement since it enabled activists to argue that battering is not just a problem for some sectors of the population, such as the poor or those with drinking problems, but for all women. Feminist scholars in the 1970s argued that violence was central to the subordination of all women. For socialist feminists such as Susan Schechter, "Woman abuse is viewed here as an historical expression of male domination manifested within the family and currently reinforced by the institutions, economic arrangements, and sexist division of labor within capitalist society. Only by analyzing the total context of battering will women and men be able to devise a long-range plan to eliminate it" (1982: 209). By defining violence as fundamental to patriarchy and patriarchy as a set of institutions and ideologies that subordinates all women, violence against one woman became violence against all. Countering this violence was not just a matter of changing the lifestyles of the poor or alcoholics but of changing women's subordination overall.

Despite the political power of this position, it implicitly foregrounded the problems of middle-class white women while ignoring the very different experiences of differentially situated women. Women of color have increasingly argued that the movement is too focused on the situations of white women, and that approaches such as criminalization fail to take into account their very different life conditions (Davis 2001; Incite! 2006). In other words, essentialism is both politically expedient and analytically flawed. This dilemma reappears in the human rights movement against violence against women, discussed in Chapter 4.

## Contemporary Conceptions of Gender Violence

Gender violence is now an umbrella term for a wide range of violations from rape during wartime to sexual abuse in prisons to insults and name-calling within marriages. International activists continue to expand the scope of violence against women to include cultural practices such as female genital cutting, illegal acts such as dowry deaths, the trafficking of women as sex workers, the displacement of women during civil wars, and the violence experienced by migrants in the context of contemporary globalization. Local, national, and regional movements around the world challenge the legitimacy of many of these practices along with the international movement. During the 1980s and 1990s, women's movements used the major UN conferences on women to solidify their definition of gender-based violence and build international political momentum for acting against it. In the early 1990s the global feminist movement succeeded in establishing that violence against women was a human rights violation. In 2001 a leading human rights NGO, Amnesty International, defined violence against women as a form of torture, and in 2004 it mounted a global campaign against violence against women (www.amnestyusa.org/ violence-against-women/stop-violence-against-women-svaw/page.do?id=1108417 &n1=3&n2=39&n3=1101).

Yet global campaigns to reduce gender violence encounter the dilemma of asserting universal standards for women's physical safety while also respecting cultural difference. This is a very complex and unresolved issue. Critiques of female genital cutting, for example, often become criticisms of cultural practices fundamental to a social system. The major documents supporting women's status globally, such as the Convention on the Elimination of all Forms of Discrimination against Women, urge governments to redefine gender roles to eliminate prejudices and customary and other practices based on the idea of the inferiority of the sexes or on stereotyped roles for men and women. More recent statements, such as the Beijing Platform for Action of 1995, urge governments not to use culture, religion, or tradition to avoid their obligations to end violence against women. On the other hand, global feminists are sensitive to cultural difference and to the importance of respecting different ways of life. The relationship between feminism and respect for cultural difference is a difficult one, constantly subject to debate and renegotiation. A strong relativist position that refuses critique in the name of protecting culture is antithetical to feminist commitments. Chapter 4 discusses this dilemma in more detail.

## Theorizing Gender Violence

### Beyond patriarchy

During the early years of the battered women's movement, activists argued that violence against women is the product of patriarchy. Patriarchy referred to family and societal arrangements in which males exercised predominant power. Men batter women, the argument went, because they can. Indeed, the initial concern with gender violence came from feminists' efforts to understand why women are subordinate to men. But, clearly, this explanation is far too simple. While patriarchy justifies and enables gender violence, many other factors account for gender violence as well. Gender violence is deeply rooted in cultural understandings of gender and power, whether it takes place within a marriage or among strangers. For example, when a woman of one ethnic group is raped by a soldier of another ethnic group during wartime, the act is a dramatic demonstration of the dominance of the rapist's group.

Moreover, the theory that gender violence is the product of patriarchy takes a heteronormative perspective that imagines all forms of violence occurring in opposite-sex relationships. However, research shows widespread patterns of violence in lesbian and gay relationships as well. Lesbian violence reflects interlocking subordinations based on race, class, gender, and sexuality rather than just gender inequality (Ristock 2002: 22).

Violence within lesbian relationships has been neglected by the battered women's movement in the past, since theories of patriarchy lead activists to see women as victims only of men. Yet stories of violence within same-sex relationships suggest that many of these incidents are also framed by struggles over power. On the basis of interviews with 70 lesbian and bisexual women about their stories of sexual assault, Girshick (2002) emphasizes the need to build a more inclusive feminist vision of domestic violence and sexual assault. Rather than placing patriarchy at center stage, she suggests examining the questions of power over others, a model which accounts for patriarchy, racism, classism, ableism, and other oppressions. Stories from the women she interviewed support this idea. Marianne's story provides one perspective on lesbian violence (Girshick 2001: 31–35).

"When Marianne (a pseudonym) was 19 she began a relationship that seemed promising. She was "awestruck" by her partner, eight years older, who seemed world-wise, confident, and safe. Her partner was well liked, had a job and apartment, and family she visited often. After about four months into this four-year relationship, Marianne realized that her partner liked controlling what she did, who her friends were, what they did together." According to Marianne:

> She'd get mad and throw things around the apartment, she'd take things of mine and throw them (or throw them out), she tossed the TV out a window and smashed it, etc. After a while she'd hit me or push my face, hard, if I did something she disliked or didn't do when she asked or demanded. She constantly threatened to leave, told me I was worthless or dumb, told me my friends (I didn't have many) were idiotic, told me I was unattractive or ugly, and so on. I was extremely anxious that she would leave. I also hated how things were going, and thought it was all my fault. After about a year she'd progressed to full-blown rampages, beating on me with things (a chair, thrown books, pans from the kitchen). I tried fighting back but she was strong and completely wild. Sometimes she would beat on me until I was crying and subdued (and hurting), then she'd tear my clothes off and force me down, then force her fingers or other objects inside of me, kiss me roughly suck on my skin to make marks that sometimes bled, hit me on the breasts, etc. She'd ask me to "do" her and I'd try to do what she wanted, but it was hard, she wanted me to almost hurt her or actually hurt her. I felt awful about this but she'd destroy stuff if I didn't, and at the time I owned very little. One time she literally raped me with a plastic dildo. This went on for several years. I finally left her when my current lover (who is not abusive at all) gave me safe haven.

For years, Marianne felt she caused or deserved what happened to her. She did not have words to label the sexual violence against her. In fact, at the time she might have called it "consensual." But today, Marianne calls what her partner did to her "rape" or "assault." It was years before she admitted she'd been hit. It took therapy and dealing with childhood incest to face the trauma of the sexual abuse within her battering relationship. The post-traumatic stress impacts of the abuse against her included

> flashbacks, fear, pain, a sense of haunting, a sense of defeat (that I hadn't managed to escape my childhood after all), incredibly low self-esteem, nightmares, a wish to die or hurt myself physically, [and] hopelessness.

Marianne wished there had been a lesbian-specific hotline and a lesbian-friendly shelter. Looking back, she realizes that if someone had noticed and approached her about the abuse perhaps she would have left sooner. Because she felt it was her fault, Marianne didn't tell others about what was happening. Without resources, including money to pay for therapy, Marianne was alone.

Ristock (2002) argues that feminist theories of battery construct a series of binaries – such as perpetrator/victim, male as batterer/female as passive victim, powerful/powerless – that are too restrictive and heterosexist to understand violence against women. Work by scholars on gay/lesbian identities has brought these binaries into question. For example, Ristock's interviews with lesbians who have experienced abuse indicate some shifting between abuser and abused roles and shows that there are situations in which violence is not about control. Abused lesbians sometimes attack their abusers, just as abused women do in heterosexual relationships. A widely used legal defense for women who kill their batterers, the battered women's syndrome, claims that the experience of battering creates such feelings of helplessness, fear, and desperation that the victim is driven to kill. This theory replicates the powerful male batterer/helpless female victim binary and ignores the role of anger and desire to retaliate on the part of the murderer. The feminist framework which looks to patriarchy as the explanation for violence also relies on the binary of powerful males/powerless females and does not describe the complexities of violence or the experience of violence within gendered relationships.

In her ethnographic study of violence in a poor community in Brazil, Sarah Hautzinger (2007) complicates the offender/victim binary. She finds that men's violence is both an effort to assert honor by controlling their women and a response to their own vulnerability in economic and social terms. Moreover, women are battered both because they are in highly subordinate and vulnerable positions and because they are attempting to contest their gendered positions of inferiority. Thus, violence can be "contestatory," as couples struggle for dominance in the relationship, rather than only one-sided. Hautzinger refers to the latter form of violence, when it is extreme and imposed on a hapless victim, as "intimate terrorism." Her analysis suggests areas of women's agency as well as domains where men live with substantial constraints on their lives which they manage through violence against their partners. Hautzinger is clear that paying attention to men's vulnerability does not excuse their violence, but it does help to understand it.

## Anthropological Perspectives on Gender Violence

Much research on gender violence considers its causes within family dynamics or childhood experiences. There is a rich body of research on psychological dimensions of gender violence. While recognizing the importance of interpersonal and psychological factors, this book examines the social contexts within which gender violence takes place. Using an anthropological approach, it examines gender violence from the perspective of family, community, state, and world. The anthropological perspective emphasizes culture and context rather than psychological or biological dimensions of violence. It focuses on the meanings of gender violence in various situations. Its comparative approach shows how gender violence is related to larger patterns of social inequality such as class and racial discrimination, histories of colonialism, and ethnic inequality and hostility as well as patterns of gender inequality, family organization, and marriage arrangements. There are connections between racial violence and spouse abuse, between ethnic conflict and rape, between nationalism and male aggressiveness, between living in an occupied state and beating up wives. There are many forms of gender violence, but all are embedded in larger structures of power and violence and shaped by cultural meanings of race, class, nation, family, and marriage as well as gender. Understanding gender violence requires looking both at the intimate details of family life and at geopolitical considerations of power and warfare. In order to understand gender violence, it is necessary to understand the world.

The anthropological perspective on gender violence has four dimensions. First, it sees this issue as created by social movements and political debates, subject to change over time. Rape and violence within intimate relationships are of course ancient practices with a global distribution; what is new is the creation of a global social movement which names these phenomena, links them to gender practices, and sees them as basic to gender subordination. But the violence which is targeted in this movement changes over time. The early movements focused on specific cultural practices, such as female genital cutting or husbands hitting and killing their wives. More recent conceptions have expanded to include state actions such as the treatment of women in prisons and during warfare as well as more indirect forms of violence, such as the disproportionate number of women who become refugees, the cutbacks of social services for poor women with children, or sex-selective abortion and infanticide.

Second, an anthropological perspective recognizes that gender itself is not fixed but performed for audiences in various contexts. Gender is defined by kinship systems and forms of marriage as well as nationalisms which see women as mothers of the nation and men as its soldiers and defenders. During the height of British militarism and imperialism, for example, there was an effort to improve the number and health of children in order to strengthen the nation. Working-class women were targeted by the government as caring for their children inadequately and therefore failing to serve the empire (Davin 1997). In the early twentieth century Congolese women were similarly trained in practices of motherhood in order to reduce infant mortality and to increase the number of laborers available to the colonial masters (Hunt 1997: 288–289).

Third, an anthropological perspective means that interpersonal behavior must be understood within wider contexts of power and meaning. For gender violence, this means that it is critical to understand how violence between individuals is a dimension of violence by states, by communities, and by institutions. For example, men who live in an occupied country may become more violent both to occupiers and to the women they live with. Those who routinely use violence in their lives, as police or as soldiers, tend to use violence interpersonally as well. People for whom denigration on the basis of race or class is a familiar experience are less likely to resist when they experience abuse on the basis of gender as well. These are only a few examples of the way larger structures give meaning to interpersonal, intimate violence for perpetrators and for victims. These structures also determine relative power and ease of exit in relationships and the forms of recourse available to those who suffer violence. They define the meanings of masculinity and femininity and provide the contexts within which they are performed.

Fourth, an anthropological perspective is comparative. Gender violence is a global phenomenon. It takes place all over the world, although at different frequencies and in different forms. For example, gender violence in the USA tends to be male battering of women in intimate, romantic relationships, while in China an important part of gender violence is battering of elderly parents and children, reflecting the different patterns of family life. Gender violence in China includes mortgaging or selling wives or children, infanticide, abandoning wives, and kidnapping women to sell as wives. As the economy shifts from a planned socialist system to a market one, the radical disruptions in work and social security have increased levels of violence against women (Human Rights in China 1995). Women in some parts of India face violence in the context of disputes over the dowry they have brought to the marriage as dowry becomes an important form of cash income for grooms and their families. Military and police in the USA use violence against their partners at far higher levels than the general population. This is a global phenomenon, but its manifestations are highly variable, depend on local systems of meaning, kinship structures, gender inequalities, and levels of violence in the wider society. As we shall see, societies vary greatly in the extent to which gender violence is defined as a legal violation and in the availability of help from the law. The rest of this book examines the variability of gender violence and its relationship to structural violence in various parts of the world.

## Measuring Gender Violence

Studies all over the world report gender violence, but it is very difficult to develop any numerical measure of its frequency. Part of the difficulty is the fact that often the same incident can be interpreted as abuse or as discipline. Surveys that rely on asking people how often they have experienced violence will miss these events. It is widely recognized that rape victims are very reluctant to report this violence, and it is likely that women in many parts of the world share this concern with reference to violence as well. The other approach to measuring gender violence is to count how many cases come to some official agency for help. Clearly this shows how often women define their problems as warranting help and are able to or choose to ask for assistance, but such an approach clearly misses many cases where women think the violence is their due, they fear retaliation for complaints, or they lack state institutions that will show sympathy and act on their complaints. Chapter 5 discusses these measurement issues in more detail.

Despite these difficulties, there are many efforts to survey the frequency of gender violence worldwide. WHO published a report in 2005 on violence against women by male intimate partners based on interviews with 24,000 women in 15 sites in 10 countries: Bangladesh, Brazil, Peru, Tanzania, Ethiopia, Thailand, Japan, Samoa, Namibia, and Serbia and Montenegro (World Health Organization 2005). Earlier studies from 35 countries had reported that between 10 and 52 percent of women had been physically abused by an intimate partner at some point in their lives and between 10 and 30 percent had experienced sexual violence from an intimate partner (WHO 2005: 1). The WHO study, initiated in 1997, found significant national and urban/rural variation, with between 15 and 71 percent of women who had ever been in an intimate relationship experiencing physical or sexual assault during their lifetime (WHO 2005: 5). Most sites fell between 29 and 62 percent, with the lowest rates in Japan and the highest in rural areas of Bangladesh, Ethiopia, Peru, and Tanzania. Rates for intimate partner violence in the last year ranged from 4 percent in Japan and Serbia and Montenegro to 54 percent in Ethiopia (WHO 2005: 5). The most common act of violence was being slapped and the next most common being hit with a fist. Most of these acts represent a continuing pattern of abuse, with over half of the women who had experienced a violent act in the past 12 months reporting that it had happened more than once. Moreover, the research found a significant overlap between physical and sexual violence in most sites, with between 30 and 56 percent of women who had experienced any violence reporting both physical and sexual violence (WHO 2005: 7).

Women also reported high levels of emotional abuse such as insults, belittling, intimidation by smashing things, or threats of harm: between 20 and 75 percent of women reported one or more of these actions, mostly within the past 12 months (WHO 2005: 9). It is, of course, very hard to reliably count these events by asking women to recall incidents because they may or may not interpret them as emotional abuse. Women frequently reported their partners engaging in controlling behavior such as isolation, ignoring them, or accusing them of being unfaithful, with a frequency of 21 percent in Japan to almost 90 percent in urban Tanzania. This behavior tends to accompany physical and sexual violence (WHO 2005: 10). Women also reported high rates of physical and sexual violence by non-partners after the age of 15, particularly in Samoa (65 percent) and Peru (28 percent urban, 32 percent rural). Surprisingly, only 5 percent of Ethiopian women reported this problem. Finally, few abused women turn to formal services such as shelters or authorities such as police, religious leaders, or NGOs: between 55 and 95 percent of physically abused women said that they had never gone to these agencies for help (WHO 2005: 18). Clearly, the pattern of intimate partner abuse is widespread globally, but its incidence is also quite variable among countries and between rural and urban settings. No simple explanation seems possible.

In practice, what actions constitute gender violence depends on how these actions are made meaningful. Cultural interpretation makes everyday events meaningful. Recognizing an act as gender-based violence depends on judging the behavior as an offense. Who the offense is against, why it happened, and who is responsible for redressing it are all matters of cultural interpretation. Even the boundary between acceptable and unacceptable violence is a cultural one which is subject to change over time. Some forms of violence are viewed as appropriate discipline while others are seen as excessive violence. Paradoxically, violence is both solidly observable and infinitely open to interpretation. The physical substrate of violence is about pain, injury, and death but its conversion into a social offense depends on culturally embedded understandings of gender, family, community, and nation. It is both physical and cultural at the same time.

Within family relationships, some forms and situations of violence are seen as legitimate discipline while others are interpreted as abuse. Whether or not a person will describe herself as abused depends on how she interprets a slap, a blow, or an insult. The same act of violence by a husband toward his wife can be defined as acceptable discipline for her misbehavior or as a crime. The context and the prevailing norms of gender performance distinguish them. Moreover, the line between what is abuse and what is discipline can and does change over time. In a dramatic example of the interpretative nature of gender violence, staff at the women's center I studied in Hawai'i said that when women first came to the center, they would minimize the violence they experienced. After several weeks or months of participating in a support group, they reinterpreted their experiences as violence. Before, the blows had appeared natural or even as a sign of love, but as they discussed them with other women and staff, they came to see them as abusive, as violations of their rights, and even as crimes. Many women accept some forms of violence as justified if they feel they have violated rules or expectations. For example, a nationwide study in India in the late 1990s indicated that over half the women (56 percent) questioned thought that some of the things women did merited violence from their husbands.[1]

## Conclusions

Violence is part of the performance of gendered identities, whether as men attack their wives to prove to other men that they are in control of their sexuality, or as men attack other men defined as enemies to escape accusations of cowardice. Gender

[1]   The National Family Health Survey, a major study of 90,000 households, asked questions about domestic violence for the first time in the 1998–1999 survey. It reported that 56 percent of ever-married women thought it was legitimate for their husbands to beat them for infractions (International Institute for Population Sciences 2000: 73). The same study reported that 21 percent of women have been beaten or mistreated since they were 15, and 19 percent of women by their husbands, although it is likely that this figure is under-reported because of shame and fear (International Institute for Population Sciences 2000: 74–75).

violence is a highly variable phenomenon that takes shape within particular social arrangements. It is never distinct from larger systems of social inequality and power based on race, class, and strength, nor is it distinct from other forms of violence such as warfare, state oppression, racism, or caste differentiation. The identification of any act of violence or threat as gender violence is always a matter of interpretation within a particular social and cultural context. It is clear that this identification can and does change over time with the introduction of new ideas about what gender violence is. It also changes with new political and economic relationships. For example, shifting from subsistence life in a village to an insecure urban squatter settlement that lacks the support of friends and kinsmen may increase gender violence.

Despite claims that there is a simple, widely applicable explanation of gender violence rooted in the power of men over women, it is not possible to develop any simple model that adequately describes this diversity or the way it changes over time. Instead, it is important to locate interpersonal violence within wider social patterns of power and inequality. The main theme of this book is the continuity between interpersonal and societal violence. Societies define acceptable and unacceptable forms of violence and determine which kinds of violence should be punished. Any person's vulnerability to violence depends on the extent to which social institutions define this violence as illegitimate and set up mechanisms for controlling it.

The rest of the book explores gender violence from the perspective of the cultural meanings of this violence, the social conditions that produce it, the social movements that have defined it, and the approaches that deal with it. Chapter 2 describes the way social movements in India, China, and the USA raised public awareness of the issue and defined it as a serious social problem. Chapters 3 and 4 look at forms of intervention. Chapter 3 explores how the legal system in the USA works to control gender violence through the criminal justice system and Chapter 4 describes the emergence of a global human rights movement focused on violence against women. Chapters 5, 6, and 7 examine some of the conditions that produce gender violence: Chapter 5 focuses on the effects of racism, poverty, and migration; Chapter 6 on violent cultural practices in families; and Chapter 7 on war and the dilemmas of refugees. Chapter 8 concludes with the argument that gender violence cannot be changed without working to transform the relations of inequality and violence in the larger society as well.

## Questions for Further Discussion

1  What is the difference between interpersonal violence and structural violence? How are they connected? Explain how social and cultural systems give violence meaning, and consider the way the meaning of violence changes over time and across contexts.
2  Explain why each shift – from sex to gender, from roles to performances, from essentialized gender identities to intersectional ones – has shaped the way we understand gender violence today. Do you think these shifts have moved activism forward? Why or why not?

3  Analyze the vignettes by Dora, Marianne, and the Wellesley alumna like an anthropologist. How is gender performed, violence understood, and power produced in their narratives? How do they describe the role of the family, the community, and the state? How do other forms of identity (including race, age, sexuality, and class) inform their stories? When did they come to understand their predicament as gender violence? What similarities and differences do you see?

## Video Suggestions

*Ferry Tales*, by Katja Esson (USA, 2003), 40 minutes

Academy Award Nominee for Best Documentary Short, *Ferry Tales* speaks to the various ways gender is performed. Every morning in their commute to Manhattan, a group of women – suburban and urban, white- and blue-collar, black and white – come together in the ladies' bathroom of the Staten Island Ferry to put on make-up and discuss anything from handbags, divorce, sex, domestic violence, and their experience with September 11th. These straight-talking, no-nonsense women illustrate how the intersections between race, class, gender, and age inform their identity as they leave their roles as mother, wife, and professional behind.

*Georgie Girl*, by Annie Goldson and Peter Wells (New Zealand, 2001), 70 minutes

In 1999 a mostly white, conservative, rural constituency elected a former prostitute to New Zealand's Parliament. Georgina Beyer (born George Beyer) became the world's first transgendered person to hold national office. *Georgie Girl* chronicles the life of this one-time sex worker of Maori descent, from farm boy to celebrated cabaret performer to grass-roots community organizer. Interviews with major government officials, everyday voters, family, and friends are intertwined with footage of her on stage in nightclubs and in Parliament, which together make for an engaging story of identity, politics, and the overcoming of prejudice.

*State of Denial*, by Elaine Epstein (South Africa/USA, 2003), 83 minutes

*State of Denial* is a sensitive portrayal of the everyday violence – both interpersonal and structural – that HIV/AIDS patients encounter in post-apartheid South Africa. Racism, poverty, a struggling middle class, poor sanitation, limited access to education and health care, social stigma, labor demands, and, not least, an unresponsive president and powerful drug cartels contribute to what has become the leading killer in South Africa. Embedded in the film are insights into how the epidemic impacts women in particular as mothers, daughters, nieces, volunteers, and sex workers.

# 2

# Gender Violence and Social Movements

The contemporary definition of gender violence comes out of political struggles. In general, social issues are created when a social movement carries out a campaign to define some form of abuse as a serious problem and manages to raise public awareness about this new definition. Over the last 30 years, women's movements have redefined gender violence as a serious problem, one that affects all women and is at the core of patriarchy. Until the battered women's movement of the 1970s, violence against women seemed either natural and inevitable or a product of social class and lifestyle. Nineteenth-century activists focused on the drunken brute while mid-twentieth-century activists and scholars attributed violence to working-class lifestyles. In their efforts to understand why women are everywhere subordinate to men, feminists of the 1960s and 1970s began to focus on the role of violence in gendered relationships. As Chapter 1 showed, feminists argued that patriarchy was a manifestation of inequality, and that violence supported patriarchy. The women's movement came to see violence as a means by which men establish power and control over women. When important social institutions such as the law fail to take it seriously, the violence is excused and normalized. To counter that tendency, the battered women's movement argued that a woman never deserves to be hit, no matter what she does.

During the 1970s and 1980s, national and local movements about gender violence emerged in many parts of the world, often influencing each other in significant ways. By the 1990s, these national movements began to coalesce into an international human rights movement, a form of transnational collective action (Keck and Sikkink 1998; Thompson 2002). Gender violence became a global feminist issue, interpreted as a violation of women's human rights. The worldwide movement grew out of distinctive national issues, producing an eclectic set of specific concerns that now constitute the global movement.

In many ways, the contemporary movement is the descendant of nineteenth-century reform efforts. During the imperial era, activists from colonizing countries sought to reform the status of women at home and in their colonies. To some extent, colonialism was justified by the need to improve the degraded status of women. British women worked to eliminate the sale of maids in Hong Kong (Pederson 1991), for example, and to end child marriage and *sati* (widow immolation) in India (Kumar 1993; Mani 1998). At the same time, movements developed in colonized countries, often associated with nationalist independence movements and influenced by transnational ideologies. For example, Chinese women influenced by international movements pressed for reform of women's status in the 1920s and 1930s. Many of these issues were taken up by the Chinese Communist Party and served as the basis for campaigns against foot-binding in the early twentieth century and in favor of marriage reforms in the 1950s.

Imperial era reformers from Europe and North America used the subordinate status of women as a measure of backwardness. Ironically, this perspective ignored the ways that British and European women of the nineteenth century were also subordinated, denied the right to vote, to a large extent excluded from education, and trapped within family structures that defined the role of women as wards of their husbands. It also tended to neglect the activism of women in Africa, Asia, and Latin America. This history has left significant legacies for contemporary reform movements. The critique of women's subordinate status frequently generates nationalistic forms of resistance, particularly among male elites. Describing some forms of gender violence as "harmful" traditional practices locates them in an unchanging culture implicitly assumed as backward and needing the "civilizing processes" of modernity. Global feminism at times replicates older ideas of intervention and salvation that are reminiscent of missionary work. On the other hand, it also provides a rich array of ideas of reform and transformation in gender hierarchies. Some scholars prefer the term "transnational feminism" to "global feminism" since it emphasizes the circulation of ideas and practices across national borders rather than the movement of a set of ideas generated by the global north to the periphery of the global south (Naples 2002: 6).

This chapter begins with an analysis of how social movements define problems and how this comes to reshape public awareness. It then explores women's movements in India, China, and the USA, three countries whose movements against gender violence I have studied in some detail (Merry 2006). This comparison emphasizes the multiple origins of the movement against gender violence, showing that it is a transnational rather than an exclusively American or European social movement (see Merry 2006). India, China, and the USA are not the only countries that tackled gender violence of course, but are all powerful and influential countries with strong women's movements. They differ in region, religion, family patterns, and government, yet they have pursued similar approaches in the last 30 years. In all three countries, husbands exercise substantial authority and control over their wives and families while the state and its laws support that control. Social inequalities such as those based on race or caste are maintained by rape and violence against subordinated and marginalized groups. All three countries have traditions of militarism that celebrate masculinity exercised through violence against women and men. In all three, violence has emerged as a critical dimension of gender subordination, although this happened later in China than in India and the USA. The intellectual currents described in Chapter 1 shaped understandings of gender and violence in all these countries. Activists have turned to the law and to the state for redress, demanding criminal penalties for violence and rape, state support for victims, and new laws condemning gender violence. And in all three places, movements against gender violence now face a backlash framed in terms of the need to maintain social order and to protect culture, family, and national identity.

The specific issues that galvanized these movements differed significantly, however. In the USA, the turbulent period of the 1960s with its widespread challenges to authority and civil rights claims for excluded groups spawned a woman's movement that challenged women's subordination. In India, concerns about dowry and dowry deaths, as well as rape by police, sparked widespread protests and demonstrations. In China, the liberalization of the economy and the rise of rights-based protests contributed to demands for redress for victims of violence as well. Of course, these are all large and complex countries with multiple, fragmented, and differing approaches to gender violence.

## Naming and Framing the Problem

To create a social movement, it is essential to develop a name for the problem. Naming the problem means developing a framework that explains it and offers solutions. As gender violence emerged as a social problem, debates over names flourished. Each name carried its own baggage, political orientation, and inclusions and exclusions. "Gender violence," "gender-based violence," "violence against women," and other terms such as "family violence," "domestic violence," "wife battering," and "spouse assault" are terms developed by worldwide social movements since the 1970s. The terms emphasize different dimensions of the problem: "family violence" refers to acts within a family context but downplays the gendered dimension, while "wife battering" emphasizes gender but excludes violence between unmarried people. "Spouse abuse" broadens the form of violence under consideration from "spouse assault," but still restricts the term to marriage.

Early research referred to family violence or domestic violence. "Family violence," still a term widely used globally, fails to specify the gendered nature of the family relationships in which the violence takes place. "Domestic violence" also does not specify the perpetrator or the victim in gendered terms. At the same time, by focusing on the domestic location of the violence, it appears to tame the violence itself. It reaffirms that it is taking place in a private space that is under the control of the husband/father. It ignores forms of violence that occur outside the domestic sphere. Another term is "spouse assault," which emphasizes the criminality of the behavior but excludes non-marital relationships and does not specify the gender of the offender or victim. "Spouse abuse" covers a wider range of behavior than "spouse assault," incorporating forms of insult, humiliation, and threats that are not physically violent. The term "woman abuse" is not limited to spouses.

Feminists in the 1970s and 1980s pointed to the neutral and degendered meaning of these terms and advocated using the term "wife battering" instead (Yllo and Bograd 1988). But this term referred only to violence against wives. The term "intimate partner violence" highlights the intimacy of the relationship but ignores gender as well as acts that are not embedded in intimate relationships. "Violence against women" is a broader term, incorporating actions outside the context of the family, but it leaves the perpetrator of the violence unspecified and even missing. Some suggest talking about "male violence against women." Activists in the international movement refer to "violence against women," "gender-based violence," or simply "gender violence." "Gender-based violence" is the term used in major international documents such as the 1995 outcome document of the Beijing World Conference for Women. This term emphasizes the importance of gendered identities to the violence, and does not restrict the sphere of concern to heterosexual encounters or to female victims. However, "gender-based violence" does not highlight the disproportionate victimization of women.

Similar terminological shifts occurred in the field of sexualized violence. The term "rape" refers only to sexual behavior, ignoring the violence that often accompanies the action. But sex within intimate relationships can be violent while violence in intimate relationships is frequently sexualized. Increasingly, rape is referred to as "sexual assault," reflecting the violence that accompanies the sex act, and "domestic violence" is understood as including sexual assault. The terms "sexual violence" and "sexual assault" are increasingly used to foreground the linkage between sexuality and violence.

Why does the name matter? Naming a problem is essential to organizing politically to do something about it and creating a social movement. Each term has a slightly different scope and suggests a different political orientation and solution to the problem. Creating a name for a problem is one of those subtle cultural technologies that defines an issue and channels responses to it. As we shall see, the modes of intervention commonly used in the USA are premised on a particular understanding of the phenomenon, often embedded in the term used to describe it.

Sociologists who study social movements talk about developing a frame for the movement, which then expands to include other things over time (Snow 2004). The history of the movement can be tracked by the terms used to describe the phenomenon. Indeed, the creation of a movement depends on developing a core term that makes sense to people and can be used to understand their experiences. For example, I watched a woman in a battered women's support group grappling with her experience of being forced to have sex with her husband. One of the women said, "That is rape." After a long pause, the woman said thoughtfully, "I guess it was, that makes sense. It felt like rape." Naming the behavior implies an analysis of what it means and a judgment about whether it was wrong.

The term "domestic violence" does not travel easily across cultural boundaries. In China, two quite different terms cause significant disparities in survey data.

One word, *bao-li*, refers to brute force, while another, *nue-dai*, refers to cruel treatment or abuse and and a third, *qin-fan*, refers to violation. A focus group in Hong Kong found that using the latter terms helped group members expand their definition of abuse (Tang et al. 2000). The term used will clearly affect reported frequencies. A 2002 survey of 3,692 rural and urban men and women in China found 2.7 percent reported violence by their spouses, 1.3 percent of men and 3.9 percent of women, using the term *bao-li*. Of the 80 percent who quarrel, 35 percent said they used violence in the quarrel, using the same term (Liu and Zhang 2002). A 2000 survey of 2,500 men and women reported that 33.9 percent of families face domestic violence, probably an underreported statistic because of the "traditional" Chinese idea of keeping family problems within the family (*China Women's News*, March 25, 2000, trans. Wei-Ying Lin). Only when respondents understand and recognize a term, however, will they report the experience to survey researchers. Thus, survey research can document the frequency of forms of violence against women more effectively after a social movement creates awareness of the issue and its terminology. Of course, surveys are also critically important in showing how widespread and serious the problem is in the first place.

## Histories of Social Movements against Gender Violence

### India

India has a long history of women's activism focused on issues such as union organizing, access to micro-credit, and widow remarriage, but violence against women has been a central concern for the last three decades. In the pre-independence period, women worked with men in the independence movement, but they were largely regarded as wives and mothers (Kumar 1993). Campaigns focused on anti-alcoholism, anti-*sati* (the practice of burning widows on their husband's funeral pyre), and promoting the remarriage of widows. The contemporary movement began in the 1970s, largely inspired by educated urban women with a left political orientation, some of whom were involved in the labor movement. Many were inspired by socialism. A major debate concerned whether to focus on political reform or social reform. Although there was a long tradition of women's affiliation with political parties, these new activists sought to create an autonomous women's movement separate from political parties and more focused on social reform (Kumar 1993; 1999 [1995]: 64–65; Butalia 2002). This movement focused on women's empowerment and economic and educational conditions. The movement was inevitably fragmented, with multiple issues, but gradually coalesced around violence as a theme that united various groups of differing educational level, rural/urban residence, and class position.

During Indira Gandhi's term as prime minister, she commissioned a report that profoundly influenced the women's movement. Published in 1974, *Toward Equality: The Report of the Committee on the Status of Women in India* was produced by a committee appointed in 1971 by the Ministry of Education and Social Welfare. The report pointed to the continuing inequality of women since independence and emphasized how much needed to be done to achieve women's economic and social equality. It helped to encourage the development of women's studies centers and literature by women. The concept of gender came into common usage and more and more middle-class women took up leadership positions in the movement.

Beginning in the 1970s, the women's movement pushed for reforms in the area of economics and politics. For example, in 1972, the Self-Employed Women's Association (SEWA) worked to organize home-based and informal women workers into trade unions and cooperatives for marketing and credit cooperatives. By the early 2000s, SEWA had almost 2 million members in cities in India and in rural areas of Gujarat (Desai 2002: 19). In 1974, recognizing that village panchayats, or councils, tend to consist of men of the dominant castes, the Government of India's Committee on the Status of Women issued a report that advocated creating women-only councils, or panchayats, at the village level as a transitional measure to ensure women's political participation. In subsequent years the idea of creating reservations for women in existing panchayats became a major issue for the Indian women's movement, and in a 1992 amendment to the Indian Constitution, 33 percent of the seats in village panchayats were reserved for women. These quotas have opened panchayat participation to women to some extent (Mayaram 2002: 396–397; Narayanan 2002: 295), but there have been differential levels of implementation around the country and substantial resistance from males of dominant castes (see Kapadia 2002). During the 1990s, the government of India and the women's movement together created Mahila Samakhya (MS), an education program for women focusing on consciousness-raising and empowerment. The MS program developed *sanghs*, or collectives, for poor rural women in six states in India (Desai 2002: 21; Sharma 2008).

Two issues in particular galvanized the movement against gender violence in the 1970s: dowry murders and rape in police custody (Kumar 1993: 128–129). Dowry murders are a consequence of the practice of endowing a bride with substantial wealth from her own family as a gift to her husband's family. Historically, it was practiced largely by upper-caste Hindus in northern India and the gifts were relatively small. It was part of a system in which women married higher-status men but still within their caste. In the last 30 years, however, the practice has spread throughout India, despite resistance and concern. Families promise dowry gifts to the groom's family in order to finalize the marriage. If there are disputes about the money, either because it is deemed to be insufficient or because it is withheld, the groom's family may threaten violence against the bride if her family does not fulfill its promises or acquiesce to ever-increasing demands. Dowry deaths, or dowry murders, are sometimes the unhappy consequence.

Before the women's movement, these deaths were regarded as private family affairs, ignored by the police. During the 1970s, however, feminists became concerned about a growing rash of murders of young women by burning. Often these women were standing in front of an open kerosene cooking stove when their sari caught fire. Whether this was accident, suicide, or murder as a result of a push by the husband or his family was often impossible to determine. Feminists showed that they were murders rather than suicides and part of dowry harassment (Kumar 1999 [1995]: 67). Women are sometimes murdered when their parents are unable or unwilling to meet the dowry demands of their husbands and their families (Karlekar 1999: 63). Despite official prohibition, the practice of giving dowry is on the increase and expanding from northern into southern India, where marriage was traditionally arranged within closer kin groups by the payment of bride price, or a gift from the groom's family to the bride's family (Kapadia 2002). It is also becoming more common among lower-caste, not just upper-caste families, fueled by the transition to a cash economy in which social status can be acquired through wealth as well as birth. The dowry payment, which has been a crucial boost for men in establishing themselves as small businessmen or in a trade or even to migrate, is therefore becoming more widespread and important rather than less (Butalia 2002: 214; Kapadia 2002). Activists campaigned for greater police intervention into dowry murders, the creation of dowry police cells, and laws shifting the burden of proof of dowry deaths. They challenged the assumption that such deaths were private affairs, under the authority of the husband, arguing instead that the state had a duty to intervene. Thus, the idea of opening up the domestic space to government scrutiny (fundamental to the US movement) paralleled this initiative.

A second major issue for the women's movement in India is rape, particularly police rape of women in custody. Police rape, landlord/employer rape, and rape of lower-caste women by upper-caste men are all common and widespread practices, although underreported (Kumar 1999 [1995]: 68–69; Butalia 2002: 208). As in many other parts of the world, including Fiji and the USA, the anti-rape movement began quite independently of the domestic violence movement. During the late 1970s, women's and community groups began to hold large rallies to protest the common practice of rape by the police (Kumar 1993: 129). Police rape took two forms: one was mass rape directed against a community or class group as part of a political struggle, while the other was the rape of individual women who were relatively powerless or marginal as an expression of the seigneurial right of the police. Public attention was galvanized in 1979 when the Supreme Court of India acquitted the police officers who in 1972 had raped a young tribal woman, Mathura, then 16 or 17 years old, while she was in police custody (Kumar 1999 [1995]: 69–70; for a full account, see Baxi 2004: 281–286). Her brother had filed a criminal complaint against her lover on the charge of abduction, and she and her brother and lover were brought to the police station at 9 p.m. to record her statement. When she failed to reappear, a crowd gathered outside the police station, including her lover and brother. When the crowd found out that she had been raped by police officers, they insisted that her complaint be registered. A medical test (the ease of inserting two fingers into the vagina) showed she was "habituated to sexual intercourse." The lower court judge acquitted the policemen and accused her of being a "shocking liar."

The Bombay High Court reversed the acquittal and argued that lack of injury did not mean consent. The police officers appealed to the Supreme Court of India, which acquitted the two policemen in 1979, arguing that Mathura did not raise an alarm and meekly submitted, indicating her consent. The defense argued that Mathura had a boyfriend and was therefore a "loose" woman and could not be raped (Kumar 1999 [1995]: 70). Outraged at this judgment, four professors of law composed an open letter to the Chief Justice criticizing the judges' interpretation that this custodial rape was based on consent and accused the Supreme Court of offering legal help only to affluent urban and educated women. The letter was published widely throughout India. The overwhelming response to it included the formation of the Forum against Rape in Bombay, an important beginning for the autonomous women's movement, and many demonstrations and rallies by women's groups, some outside the Supreme Court in Delhi. Although the women's organizations filed a petition for review, the court decided that they had no standing and acquitted the police officers (Baxi 2004: 281–286).

However, this issue and the attention it received energized women's groups to conduct a major anti-rape campaign from 1980 to 1983, with mass demonstrations in several cities (Kumar 1993: 130). Rape became defined as an act of power, a mechanism through which patriarchy maintains its control over women rather than the action of a perverted individual (Baxi 2004: 4–5). The movement emphasized the complicity of the courts as a place where rape is redefined as consensual sex. In response to these demands, the rape law was amended in 1983 for the first time since 1860. Women's groups have continued to campaign for further reforms of the rape laws in the last two decades, including expanding the definition of rape from penile penetration of the vagina to other forms of penetration and abuse and including marital rape. They have also focused on challenging norms that treat rape survivors as stigmatized (Baxi 2004: 6–7).

The Indian women's movement has also promoted the elimination of *sati*, or widow immolation. Although it is very rarely practiced now, a celebrated case in 1987 in the state of Rajasthan reflected revived political support for the custom among certain groups. An 18-year-old woman, Roop Kanwar, who had been married for eight months, was apparently forced to jump on her husband's funeral pyre and burnt alive as thousands of supporters watched, seeing her death as a sacred act that brought honor to her family (Mathur 2004: 171–174). However, this event set off a major regional and national protest by women's groups and led to the passage of state and national laws in 1988 prohibiting *sati* and providing stringent punishment for aiding and abetting the act.

During the 1980s, the women's movement established centers to provide women with legal aid, health care, and counseling. It branched out into a wide range of issues such as employment generation and slum improvement work. At the end of the twentieth century, the movement addressed such varied problems as work, wages, environment, ecology, civil rights, sex, violence, representation, caste, class, allocation of basic resources, consumer rights, health, religion, community, and individual and social relationships (Kumar 1999 [1995]: 75–83). More recently, women's groups have focused on the increasingly prevalent practice of female feticide and infanticide, in which families preferring sons abort or fail to nurture daughters. The 2001 census revealed 967 girls to every 1,000 boys in the 0–6 age group. As sex ratios plummeted in the early twenty-first century, women's groups talked about the number of "missing women" and campaigned against the practice of killing girl fetuses, which they referred to as "sex selection."

Until 2006, domestic violence was covered by the Indian Penal Code Section 498A which defined it as cruelty by a husband or his relatives to his wife (Lawyers' Collective 1992: 36). This law, passed in 1983, was the "first time the crime of violence specifically against a woman by her husband was recognized in law" according to a legal aid handbook (Lawyers' Collective 1992: 36). Until recently, the term "cruelty" was used instead of "domestic violence." The latter term is now becoming far more widespread and the number of complaints has increased dramatically. A police officer I interviewed in Delhi in 2001 who handles domestic violence cases said that under section 498A, the sentence is a fine plus up to three years in prison, and some men actually do go to jail. In 2006 India passed a new law targeting domestic violence as a crime and creating the victim's right to stay in the marital home. It focused on emergency protection orders and created a system of civil protective officers. According to this law, domestic violence includes sexual, verbal, and economic as well as physical abuse. It took six years of activism and mobilization by the Indian women's movement to frame this law and get it passed.

Dowry murders continue to be a serious concern for the women's movement (Karlekar 1999: 63–64). Quarrels over dowry gifts often last years into the marriage, contributing to abuse of the woman and possibly murder. The Dowry Prohibition Act of 1961 made asking for dowry illegal, while amendments in 1984 and 1986 provided stringent punishments for giving and taking dowry (Poonacha and Pandey 1999: 179). A law passed in 1980 required a police investigation into the death of any woman within five years of marriage while more recent laws allow the courts to draw inferences about whether others in the family have contributed to apparent suicides. According to an amendment to the Indian Evidence Act, if a woman commits suicide within seven years of the date of her marriage and her husband or husband's relatives have subjected her to cruelty, the court may presume that the suicide was abetted by the husband or his family, and if a woman dies within seven years of marriage and she has experienced cruelty, her husband and relatives are assumed guilty unless it is proven otherwise (Lawyers' Collective 1992: 41; Jethmalani 2001: 60–61). Nevertheless, it is still hard to prosecute dowry deaths and the practice continues (Kumar 1999 [1995]: 67–68).

In order to handle these cases, special police stations focused on dowry conflicts were established starting in 1989 in Bangalore as a branch of the detective units (Poonacha and Pandey 1999: 76–77) and since 1983 in Delhi (interview, Special Cell, 2001). Each of the nine police districts of Delhi has such a cell. Special police stations tend to reconcile couples rather than punishing violence. One problem with the focus on dowry as the cause of violence is that police officers tend to assume that all marital fights and injuries are about economic issues and try to settle these cases in terms of money rather than morality.

By the 1990s and 2000s, the women's movement faced a growing backlash, the rise of a nationalist Hindu right-wing political movement, and the eruption of ethno-religious conflict within the country and on its northeastern and northwestern borders. Politicians of the right seeking to develop a Hindu-based nationalism and inflame communal tensions used women's issues to support these agendas. Feminists found that some of their key demands, such as a secular uniform civil code for laws governing family relationships, were used to condemn Muslim family law as retrograde in comparison with Hindu family law. As increasing communal tensions led to outbreaks of violence between Hindu and Muslim religious groups in the 1990s and 2000s, women's groups highlighted the use of rape and violence against women in the riots (International Initiative for Justice in Gujarat 2003; see Chapter 7). Thus, the movement is continually taking on new challenges, new forms of violence against women, and new issues. It does not act as a unitary body and faces multiple internal divisions, but is nevertheless vibrant and engaged. It has a long history of tackling the problem of violence against women in domains such as the family, the kinship system, the political system, structures of class and caste inequality, and communal violence. This movement is connected to feminist movements around the world but has developed in particular ways as a result of India's history of British colonialism, its anticolonial struggles, Gandhian self-help, and socialism as well as its distinctive religious and kinship systems.

## China

The contemporary women's movement in China grew out of urban men and women's demands for gender equality in the 1920s and 1930s. Throughout the period leading up to the 1949 revolution, nationalism and anti-imperialism were inextricably connected to the movement for gender equality (Zhang 1995: 28–29). Most leaders were men seeking to mobilize women to achieve military victory for the communists, and women's rights were a by-product of the socialist revolution. In the early years, it was men rather than women who fought for women's rights.

After the revolution and the founding of the People's Republic of China in 1949, the Constitution stated that Chinese women "enjoy equal rights with men in all spheres of life, political, economic, cultural social, including family life" (Wang 1999: 13). The policy of gender equality was fundamental to the New China established by the Chinese Communist Party (Hecht 1998: 72). Reforming family laws was a central concern of the new government, and in 1950 the new Marriage Law represented a dramatic turning point in the conception of women's family roles, attacking "feudal" elements of marriage such as forced marriage and bride price. Early post-revolutionary efforts to improve women's roles, collectivize domestic labor, and get women into the labor force substantially improved women's position, but efforts to transform women's roles stalled as the government confronted opposition from poor peasant men and the demands of socialist transformation took center stage. By the late 1950s the government declared that the socialist transition was complete and that equality between men and women had been achieved (Croll 1978; Johnson 1983; Zhang 1995: 31). In the subsequent years of the Great Leap Forward (1958–1960) and the Cultural Revolution (1966–1976), women's struggle was submerged by the class struggle.

Since the economic reforms and move toward privatization in 1978, China has experienced rapid economic and social change and an increasing openness to international ideas. A new women's movement has emerged, inspired by a more open, liberal, and pluralistic environment, more access to Western ideas, a revival of academic studies, and a greater freedom to form new networks and groups (Zhang 1995: 34). The 1980s and 1990s witnessed the growth of women's NGOs in cities, a women's press, women's studies as an academic discipline, and some increases in women's political representation. However, the shift to a more capitalist economy and the closing of many state-owned enterprises has hurt women's economic status, as they are often the first fired and last hired and are forced to retire at younger ages than their husbands. The disruption of economic relationships and kinship ties caused by these economic upheavals and the migration of many poor peasants to the more affluent cities has probably increased the levels of violence women experience in the home. Studies show that unemployed women tend to be victims of domestic violence more than employed women (Wang 1999: 26). Human rights groups claim that the one-child policy, instituted in 1979, has produced forced sterilizations and abortions, kidnapping of women, and forced marriages (Human Rights in China 1995). As in India, the preference for sons in China has meant that it also faces a severe shortage of young women.

In 1980 China ratified the Women's Convention – the Convention on the Elimination of all Forms of Discrimination against Women (CEDAW) – and in 1992 it passed a sweeping law protecting women's rights and interests. This law, created through three years of investigation and refinement, was intended to bring CEDAW principles into Chinese law (Hecht 1998: 72–74). It clearly articulates a policy of gender equality, but it specifies that men and women should be treated equally rather than that their conditions of life or social status should be equal. The law protects women's bodily integrity and contains considerable protective legislation for the workplace which emphasizes women's biological differences and the need to protect pregnant women (Hecht 1998: 76–77). However, it does not define discrimination or provide an enforcement mechanism (Human Rights in China 1998: 13). It prohibits violence and abuse against women, but does not specifically mention violence in the family, nor are remedies provided. Instead, the language is abstract and general. Although the implementation of this law was not spelled out, it has great symbolic significance (Zhang 1995: 34).

The All-China Women's Federation, founded in 1949 as a mass organization to mobilize and represent women's interests, serves to interpret and implement state policy on women. It has no administrative or legislative power, but relies on hundreds of thousands of grass-roots activists. It is a mass governmental organization representing women's interests and the main organization protecting women's rights and providing legal aid. Abolished in 1966, it was rehabilitated in 1978 to play a major role in solving China's social problems. In the early 1980s it launched a major campaign to protect the rights and interests of Chinese women and children (Zhang 1995: 30–34). In 1983 Rights Departments were established within every Women's Federation branch down to the county level (Hecht 1998: 79). Although it represents the interests of the state as well as of women, it is still the place to which many women turn for help outside the family. The Federation receives complaints from individual women, a large proportion of which concern violence in the family. In the late 1990s in one district, for example, 41 percent of complaints concerned domestic violence (Wang 1999: 24) and by 2002, in some areas 57 percent of complaints to the Women's Federation concerned violence (Guo 2005: 50).

Because women in China have relatively high status, domestic violence was not seen as a serious social issue until the mid-1990s (Wang 1999: 13). Until then, government and public awareness of the problem had been very limited (HRIC 1995: 25). As late as 1990, the government was able to deny that it was a problem in China (see Liu and Chan 1999; 2000). It was viewed as a traditional practice, largely outside the concern of police officers and state judicial institutions. Given China's long history of patrilineal, patrilocal kin groups in which senior males exercised authority over the family, male superiority and female inferiority were taken for granted. The family was seen as a hierarchical structure with male authority and female obedience. Individual rights were subordinated to family duties and national interests.

The World Conference on Women held in Beijing in 1995 had an electrifying effect on women in China, however, spawning a number of independent women's groups working on a range of issues, including violence against women. It mobilized public concern about violence against women and led to the development of women's hotlines, legal services clinics, and counseling centers in urban areas. News media contributed to this explosion of interest. For example, in 1996 the China Women's News reported a case in which a 37-year-old woman who had been beaten by her husband for three years during their marriage was thrown to her death from a six-story building (Wang 1999: 16–17). He had beaten her black and blue with clubs, tongs, a kitchen knife, and a bicycle pump, but when she finally fled to her parents' home, he followed and fired at her, hitting her 85-year-old mother as she tried to protect her. He then grabbed her and threw her off the balcony. The incident initiated a discussion in the *China Women's News* about the problem of domestic violence and how to deal with it. Newspapers in other cities and provinces joined in. It gradually became clear that domestic violence was not simply a matter of a few isolated incidents but was a serious social problem. A series of surveys by scholars and the Women's Federation in the 1990s provided evidence that wife battering was widespread and common. In 1990 almost 30 percent of women in a national survey said that they had some experience of beating by their husbands (Wang 1999: 14).

Since 2000 governmental and nongovernmental organizations have paid more attention to this issue, but institutional support has grown only slowly. Hotlines and complaint mechanisms are well established in China, and the number dealing with domestic violence has grown. A few shelters have been created but fail to last because of lack of resources, whereas in tiny Hong Kong there were four operating shelters by 2002. A report on police effectiveness at a domestic violence conference in Beijing in 2002 said that neither the police nor the public is aware of the problem and that the police are often reluctant to intervene. Even many women police officers think the anti-domestic violence movement is too "feminist" (Rong 2002). A long-time employee of the Women's Federation who handles complaint cases for women told me in 2005 that she was not a feminist but just wanted to help women. In the rural areas, the All-China Women's Federation (ACWF) still provides one of the few places of recourse beyond a woman's family, yet interventions often encourage women to go along with their situation rather than attempt to leave their abusers.

The revised Marriage Law of 2001 prohibits domestic violence but does not define it or specify any mechanisms for preventing or punishing it. Some worry that the law does not expand the concept beyond hitting to threats and mental and sexual abuse (Wang Xingjuan, *China Women's News*, November 16, 2000, trans. Wei-Ying Lin). Since it is civil law, it does not delineate punishments, but offers the victim mediation and the opportunity to press criminal liability claims (Article 43, trans. Wei-Ying Lin). The victim has the right to bring a lawsuit to the people's court. The public security division will carry out the investigation and the people's court will bring the lawsuit (Article 45). Despite the efforts of activists, the law does not include provision for a protection order and it requires the victim to take the initiative in going to the law. Nevertheless, a 2000 survey of ten provinces and cities by the ACWF reported that 96 percent of respondents thought this revised Marriage Law should include regulations on domestic violence (*China Women's News*, August 3, 2000, trans. Wei-Ying Lin) and activists think that it is very important that this law at least names domestic violence as a problem rather than as a necessary form of discipline.

Between 2000 and 2002, a Domestic Violence Research and Intervention Project (DVRIP) run by the China Law Society in Beijing engaged in major research and intervention initiatives concerning violence against women. Funded by the Ford Foundation, NOVIB of Holland, SIDA of Sweden, and the Human Rights Center of Oslo University in Norway (DVRIP newsletter, 2, October 2000, typescript), it culminated in the first international conference on violence against women held in Beijing in 2002 and a report in 2005 (Huang and Rong 2005). At the final session of the 2002 conference, the chair presented a draft bill on domestic violence prepared by the research team. The team worked intensively for two years and consulted domestic violence laws collected from 40 countries (Huang and Rong 2005: 281–284). Many of the conference participants expressed the need for a strong and effective domestic violence law in China. Despite the efforts of the women's movement, however, as of 2006, a national law governing domestic violence has not yet been passed.

Cases of domestic violence are handled in court, but they pose dilemmas for victims. The DVRIP reported some of its research findings on the legal situation of domestic violence victims in its third newsletter. In a typical case reported in 2003, a woman who had been severely injured by her husband had great difficulty getting help from the police and the courts (Qi 2003: 172–176). In this case, a new NGO established after the 1995 World Conference, the Center for Women's Law Studies and Legal Aid of Beijing University in Beijing, played a critical role in helping the victim get redress from the legal system. In 1998 a 35-year-old woman, Zhang, described as a farmer from Beijing, quarreled with her husband of ten years, Wang. He "flew into a fury" and poured gasoline on her body and set fire to her, seriously wounding her. Her sister tried to report this to the local police station, but the police refused to respond, saying that it was a family conflict. The Center decided to help, but its lawyers confronted many difficulties using the legal system. In order to file the case, they had to provide a forensic authentication of the injury, and to apply for this authentication, the victim needed a written authorization by the police station or the court. The police station refused to provide this and the court could not before the case began. After getting evidence from the hospital, the Center's lawyers went to the Women's Federation of the district and asked them to help obtain forensic authorization, an unusual procedure. They agreed, and with this authentication the lawyers returned to the police station and had Wang placed into custody.

At the same time, they instituted a civil case for financial loss of medical costs, loss of work, costs of cosmetic surgery, and subsidy for the injury and disability. The judge asked Zhang's sister to withdraw the civil proceeding, which she did, not understanding the law. At the trial, the judge thought that, since Zhang had not initiated divorce proceedings, the property of both was held in common and could not be divided. However, with much negotiation, the attorney persuaded the judge that the man should pay from any property he owned alone and that if he had none, he should pay from his part of the property which should be recognized at the time of divorce. The judge acquiesced, and Wang was sentenced to 15 years in prison and to pay compensation of 80,000 yuan. This outcome required great effort by the attorneys at the Center, however and, according to the judge, was the first time that a court had made a judgment compensating a wife for her financial losses. Clearly, the legal system in China needs further reform, although there are important movements in this direction such as the Center and the support of the Women's Federation.

Another case shows the difficulties of criminal prosecution (Qi 2003: 181–185). According to the present laws, the relevant criminal charges are intentional injury or abuse. The first charge requires that the woman have at least a flesh wound and call the police in time, and that the police provide her with written authorization for forensic authentication. Yet women are often reluctant to call the police and, as we saw above, the police often do not respond. Abuse requires "evil circumstances" which means regular, continuous, and consistent maltreatment with "wicked means." Li, a 49-year-old woman was a college graduate, married to Zhang for 21 years. He began to beat her just after they were married, and frequently intimidated, cursed, and beat her, damaging her eyesight and breaking two of her ribs. She became depressed and contemplated suicide, but also tried to preserve her family by putting up with the violence. Her husband applied for divorce, however, removed the family property, and moved out of the house. When the judge refused the divorce, he filed again.

Li then began criminal prosecution of Zhang for intentional injury and sued civilly for compensation. The court refused to accept the case for lack of evidence, and Li appealed. The divorce petition was granted during this process. The county court denied the criminal charge, finding that there had only been ten incidents of beating over 20 years of marriage and that it was not regular, continuous, and consistent, and that there was a good reason for it. The accused had no intention of abusing his wife, and therefore this did not constitute abuse. Nor were medical expenses paid because the property was joint, and had been divided by divorce. Li appealed this decision to a higher court, which determined that there had been 13 incidents of abuse but still considered that they were not regular, continuous, and consistent. Although the Center's attorney helped Li appeal to higher courts, the case is still pending. Despite her considerable injuries, under the existing law Li's husband was not found guilty.

In some cases, women as well as men do not support the efforts of battered women to prosecute their attackers. The newsletter of the DVRIP project describes a case observed in the appeal court in Tianjin in 2000 (Wang 2001). The court of first instance had already decided in favor of the battered woman, a 26-year-old housewife married to a young peasant living in Tianjin City for almost two years. She was said to be battered by her husband because she had been slow in caring for her ill mother-in-law. She filed a criminal suit and a civil claim against her husband in the Jing County People's Court with a private prosecutor. Forensic evidence confirmed that she had a fractured rib, and the court convicted the husband for ten months' imprisonment with one year's probation and a fine of 2,000 yuan for medical expenses, damage compensation to the plaintiff, and a lawsuit fee. The husband appealed the judgment. He claimed he had not beaten his wife's chest and caused the fracture. The case was the first heard in the Domestic Violence Criminal Collegiate Tribunal since its establishment within the intermediate court. A legal aid agency lawyer was appointed for the husband and the Tianjin Women's Federation recommended two lawyers from its affiliated law firms for the wife.

The appeal was witnessed by over 100 visitors including family members, women's federation leaders, judicial administrative officials, and law school students and was broadcast live by Tianjin television. The court upheld the earlier judgment. The woman was successful because her husband confessed that he had beaten his wife and the village clinic doctor and other villagers testified to the violence. Finding witnesses willing to testify would have been far more difficult in a city. The audience had some sympathy for the man, however. An older woman said, "I found the woman too aggressive and deserves beating. The husband looks really pitiable!" Even though the woman won the appeal, the fine will probably be paid out of family resources, which are jointly owned by husband and wife, so that he will use part of his wife's property to pay for the damage he has inflicted on her. Wang, the author of the newsletter article, concludes that there are still problems in the legal resolution of domestic violence cases (Wang 2001: 4–6).

In the same newsletter, a lawyer who handles domestic violence cases in court notes the many difficulties battered women face in court: a lack of concern by law enforcement officers in comparison to other criminal cases, a lack of effort by police and court to gather evidence, and an unwillingness on the part of other family members, neighbors, friends, workmates, and relatives to serve as witnesses. They may be afraid of the perpetrator or reluctant to interfere in other families' business.

Even brothers and sisters of the abused woman may feel intervention is inappropriate (Liu Donghua 2001: 6–7).

Activists in China are currently examining programs for dealing with domestic violence in other countries and relying on the social science literature produced in North America for its theoretical framework (see Liu Meng 2001: 8–9). However, they are seeking to develop an approach with Chinese characteristics. The leaders of DVRIP as well as other domestic violence activists want to develop a Chinese model of violence against women, more kin-based and less focused on spouses and romantic/sexual relationships than are Western models (see Li 2000: 75). Because Chinese families are typically three-generational, violence is not restricted to husband/wife battering but occurs among a variety of relatives and often against elderly parents or children. In rural areas, the husband's family is very important, and if a woman sues her husband she risks alienating his entire family, with whom she lives and works. She has often lost ties with her natal family and has no place to go if she leaves her husband's family.

These family conditions affect patterns of violence and forms of intervention, making recourse to shelters or the use of restraining orders very difficult. Instead, domestic violence intervention programs focus on raising awareness among the police about their responsibility for domestic violence and working with local hospitals and women's federation workers (Huang and Rong 2005). A Beijing NGO, the Maple Women's Psychological Counseling Center, recommended strengthening the Peoples' Mediating Committees to prevent and halt domestic violence since they are a mass organization with a long history and are spread all over China (China Working Group against Domestic Violence 2000: 9). People's mediation committees numbered over 1 million by the early 1990s and handled over 2 million marriage and family disputes in 1995 (Wang 1995: 34–35). There are also neighborhood committees made up of retired people and chosen by the party. Sometimes these committees get involved in domestic violence. The work unit, or *danwei*, exercises considerable authority over the work, housing, and family lives of workers. However, most local organizations do not view domestic violence as a problem that is their responsibility.

In sum, even though the movement for women's equality has a long history in China, the idea that domestic violence is a social problem is relatively new. It was inspired to a significant degree by the growing international movement against violence against women. The Beijing Conference and international funding have supported the efforts of Chinese feminists to develop indigenous Chinese approaches and mechanisms to deal with the problem. Segments of the ACWF are addressing the problem more seriously, and the government is beginning to acknowledge the problem. Recourse to the law is still very difficult, however, and battered women face serious barriers to winning protection from the courts. Although urban middle-class women are less subject to patriarchal family structures, they now face new difficulties as a result of economic changes that have raised women's rate of unemployment. The idea that gender-based violence is a social problem is clearly becoming more widespread, however, and there are important new initiatives taking place. As in India, transnational influences have been important in raising awareness of the problem, but it has been the activities of a national women's movement grappling with specific national issues, such as dowry in India and what are called "feudal" marriage practices in China such as child marriage and the prohibition on divorce, that have adopted and carried forward the international ideas. And in both countries, activists have turned to public awareness campaigns and reforms of the law.

## USA

In the United States, gender violence emerged as a social issue in the 1970s and 1980s under both domestic and international influences. Both the 1960s civil rights movements and transnational socialism and Maoism contributed to the emergence of the women's liberation movement. The four world conferences on women organized by the UN in 1975, 1980, 1985, and 1995 had powerful effects in the USA as in India and China. As with the situations in India and China, gender violence was generally ignored in the nineteenth and early twentieth centuries. There were intermittent demands for punishment in the last third of the nineteenth century, including a movement to impose flogging on batterers (Pleck 1987; see also Gordon 2002 [1988]). Child abuse and woman abuse elicited periodic concern, but intervention was inhibited by conceptions of coverture: the legal construction of the family as an enclosed unit under the authority and control of the husband/father, much as notions of the private patriarchal family inhibited intervention in China and India.

One of the earliest efforts to confront the problem was in the late nineteenth century, when the temperance movement focused on the evils of the drunken brute who beat his wife (Pleck 1987). Much of the campaigning against wife battering joined with that of the social purity and temperance movements (Gordon 2002 [1988]; Valverde 1998; Hunt 1999). These movements sought to strengthen the family in which men were heads of the household but were not violent. "The new bourgeois norms of masculinity required self-control, containment, rule through authority – i.e. symbolic force – which required no violence to impose itself" (Gordon 2002 [1988]: 255). By the turn of the century, the problem had again lapsed into invisibility (Pleck 1987). Wife battering was made illegal in most states by 1870, but it was not prosecuted seriously until the 1970s. After 1890 the problem virtually disappeared from public view (Pleck 1987).

However, the courts did intervene with domestic violence cases in the nineteenth century. For example, in the second half of the nineteenth century Hawai'i, an independent kingdom with an American legal system, judges heard a substantial number of cases of domestic violence (Merry 2002). In 1853 a court heard the following case in which a white man was accused of assault and battery on his Hawaiian wife the day before (Hawai'i State Archives, Honolulu). The court records, written in English by an American judge working for the Kingdom of Hawai'i, report:

> Hulu testified that he heard the defendant's wife crying and looked into the house and saw defendant beating her and kicking her. Defendant drove Hulu away. Defendant was holding wife down and trampling her with his feet; her forehead was bleeding.

Hulu had not heard them fighting but had heard the sound of blows and the defendant's wife crying murder.

Apukaia heard the wife crying out she was being killed and heard the blows. The fight was still going on when the other witnesses reached the door. Deft. then drove the woman off. Saw the blood on her forehead.

Holokahiki (wife of deft.) testified that she came home from church and the deft. came home to change clothes and intended to go to one of the eating houses. Foreigners came to the house and they went off. When the husband returned he asked Holokahiki if Makina had been there during his absence and wife told him no, but the husband insisted he (Makina) had been there. Husband left and wife said she left soon after. Deft. returned and again made the accusation that Makina had been there and again she denied it. She then described how deft. beat and kicked her as two women witnesses had testified. She said she's still weak and in pain from being beaten.

Deft. admits kicking his wife and pushing her against the wall and that the bruises on her head were the result of that punch.

Deft. is fined $30 or in default imprisoned until paid.

This is a very high fine for assault, but the defendant Smith had been to court for another assault earlier in the year. The courts in this town typically prosecuted domestic violence cases the day after they occurred and generally imposed fines of about $6 (Merry 2000).

Research on the court records of this town, as well as other studies of nineteenth-century records in Boston (Gordon 2002 [1988]), Philadelphia (Steinberg 1989) and Ottawa (Backhouse 1991) indicate that battery and rape were common and were often prosecuted as rape or assault. These cases typically came from the working class and the poor, while wealthier people managed to escape court scrutiny. Even when abuse occurred in wealthy families, it rarely made it to court (Hartog 2000). Thus, despite the existence of legal penalties and convictions, because social class affected which cases were taken to the police and courts, it appeared that only the poor and the drunkards were guilty. As late as the 1970s, violence in domestic relationships was generally understood as unfortunate but a matter of lifestyle or alcoholism (Field and Field 1973).

My own interviews with a variety of older people from many ethnic backgrounds in Hawai'i confirm that, in the past, family violence was very common and generally ignored by neighbors and other adults. For example, one woman born in 1926 of Portuguese ancestry who grew up as a worker on a sugar plantation said that when she was young, nobody talked about men hitting women, although it was common. Mothers told their daughters, "You made your bed, now you lie on it," and "If a woman leaves her husband, it is big gossip." When I asked, "Why do men hit their wives?" she replied, "Some men are just vicious, just jump on their wives." During this period, she said that about half the plantation overseers were violent and hit workers, but again nobody complained. Kids did not get into trouble because if they did their parents hit them with the buckle end of a belt or a guava switch which, she said, hurts! "You could go to school black and blue from your parents hitting you," she said, "and nobody said anything." I asked her how the kids turned out, and she said fine.

It was not until the feminist movement of the 1970s that public consciousness of wife beating as a problem was rekindled (Schechter 1982). This movement focused first on rape and then on violence against women. It defined gender violence as a systemic, cultural problem instead of one of drunk husbands or poverty. The socialist-feminist activists developed the radical perspective that this behavior was central to the processes of subordination that all women experienced (Schechter 1982). Violence was one of the critical mechanisms for maintaining the universal subordination of women. Therefore, violence and rape are problems for every woman, not just the poor. The movement promoted the theory that men batter because they can and that battery and rape are acts of power and control.

The feminist movement challenged the idea that the family was a private sphere under the control of husbands who had the right to rape their wives and to use violence as a form of discipline. Wife beating was already a crime under the categories of rape, assault, and murder, yet in the absence of social movements, these crimes had been lightly prosecuted and marginally punished. They were all treated by police and courts as less serious if they took place within the family. Using the notion of the personal as political, feminists struggled to extract this form of violence from its protected space in the family and open it to public scrutiny as a crime warranting the intervention of the state (see Schneider 1994). They argued that physical and sexual violence in the family and outside of it both contributed to women's subordination. Like movements in other countries, the US violence against women movement focused on changes in public awareness and in the law. It pressed for greater attention to the problem by the police and courts and worked to develop more stringent laws and penalties for these forms of violence. They also challenged police inaction and willingness to mediate such conflicts rather than arresting the perpetrator.

Because many of the early activists began from socialist-feminist critiques of American society, they emphasized approaches which were egalitarian and community-based. They began opening women's centers and shelters to provide safety for victims of violence. The first shelters opened in the 1970s and were often run as collectives, staffed by formerly battered women. They were resistant to hierarchy and professionalization. The shelters focused on helping women develop independent lives away from their batterers. They tended to be socially homogeneous, however, not open to people of varying ethnic backgrounds, language skills, and sexual orientations. They encouraged battered women to leave their spouses rather than working through the relationship, viewing those women who resisted as troublemakers (Ferraro 1983). By the early 1980s, many groups opened women's centers that offered legal assistance and counseling to help victims use the legal system.

Over time, however, government support became increasingly important to maintain shelters, and they gradually became more professionally staffed and more hierarchical. The focus on empowerment and sisterhood gave way to a greater emphasis on providing services and legal advice to women. Although there is still a strong feminist current to the movement against sexual violence, there are also psychological approaches engaged in research and counseling to understand and ameliorate what are defined as family violence problems. Such approaches look both toward the psychological features of those who use violence against their partners and at the dynamics of family interactions. Interventions focus on teaching mechanisms of managing violence and improving relationships rather than changing society. This research has demonstrated the deleterious effects on children of witnessing violence in the home, leading to efforts to remove children from families that refuse to separate despite the violence.

While socialist-feminist groups were eager to transform society as a whole, liberal feminists focused on protecting the rights of victims of violence through legal reform. They sought stronger laws and more effective intervention. As battered women and their advocates tried to use the courts, they discovered that police typically asked batterers to take a short walk to cool down, prosecutors rarely pressed charges, and judges imposed lenient penalties. During the early 1980s, an experiment in policing domestic violence indicated that recidivism rates were lower when police arrested batterers (Sherman and Berk 1984). Activists worked to establish mandatory arrest programs for police and by the early 1990s, advocated no-drop prosecution policies (Hanna 1996). Penalties for violations were increased significantly. These efforts improved the likelihood of arrest and prosecution, but penalties are still relatively light. Significant police training has improved intervention, yet many still fail to take the offense seriously.

Although the battered women's and rape movements emphasized criminalization, by the mid 1980s there was growing interest in civil protective orders as well (Schechter 1982; Fischer and Rose 1995; Ptacek 1999; Schneider 2000). These orders are typically called temporary restraining orders. They may be no-contact orders that require the batterer to stay away from his/her victim or contact orders that require the abuser to refrain from using violence against a person. Since these are civil orders, they do not have criminal penalties, but those who violate restraining orders are subject to criminal penalties, at least in theory. They are often used in conjunction with a variety of anger management, violence control, or batterer treatment programs and support groups. In my research in a small town in Hawai'i, I found that a woman getting a contact restraining order can still have contact with her violent partner, but he will probably be required to attend a psycho-educational violence control program (1995a; 1995b). If he fails to attend or violates the order, he will usually be sent back to the program but could be criminally prosecuted. Many battered women I talked to in Hawai'i did not want criminal penalties imposed on their partners but preferred to get a protective order and send them to a program that tries to train them not to be violent. Training programs focused on teaching batterers to manage their anger and avoid violence, and support groups for those who are battered became increasingly important to the treatment of domestic violence during the 1990s (see Anderson and Umberson 2001; Merry 1995b). Whether this is an effective approach is still unclear, but for many who experience violence, it promises what they are looking for: a way to maintain the relationship without violence.

In recent years, there has been an expansion in the forms of gender violence considered by social movements. Sexual harassment and teen-dating violence have emerged as major new concerns. Studies have highlighted violence in fraternities, in military hazing, in torture practices, and in prisons. The role of violence in US conquest and in the treatment of indigenous peoples, as well as the violence of colonialism, have received new attention (Smith 2005).

In a similar way to developments in India, the gender violence movement in the USA began under the leadership of middle-class, educated urban women but struggled to expand its framework to a more diverse population. African American women in particular were central to the early anti-rape movements, but have been insufficiently recognized for their contributions. As feminists shifted their analytic framework from sex to gender, essentialism to intersectionality, and roles to performance in their analytical frameworks, their conceptions of gender violence and forms of intervention broadened. As activists began to rethink gender as a performance rather than a biologically based distinction between two sexes, the bias toward heterosexual ways of thinking about violence became more obvious and fostered a broader understanding. Women of color began to contest the emphasis on a criminal justice approach to gender violence given the historically disproportionate incarceration of African American, Native American, and Latino men. In 2000 a major conference organized by women of color in Santa Cruz, California argued for a broader, more socially grounded approach. The conference was inspired in part by Angela Davis and her work on what she termed the prison-industrial complex. This conference spawned an organization, Incite!, which has subsequently held several conferences and published collections of writings, and has an active Internet presence (see INCITE! Women of Color against Violence 2006). Leaders of Incite! have recently targeted the role of funding organizations and nongovernmental organizations as inhibiting more radical social change (Incite! Women of Color against Violence 2007). Indian feminists confronted similar suspicions against police and advocated creating a new set of civil protective officers in their landmark domestic violence law rather than relying on the existing police forces.

Since the mid 1990s, the gender violence movement in the USA has started to incorporate a human rights framework, following developments elsewhere in the world. This framework focuses on the range of social, economic, and educational needs of victims of violence rather than only on punishment for the perpetrators (Schneider 2004). The turn to a human rights framework, inspired by American activists such as Dorothy Thomas and Charlotte Bunch has created deeper connections between the US movement and that of other countries around the world (Bunch 1990; Thomas and Beasley 1993). There is still resistance to applying the human rights framework domestically, led by neoconservatives in particular, but the US movement is growing nevertheless.

As in other parts of the world, the success of this movement has generated a backlash from more conservative groups that claim to stand for the family, such as some Christian social conservatives, and from political leaders who denigrate feminism and see the increasing power of women as a threat. There is some tendency to see domestic violence as a problem of the poor, as it has been in the past, rather than as a problem for all women or for all humans. While there is greater concern for violence in same-sex relationships, attention to the way violence serves to police homosexual gender performance has not developed significantly. The courts and police are far more effective than they were in the 1970s and earlier, but there is some concern about whether punishments are being imposed for minor forms of violence. Indeed, international activists, including Americans, worried that the 1995 Beijing Fourth World Conference on Women represented a high point of activism on the part of women and that subsequent conferences might lead to retrenchment from the accomplishments of that time. The Platform for Action written at the 1995 conference highlights gender-based violence as a key problem for women, suggesting its importance for activists around the world. Clearly, the developments in the USA were substantially influenced by events and theoretical developments in other countries and contributed in important ways to the global social movement.

## Conclusions

As the study of these social movements indicates, the concern with gender violence has developed along distinctive paths in different countries, responding to the particular difficulties victims of violence face and the texture of race/class/gender subordination in each. However, there have been significant cross-cutting influences both in conceptions of gender, violence, and gender violence and in modes of intervention. It is clear that the movement against gender violence is not an exclusively American or European phenomenon. While the law seems an ideal mode of intervening, it has significant limitations, as the activists in all these countries discovered. Nevertheless, it remains an essential ingredient in a social transformation that requires a broader attack on all forms of inequality and marginalization.

The next chapter describes the impact of this social movement on approaches to gender violence in the USA. Using a small town in Hawai'i as a case study, it examines a range of approaches to domestic violence commonly used in the USA. These approaches focus on punishment by police and courts; creating security through civil protective orders, safety counseling, and shelters; and reforming violent people through batterer intervention programs and women's support groups that encourage women to see themselves as having the right not to be hit. Each of these interventions depends on the others. Although they have not succeeded in ending gender violence in intimate relationships, they have clearly reshaped public attitudes toward its acceptability.

## Questions for Further Discussion

1   Consider the ways in which naming and framing the problem of gender violence affects a social movement. How does the name of a social movement shape the way problems are imagined and the kinds of remedies sought?

2   Compare feminist social movements in India, China, and the USA. When did activism begin in earnest in each place? How did the transition to a cash-based,

consumer economy affect women in India and China? Who participated in these movements, and how did they in turn define their movements' form and content? How did each country's distinctive history shape how gender and violence are conceived? Alternatively, what are some overlaps between these three examples?

3  Cite evidence from Chapter 2 to explain whether you think law is an effective mechanism for social change. Do you think law has helped or hindered activists' efforts?

## Video Suggestions

*Made In India*, by Patricia Plattner (Switzerland/India, 1998), 52 minutes

*Made in India* is a portrait of SEWA (Self-Employed Women's Association), a grassroots organization that asserts that women need organizing, not welfare. Headquartered in Ahmedabad, on the edge of the Gujarati desert, SEWA offers membership to over 217,000 self-employed women in the informal economy, many of whom are poor and illiterate. Inspired by the activism of Mahatma Gandhi, SEWA offers a vision of global feminism contoured by India's history, politics, and socio-economic conditions. The film illustrates that as women advocate for labor reform and access to banking and education they change gender and family dynamics too.

*Step by Step: Building a Feminist Movement, 1941–1977*, by Joyce Follet
(USA, 1998), 56 minutes

Though feminism as a social movement took root in earnest in the USA by the late 1960s, this film documents the players who in the 1940s and 1950s set the stage for action in their calls for equal pay and fair labor for women. Through archival footage, still photographs, and first-hand interviews, the film traces the lives of eight Midwestern women, six of whom became founders of the National Coalition for Women (NOW), and weaves into their stories decades of war, prosperity, and civil rights reform. We see from the front line how the women's movement changed over time to incorporate other issues, including gender violence and concerns of the gay and lesbian communities.

*Through Chinese Women's Eyes*, by Mayfair Yang (USA, 1997), 52 minutes

From state-sponsored feminism under Mao to the UN's Beijing Conference in 1995, this film presents the stunning transformation of gender in China. Through state propaganda, operatic performances, news footage, and advertisements, we learn about the historical memory and contemporary experiences of gender in Chinese women's own words. Academics, activists, public relations specialists, and common workers, among others, emphasize that Chinese feminism is by no means stable. Rather, the transition from a command to a market economy has formidably reordered gendered identities and the nature of Chinese activism.

# 3

# Punishment, Safety, and Reform: Interventions in Domestic Violence

Communities have always made efforts to control gender violence, usually through kin groups or community leaders. In recent decades, urbanization, migration, and the shift to cash-based economies have weakened these institutions. Law and government services are now more important. The social movements focused on gender violence developed three approaches, emphasizing punishment, safety, and reform. The first sought to punish the violator, the second to protect the victim, and the third to reform the violator and encourage the victim to recognize the violence as abuse. This chapter discusses these American efforts as well as similar projects in other countries.

The three approaches follow fundamentally different logics. Punishment seeks to deter violent acts through the authority of the law. Safety focuses on the victim, seeking to improve her life by separating her from her batterer. Reform programs endeavor to change batterers and their victims, to reshape the way both men and women understand and enact their gendered identities. They teach new ways of thinking about what it means to be a man or a woman. Women are taught that they have rights and men are told that hitting their partners is a crime.

The US movement initially focused on punishing perpetrators of violence and creating safe spaces for victims. They hoped that more severe punishments would deter violence. At the same time, they started hotlines and women's centers to teach women how to escape violent relationships and formed shelters to give them a place to go. The third approach, developed somewhat later, focused on reform and re-education. At the end of the 1970s, activists began to set up programs to teach angry people to control their violence. These programs were designed to teach batterers to treat their partners more equally and with greater respect. They endeavored to teach batterers to handle differences with their partners through negotiation rather than hitting. Emerge was the first psycho-educational program for men, formed in 1977. At the same time, women's centers started support groups to provide emotional support for women and to teach them that they have rights, including the right not to be hit no matter what they do.

This combination of strategies is a radical departure from past practices. Historically, punishment was the major form of intervention. For example, 150 years ago in the town of Hilo, Hawai'i, the courts simply imposed fines on wife batterers and exhorted husbands and wives to get along. There was no effort to teach the offender to control his violence or to rethink his ideas about masculine privilege. Rather than protecting a woman's safety by requiring him to stay away from her, courts insisted that she return to her violent husband. Women were never encouraged to leave their batterers and those who did were forced to return home or were thrown into prison if they refused. Preservation of the marriage was prized above all else, even when there was violence and fear (Merry 2002).

The present situation in Hilo is dramatically different. If a man hits his wife, she can call the police. They will arrive more or less promptly, and if there is clear evidence of violence, they will arrest him. At a court hearing, he can be required to attend a batterer intervention program for six months and to spend two nights in jail. If he refuses to go, he faces criminal charges. Instead of telling the wife she must strive to get along with him and forcing the couple to stay together, the court now requires the batterer to attend training sessions for violence and sends the victim to a support group that will help her to leave him. Instead of reinforcing male authority within the marriage, these interventions seek to diminish patriarchy. Thus, modern punishment is tied to a variety of social services and reform programs, while in the nineteenth century punishment stood alone. Survivors are now told they have rights, while in the nineteenth century they were only reminded of their responsibility to get along better.

This wide array of approaches to gender violence offers survivors much that punishment alone does not. Many survivors live in continual fear of their batterers and are more interested in the security provided by shelters or civil protective orders than they are in punishing their batterers. Many want their batterers to stop the violence but do not want to leave them. Yet, punishment is still the backstop. Shelters and restraining orders require punishment to keep batterers away, and batterers often refuse to go to therapeutic programs unless they are required to by threat of jail. In modern society, controlling social behavior through a combination of punishment, mechanisms to produce safety and security, and reform through therapy is common. This combination has been used for drug abuse, alcoholism, gambling, and other social problems (Feeley and Simon 1994; O'Malley 1999). A similar conjunction of approaches is becoming dominant in the global movement as well.

These new approaches require close collaboration with the police, courts, and social service agencies. Although the first initiatives against gender violence in Europe and North America were grass-roots, self-help efforts concerned with victim safety, activists soon recognized that they needed the resources of the government for shelters as well as for punishing violators. As the government began to fund NGOs and women's groups, however, changes occurred. Approaches to gender violence shifted from a radical critique of patriarchy, racism, and other forms of inequality to a more therapeutic stance that focused on helping individuals get along in their family and work lives but not on changing society. Gender violence was increasingly viewed as an aspect of family functioning.

This chapter discusses the three strategies and their interconnections. After outlining their general structure and the way they have been implemented in the USA and around the world, it describes how they work in Hilo, a small town in Hawai'i where I studied many dimensions of domestic violence interventions from 1991 to 2000. Although some features of Hawai'i are distinctive, the social programs and legal reforms parallel those of the rest of the USA. I studied family courts, criminal courts, women's support groups, and batterer intervention programs, interviewed participants and staff, prosecutors and judges, and community leaders. I analyzed the race, education, income, and social class of batterers and survivors in these programs.

## Punishment

Early in the battered women's movement, activists turned to the law as a strategy for eliminating violence, advocating tougher laws and more active policing, prosecution, and punishment (Schechter 1982). Before this, wife battering was often seen as a social problem for which the law was inadequate and inappropriate. In Europe and North America, the battered women's movement demanded that gender violence be taken more seriously as a crime. Using the notion of the personal as political, feminists struggled to extract this form of violence from its protected space in the family and open it to public scrutiny as a crime warranting the state's intervention (Schneider 1994). They demanded that wife battering be viewed as a serious criminal offense and that the courts take responsibility for punishing violators. In the 1970s some states, such as Hawai'i, passed laws specifically targeting violence against spouses. In the 1980s and 1990s, activists demanded that police routinely arrest offenders instead of just cooling them down and that prosecutors follow through with domestic violence cases instead of dropping them. Since the establishment of mandatory arrest and no-drop prosecution policies, the number of cases of domestic violence in courts has increased dramatically. For example, arrests in California for spousal assault jumped from 757 in 1981 to 60,279 in 1995, a sixtyfold per capita increase (Rosenbaum 1998: 412). After Denver's mandatory arrest policy was implemented in 1984, arrests increased tenfold in ten years (St. Joan 1997: 264). But offenders are rarely sentenced to prison. Instead, they are commonly required to attend some form of treatment, of which the dominant model is the feminist power/control model developed by women who experienced battering in Duluth, Minnesota (Hanna 1998). A 1995 study of 140 domestic violence arrests in 11 jurisdictions found that only 44 made it to conviction, plea, or acquittal and of these, only 16 served any time (Hanna 1998: 1523).

Criminalization was not only a principal demand of the battered women's movement in Europe and North America but also the dominant approach globally. In the USA, UK, and India, early efforts focused on developing new regulations criminalizing domestic violence and encouraging the police, judiciary, and prosecutors to take the crime of rape and assault in intimate relationships more seriously. This approach emphasized mandatory police arrest, no-drop prosecution policies, and statutory requirements for incarceration as well as treatment. Increased legal intervention means more sanctions for batterers as well as the creation of a new legal consciousness for both men and women. Women are encouraged to see themselves as endowed with rights not to be hit while men discover that their violent discipline of their wives is defined as criminal. The encounter with the new, sterner law transforms legal consciousness – the way the individual understands himself/herself with relationship to law – but does so differently for men and women.

But this transformation is diminished by the failure of the legal system to punish. The law promises victims of violence rights, but in practice often fails to arrest, to prosecute, and to punish. Although the contemporary intervention in gender violence represents a repudiation of conceptions of marriage based on coverture and male protection of women, at the same time the law continues to support husbandly and parental authority in other ways. Courts may fail to intervene effectively because they are too slow, judges do not take these problems seriously, or the laws are ineffective or non-existent, as Lazarus-Black shows in Trinidad (2007). Police are often corrupt, unavailable, or uninterested in protecting women from violence, as demonstrated by research in Vanuatu in the South Pacific (Mason 2000: 131–134). Studies from many parts of the world show how these laws are subverted by local court and police officials who fail to take the violence seriously or who favor reconciliation and keeping the family together over protecting the safety of the woman. This ambivalence undermines legal intervention and its capacity to criminalize sexual violence in families.

A case from Papua New Guinea illustrates the difficulties women face with courts that fail to take domestic violence seriously. They commonly seek to reconcile marriages and ignore the violence. In this case, a woman who earned the family income wanted to divorce her husband because of continuous harassment and violence at home and in her workplace (Garap 2000: 165–166). For two years, the court hearings proceeded erratically, with the village court viewing her complaint as a minor family matter. After her brother helped her, the court agreed to the separation if she repaid half of her bride price. During the protracted court proceeding, the husband continued to lock his wife in her office and prevent her from working until she "saw reason." The court awarded custody of the son to the father and gave his twin sister and baby brother to the mother. Since the custody agreement, however, the father has punished the son still living with him severely for minor infractions. Once, after staying with his mother for a week, the son resisted going back with his father and hung onto his mother. "The mother and child were taken to the police station so that the police on duty would assist in getting the son to go with his father. The boy refused and the mother and child were kept at the police station from 4:30–7:30 p.m. It was clear that the police officers concerned were unaware of the Child Rights Convention [the international treaty that articulates the human rights of children]" (Garap 2000: 166). The mother subsequently got a court order prohibiting her husband from verbally or physically abusing her on pain of six months in jail, which seems to have helped.

Batterers often receive relatively light punishment and frequently escape any legal responsibility for their battering. The law criminalizes and disciplines batterers most stringently when they are poor or minorities. Rich white males, or wealthy men of dominant kin groups typically escape penalties. Not surprisingly, the law is most effective when batterers closely resemble the criminal population in terms of race, class, and gender identities. Since people of color and indigenous people are already disproportionately policed and incarcerated, women who call the police for help against men of these groups further criminalize their communities (Davis 2001; Smith 2005). Thus, progressive efforts to protect women from violence succeed in transforming their consciousness of rights but at the same time focus on poor men while batterers with more resources escape. Poor women win greater control over their lives, but at the price of criminalizing the men in their community.

Thus, the law occupies a complex place in its interventions into gender violence, acting in different ways according to particular race/class/gender groupings as well as colonial histories and postcolonial presents. Over time, it has redefined the boundary between acceptable and unacceptable violence and encouraged a flood of pleas for help from battered women, but it has imposed greater supervision over economically powerless groups. The law provides both an emancipatory discourse of rights along with a set of disciplinary processes that demand participation and exposure of feelings for those found guilty of battering. It provides an array of surveillance and control systems for batterers which are part of the non-state forms of capillary power which Foucault argues constitute the dark underside of modernity (1979). These new forms of control, often insufficient to prevent battering, operate on the terrain of gendered, raced, and classed identities.

## Safety

Some mechanisms promote victim safety that do not depend on punishing batterers. These mechanisms seek to protect the survivor of violence by separating her from the batterer, providing her with temporary shelter or enjoining him from any contact with her by means of a legal restraining order. Instead of preserving the family by reforming the man or reconciling the marriage, these techniques seek to protect the victim. They encourage the woman to separate from the offender and provide her with support.

Shelters, or refuges as they are called in the UK, were developed by grass-roots organizations in the 1970s (Schechter 1982). Originally conceived as safe houses, they were often simply homes where violated women could take temporary refuge. Over time, the system of shelters expanded dramatically so that it now offers a wide range of services to women who seek protection. Shelters offer assistance with jobs, housing, and legal cases as well as personal and group counseling. Maintaining security is an important concern in shelters, as angry partners have attacked shelters and set them on fire. Some shelters keep their location secret while others rely on the police. However, shelters are expensive and require either a private funder or government support. While there is an extensive network of shelters in most affluent countries, those with fewer resources have few to none. Even China and India, with their growing middle classes, have very few shelters. Tiny Hong Kong, with its greater resources, has four. As budget constraints limit the length of time a woman can stay in a shelter, new problems arise. For example, in Massachusetts, a woman may be moved every two or three months, dragging her children with her to new schools and communities.

A second strategy for improving a woman's safety is the civil protective order, often called a restraining order. This is a civil order that orders the batterer to stay away from his victim for a fixed period of time. Failure to abide by its terms leads, at least theoretically, to a criminal contempt order. Civil protective orders, often referred to as TROs or temporary restraining orders, are court orders which require the person who batters (usually but not always male) to stay away from his victim (usually but not always female) under penalty of criminal prosecution. They can be issued on a temporary, emergency basis without the presence of the complainant and extended for months at a subsequent standard court hearing where the offender is present. Some TROs, called no-contact TROs, prohibit all contact while others permit contact but not violence. The strength of these mechanisms depends on how much the parties believe in their power and on the willingness of the police to come when they are called for violations and to arrest offenders. Prosecutors must also be willing to file contempt charges when TROs are violated. Many advocates see this approach as the most effective use of the criminal justice system for domestic violence (see Fischer and Rose 1995).

In the late 1960s, activists argued for the applicability of protective orders for such situations. In the USA, protective orders were used for domestic abuse situations beginning in the 1970s, about the same time as refuges and shelters were being promoted by the battered women's movement (Schechter 1982). The first domestic violence restraining order was created in Pennsylvania in 1976 and a similar law passed in Massachusetts in 1978 (Ptacek 1999: 48–50). In Hawai'i, a law providing for ex-parte temporary restraining orders for victims of domestic violence was passed in 1979. But it was not until the late 1980s that activists succeeded in persuading courts and police to use these protective orders widely. Requests for civil protective orders for battering grew dramatically in the 1990s. My research documents the explosion of these cases in Hilo in the late 1980s and 1990s, a pattern replicated in other parts of the country during the same time period. For example, the number of restraining orders issued in Massachusetts nearly tripled between 1985 and 1993, then began to level off (Ptacek 1999: 62).

This is the most innovative feature of contemporary American efforts to diminish wife battering. It is fundamentally a spatial mechanism since it simply separates the batterer and the victim. Shelters, which provide places of refuge for battered women, are similarly novel inventions of the battered women's movement of the 1970s, although they build on older patterns of safe houses and helpful neighbors and relatives. Both of these interventions make no effort to reform the batterer but only seek to keep him away from the victim. They do so by designating spaces of safety and excluding perpetrators.

## Reform

In the last few decades, therapy and reform have joined punishment and safety as ways to manage gender violence. Batterer intervention programs attempt to change batterers through education and discipline and teach them to control their violence. They are typically closely connected to the criminal justice system. Participation is mandated after conviction for spouse abuse or after receiving a contact TRO. Thus, the legal system is the major gateway into batterer intervention programs. Moreover, such programs represent virtually the only major penalty men receive unless their violence is severe and/or repeated. Feminist activists in the USA began to experiment with retraining batterers in the late 1980s at the same time as more therapeutic approaches were developing for other offenses such as taking drugs (Ptacek 1988; Yllö and Bograd 1988; Pence and Paymar 1993).

By the beginning of the twenty-first century, the legal system in the USA had many therapeutic programs to reform batterers as well as programs for victim protection. Punishment is a distant threat for those who fail to go along. Relatively few domestic violence offenders spend much time in jail. Punishment is largely a means to force offenders to accept treatment and to stay away from their victims. The courts make mandatory referrals to a range of private therapeutic and self-development programs designed to retrain batterers' conceptions of gendered relationships and ability to control their violence. They seek to diminish violence through insight and self-understanding rather than through punishment and deterrence. Reform programs are less common in other parts of the world. There are efforts to develop them in Hong Kong, for example, but I found little work of this kind in my research on India and China (see Merry 2006).

## Controlling Gender Violence: A Case Study of Hilo, Hawai'i

The rest of this chapter illustrates these approaches through an ethnographic description of the situation in Hilo, Hawai'i. The TRO process in Hilo exemplifies an effort to increase the safety of the victim. The batterer intervention program attempts to reform perpetrators. Both depend on the threat of punishment. Thus, the Hilo case study shows how processes focusing on safety and reform work in practice and how they are connected to each other.

While no town in the USA is typical, this one is characterized by ethnic diversity, its plantation past, and its contemporary poverty. Hilo is a small town in windward

Hawai'i whose domestic violence programs I studied during the 1990s.[1] Between 1850 and 2000, Hilo changed from an industrial sugar plantation society to a post-industrial society based on services, education, and a marginalized poor population. An independent kingdom until a US-backed coup in 1893, Hawai'i was annexed to the USA in 1898 and remained a colony until statehood in 1959. In the middle of the nineteenth century, many New England institutions of law, government, and religion were adopted by the Kingdom of Hawai'i, while in the last quarter of the nineteenth century, the rapid expansion of sugar plantations fueled the importation of workers from Asia and Europe and the introduction of harsh work discipline backed by innumerable fines and incarceration for refusal to work (Merry 2000). The plantations have disappeared, replaced by extensive unemployment and a new economy of tourism. Native Hawaiians, displaced by US colonialism, are increasingly economically marginalized. In May 2000 the island of Hawai'i had a 7.1 percent unemployment rate and increased pressure on homeless shelters and food banks as welfare rolls were cut back (*Hawaii Tribune-Herald*, September 9, 2000: 1, 8). This is a post-plantation version of post-industrial society.

The sugar plantations of the Hilo region, like factories, provided an intricate and complex system ordering the details of workers' lives. The plantation provided a firm disciplinary order, often relying on violence against workers to propel them to the fields and keep them at work (Beechert 1985; Takaki 1983). Plantations hired camp police who sometimes kicked in the door to get a person to work or flicked a whip over a worker's head. But workers' violence against supervisors received stern punishment, as court records from the nineteenth century indicate (Merry 2000). Violence was linked to social status, with dominant groups using violence against subordinates, especially in reaction to their violence, while ignoring violence within worker communities.

---

[1] My ethnography of gender violence in Hilo covers both civil and criminal court proceedings, the violence control program, the probation office and prosecutor's office, church and indigenous Hawaiian alternatives, and general ethnography and history of the town. I worked in Hilo from 1991 to 2000, spending in total about two years doing ethnographic research in Hilo over a ten-year period consisting of field work once or twice a year. Thus, this project has an important longitudinal dimension. My work was supplemented by 26 months of observation in Hilo by several research assistants. Marilyn Brown, Tami Miller, Erin Campbell, Nancy Hayes, Madelaine Adelman, and Linda Andres. The research includes observations of legal processes and programs combined with numerous interviews and discussions with judges, attorneys, prosecutors, facilitators, and staff at the shelter and program and with victims and perpetrators of violence. Because I worked in this town for several years, I can chart significant changes that took place during the 1990s, a period of dramatic change in the legal management of gender violence. In addition, I did historical archival research on Hilo, on Hawai'i generally, and on nineteenth-century court cases from Hilo (see Merry 2000). In order to document gender violence interventions in the past, I collected archival data on gender violence cases from Hilo in the nineteenth century in the Hawai'i State Archives, framed by a larger sample of nineteenth-century court records from Hilo between 1852 and 1913. A close examination of the kinds of cases that appeared in court, the discourses surrounding them, and the kinds of outcomes that resulted reveals the practice of punishment by fine that was characteristic of the period and the missionary concerns about the family life and sexuality of the native Hawaiian population which shaped this intervention.

In the plantation era, the workplace provided the basic disciplinary mechanism of society through detailed control over tasks backed by an elaborate system of fines and imprisonment. In the current period, however, the workplace no longer provides such discipline (see Simon 1993b). In post-industrial society, workers must learn to manage themselves rather than obeying the order of the assembly line or the plantation work group. They must come to the workplace already skilled in self-management, interpersonal relationships, and non-violent interactions. Those who fail must be retrained, and those who cannot learn are increasingly incarcerated or abandoned as systems of ordering shift from disciplining offenders to minimizing harm to populations (see Feeley and Simon 1992; 1994; Garland 2000).

## Producing safety: the TRO process in Hilo

Gender violence incidents arrive in the legal system through two quite different processes: a criminal process of arrest and conviction and a civil process of issuing a temporary restraining order. The first leads to a trial and potential criminal conviction, the second to a family court hearing which could result in the issuance of a TRO. Both are activated largely by the complaint of an injured party, although a police officer may be summoned by a neighbor, relative, or friend. TROs are almost always issued at the request of an individual petitioner. Although the first process is a criminal one and the second a civil one, in practice there are many connections between the two. Criminal cases are often handled through plea bargaining between the prosecutor and defense attorney rather than trial. Defendants typically receive the same sentences as TRO respondents. Moreover, a civil case can be converted into a criminal case if there is a violation of the conditions of the order. Thus, civil cases often become criminal while criminal cases are typically handled through informal negotiation which takes the victim's wishes into account, paralleling civil procedures. A final important connection between these two processes is that it is common for the same couple to become involved in civil and criminal processes simultaneously. Victims and batterers are sometimes confused about the relationships between the two courts and the differences in their procedures.

The civil court process must be initiated by the victim, who goes to the Family Court to secure the order. The Family Court is itself a recent concept, created as a separate judicial entity in Hawai'i in 1989. A person can apply for a TRO against any family member, whether or not he or she is living in the same household.[2] The victim fills out an affidavit which is reviewed and signed by the judge. This initiates a temporary, emergency order requiring the named individual to vacate the premises or

---

[2]   The statute for domestic violence is in Chapter 586 of the Civil Family Law. Harm or threat of harm is sufficient grounds for a temporary restraining order. Violation of a protective order is covered under Penal Code 709–906. Violation of the protective order means a mandatory minimum two days in jail for the convicted person.

to refrain from violence, depending on the kind of order requested. There must be a hearing within 15 days before the Family Court to extend the order.

The number of requests for TROs has increased dramatically since the early 1970s. Between 1971 and 1978, there were seven protective orders, or "peace bonds," issued in Hilo for domestic violence situations. By 1985, however, the year a more stringent spouse abuse law went into effect, there were 250 in one year. In 1990 there were 338, and by 1999 471, from an area of perhaps 70,000 residents. Although there has been a doubling of the population in the last 20 years, TRO petitions have increased far more rapidly.

Observations of the domestic violence calendar during the 1990s indicate that most defendants are men and most victims women.[3] The women who bring these cases to the court are primarily young, in their twenties and thirties, and non-professional workers or non-workers. Their ethnic identities reflect the local population, including white, Portuguese, Filipino, Japanese, Hawaiian, Hawaiian Chinese, and Puerto Rican individuals. Because of the high rate of intermarriage among these groups, the majority have multiple ethnicities. Most are "local," although a significant minority are people from the mainland, many of whom follow alternative life-styles such as that of the pioneer-survivalist aspiring to live off the land. A few support themselves by cultivating marijuana. Most of the people have low incomes and often are not working.

At the hearing, victims are almost always accompanied by a woman advocate from the women's domestic violence program, Alternatives to Violence (ATV). The man appears alone, although there is always a male advocate from the ATV program present in the waiting area of the court and willing to talk to the men. The Family Court judge reads the written account provided by the victim, asks the accused if he or she acknowledges the charge, and takes testimony if the accused denies all violence. If the accused accepts the charge or the evidence is persuasive, the judge issues a temporary restraining order for a period of months with a series of conditions. If there are no children and a desire by both to separate, the respondent is told to stay away from the petitioner and both are told to have no further contact. This is a no-contact TRO. If they have children but the victim wishes no contact, the judge will arrange visitation or custody for the children and specify no contact between the adults. If they wish to continue the relationship and/or to live together, the judge usually issues a contact TRO but also sends them to ATV, requiring either the accused or both parties to participate in the program. The contact order allows the respondent to be with the petitioner but prohibits him from using violence against her. Observations of 130 cases in the early 1990s indicated that slightly under half (42 percent) of petitioners requested and received contact TRO orders.

---

[3]   Marilyn Brown and I observed the domestic violence calendar in the Hilo Family Court, which was held once a week, for 19 weeks from July 1991 to August 1992 and tabulated and analyzed these 130 cases. I continued to observe the domestic violence calendar of the Family Court subsequently every year from 1991 to 2000.

At the hearing, the judge points out that any violation of the conditions of the protective order is a misdemeanor, punishable by a jail sentence of up to one year and/or a fine of $2,000. He frequently schedules a review hearing in a month or two to monitor the situation, particularly for the contact restraining orders, and to make sure that the conditions of the TRO are being fulfilled. He also requires the respondent to surrender any guns in his possession to the local police officer for the duration of the TRO.

The Family Court judge's concerns are twofold: first, to stop the violence; and second, to protect the children involved. He endeavors to convey a clear message that violence is against the law and that it is bad for children. Any indication of violence or abuse against children elicits an immediate referral to Children's Protective Services. Protective orders commonly include the requirement to seek treatment as well as the obligation to refrain from violence and, in no-contact orders, to stay away. The judge is much more likely to refer a couple to the batterer intervention program when the woman requests a contact TRO than when she wishes no contact. When a woman requesting a TRO says she wishes to stay with her partner and they have children, the judge usually makes a referral to ATV.[4]

These legal orders are sometimes viewed uneasily by judges. Since they begin as an emergency intervention, they impose restrictions on individuals who are initially absent from the hearing. Because they are civil rather than criminal proceedings, defendants do not have the right to an attorney if they cannot afford one. Yet if a person violates the terms of a TRO, he is guilty of contempt of court and can be prosecuted for a criminal violation and theoretically face a prison sentence. Although in practice this is rare, in theory it remains a possibility. In Hilo, a violation based on a violent incident typically led to a new arrest, while a violation based on the failure to attend ATV typically led to being re-sentenced to the program.

A second difficulty with the TRO in gender violence cases is its limited enforceability. It relies on the respondent's acquiescence or an effective police response. In the hands of a skeptical batterer, it is no more powerful than the policing behind it. With a no-contact TRO, a respondent is in violation if he simply appears at the plaintiff's house or workplace. The police should remove him and charge him with a violation of order. Thus, the efficacy of the order depends on the willingness of the police to appear and take the violator away.

A third difficulty with the TRO process is that a no-contact order does not fit well with the exigencies of everyday life. A woman may wish to see her partner to exchange children, ask for financial help, or simply because she is lonely and wishes to consider restarting the relationship. If she allows him into her house, she is violating the

---

[4]   In the sample of 130 cases from the early 1990s, almost half (43 percent) of respondents in all hearings, both initial and review hearings, were referred to ATV. Of newly issued orders, 37 percent (31 of 85) included referrals to ATV and 63 percent did not. But ATV referrals were much more likely with contact TROs. Slightly under half (42 percent) of petitioners requested and received TRO orders allowing them to have continuing contact with the respondent but without violence. Of this group, 61 percent were referred or re-referred to ATV and only 34 percent were not.

TRO and he is risking a criminal penalty. In order to avoid these difficulties, many women request a contact TRO initially or ask to change the no-contact order to a contact one a few months after the incident. Under a contact order, the petitioner and respondent can be together but he is prohibited from using violence against her. There is no spatial segregation. On the other hand, a woman with a contact restraining order is little better off than one without it. A new act of violence simply places the batterer at risk of being arrested for that violence, as he would be in any case. Some judges have expressed discomfort with the contact TRO, arguing that it is too hard to enforce and should be eliminated. The Family Court judge in Hilo tried to persuade petitioners to ask for no-contact TROs. Nevertheless, almost half the TROs issued in Hilo were contact orders.

Finally, if both parties ask for a TRO and a judge issues mutual restraining orders, then any time they are together both are guilty of a legal infraction. Since it is common for an incident of wife battering to include mutual blows, it is not improbable for a judge to issue a restraining order for both parties. Yet the result is an enforcement quagmire, since both are equally, and indistinguishably, guilty at the moment of contact. A related problem is the use of TROs to deal with custody disputes. The party who retains custody of the children with a TRO has an advantage in keeping the children during subsequent divorce proceedings. Consequently, a person contemplating divorce may take out a restraining order on his/her partner in order to be in possession of the children at the time of the divorce decree. Judges are aware of this pre-divorce strategy.

Despite these difficulties, the TRO, particularly its no-contact version, is a mechanism that focuses on the safety of the woman without waiting until the man has been reformed. Because wives with restraining orders are sometimes murdered, such orders are often considered of little value. Yet many of the men I talked to took the order seriously and, although they were angry at being kicked out of their houses, they did stay away. Women felt comforted by the presence of this legal document, even though many were still harassed by their batterers at home and at work. Furthermore, the no-contact TRO shifts the evidentiary burden away from the woman, releasing her from the necessity of testifying against her batterer in his presence. His presence in a proscribed location constitutes adequate evidence of a criminal offense. The skyrocketing use of this mechanism in the 1980s and 1990s indicates its popularity with battered women. It offers what many victims want: separation from their batterer, or even prohibition of violence while they remain together, along with a program of reform. Whether or not this mechanism is always effective, it encapsulates the desire of many battered women who do not want their abusers punished but reformed or gone. Its novelty is that it foregrounds the security of the victim rather than the reform or punishment of the offender. This spatialized form of governance represents a popular new addition to legal relief for battered women.

It is possible to imagine other expansions of this logic of security for the problem of wife battering. Women could subscribe to battering insurance programs which would provide funds for emergency housing and moving costs to relocate to a different area. Violence-free zones could be established from which a person with a history of battering would be excluded. Batterers could be required to wear monitors which would emit a sound when they enter a prohibited zone. Obviously there are difficulties with aspects of these ideas, but they suggest the possibilities of governance based on security and the regulation of space rather than punishment and the regulation of persons.

## Reforming perpetrators: the batterer intervention program

In Hilo, as in other American towns, the courts send most convicted batterers who stay with their partners to some form of counseling or retraining to learn how to control their violence. They also send people who have contact TROs issued against them. Here they are taught to overcome their belief in male privilege. Instead of being fined, participants must pay a fee to attend the program. If they fail to attend, they go to jail, at least in theory. Women are encouraged to interpret violence as blameworthy behavior and a violation of their rights (see Merry 1995a; 1995b). Wife beating is viewed as not just another assault but a consequence of flawed gender ideas and an inability to control angry feelings. These interventions seek to redefine the cultural boundary between acceptable and impermissible violence.

In the mid 1980s, a women's center in Hilo developed women's support groups and batterer training programs called Alternatives to Violence (ATV). Supported at first by independent grants, it soon acquired more or less permanent support from the state judiciary. From 1986 to 1996, the ATV program closely followed the feminist approach developed by battered women in Duluth, Minnesota. Discussions in Duluth in the 1980s emphasized that battering needs to be understood in terms of power and control (Pence and Paymar 1993). This model focused on undermining the cultural support for male privilege and violence against women by exploring men's feelings and beliefs and encouraging men to analyze their own behavior during battering events. Violence against women was understood as an aspect of patriarchy. A dominant feature of group discussions was changing beliefs about men's entitlement to make authoritative decisions and back them up with violence.

In the 1990s, this model dominated batterer reform efforts in Hilo as well as in the rest of the United States.[5] The Duluth model came to Hawai'i in 1986. Men convicted of spouse abuse or given a TRO were required to attend the ATV program. ATV offered both violence control training for men and a support group for women.[6] Men were required to attend weekly two-hour group discussions for six months. In groups of 10 to 15 men and two facilitators, participants talk about their use of violence to control their partners. Discussions stress the importance of egalitarian

---

[5] Batterers' intervention programs following this model were the dominant approach to treating batterers in the United States by the end of the 1990s (Hanna 1998; Healy and Smith 1998).

[6] I observed women's support groups and men's violence control groups in Hilo from 1991 to 2000 and formally interviewed 30 men and women who participated in the program. Marilyn Brown, Tami Miller, and Madelaine Adelman provided valuable assistance with observations and interviewing.

relations between men and women and the value of settling differences by negotiation rather than by force. The men are taught that treating their partners with respect
rather than violence will win them a more loving, trusting, and sexually fulfilling
relationship and forge warmer relations with their children. Egalitarian gender
relations are modeled by the male/female team of facilitators leading the group.

If men fail to attend the program, the staff informs their probation officers: those
whose attendance is a stipulation of a criminal spouse abuse conviction face revoca-
tion of their probation; those required to attend as a condition of a TRO are guilty
of contempt of court – a criminal offense – and their case is sent to the prosecutor.
In practice, these men are typically sent back to ATV rather than receiving a jail
sentence or other criminal penalty, but the threat of jail time is frequently articulated by judges during court hearings. Thus, attendance at this psycho-educational
program is enforced by the threat of prison. The program emphasizes training in
self-management of violence but failure to accomplish this task results in the return
to a regime of punishment, at least in theory. In practice, they are returned to the
program and go to jail only after a new violation.

During the early 1990s, the Hilo program was strongly feminist. Participants were
separated on the basis of gender. The men's group provided training in violence
control, the women's group offered support and encouragement to assert rights.
Because the program viewed gender violence as a prop for patriarchy, it made sense
to provide separate treatment for men and women regardless of their own violent
behavior. At this time, the program for men consisted of eight months of weekly
two-hour meetings of groups of 10 to 15 men led by a pair of facilitators who modeled respectful, egalitarian, and give-and-take interactions between a man and a
woman. The time was later reduced to six months. The program for women consists
of ten weeks of two-hour meetings of a support group, but women were rarely
required to attend under threat of criminal penalties. My research assistants and
I observed at least 50 men's sessions and 40 support groups for women over the
decade of the 1990s and spent a good deal of time talking to program staff, facilitators,
judges, and participants.

Following the Duluth model, group meetings are designed to help men change
their beliefs and values about gender relationships. They are encouraged to consider
their partners as equals and to make decisions by negotiation. Since the program
sees violence as learned behavior, it focuses on the values and beliefs that allow men
to accept their own violence. There is an explicit attempt to change these values.
In their training sessions, men were encouraged to use "positive self-talk" – to think
positive thoughts about themselves – as a technique for diminishing their desire to
strike out. They were told the problem was not their anger but their violence, and
taught to recognize the bodily signs of anger and to pursue strategies to "cool down."
A new vocabulary is central to the teaching mission. Instead of calling the women in
their lives "old ladies" or "cunts," they were to refer to them as "partners." "Just a slap"
was a case of "physical abuse," and "battering" consisted of physical battering,
sexual battering, psychological battering, and destruction of property and pets. The
terms "lickins'" or "dirty lickins'" were replaced by "abuse." The unfamiliar term

"intimidation" (many asked for a definition of the word) is used to describe what they did when they smashed the windshield on their wife's car to prevent her from driving to town and "male privilege" to describe their assumption that men decide where women go and whether they have a job, take drugs, or buy themselves a new truck. After a few weeks in the program, men began to use these terms in conversation with each other, with me in interviews, and to judges in court. Attorneys and other court officials also noted this new language, although they, along with program staff, were skeptical about how much it signaled a change in behavior.

The men attending this program are largely poor, unemployed, and relatively uneducated. Program intake forms for 1,574 people served between 1990 and 1998, of whom two-thirds were men, provide demographic data on who is referred. About three-quarters of the men (77 percent) and women (70 percent) earned under $11,000. Men and women in the violence control program and women's support groups frequently talked about poverty, welfare, and survival by fishing, hunting, and odd construction jobs. ATV clients are also substantially less educated than town residents, with the men even less educated than the women. Half are high school graduates (46 percent) and one-quarter started college (25 percent), but only 3 percent have a college degree. While 29 percent of Hilo's population has an associate's, bachelor's, or higher degree, only 5 percent of the ATV population does.[7] Thus, the men sent to the violence control program as well as the women they batter are significantly poorer and less educated than the town overall. Those who attended the feminist programs for men and women were largely people living on the fringes of the town's economy. Many are on welfare or living with partners who are; many camp in forests or beaches; many are embittered by a colonial past and present poverty.

Many suffer from emotional scars of childhood physical and sexual abuse. Most (three-quarters) had some experience with violence in their homes, either witnessing it or experiencing abuse as children, or both. Those with histories of abuse were significantly more likely to have had previous abusive relationships than those without. The experience of being abused as a child or seeing violence in the family normalizes the violence, so that those with these experiences are less likely to leave batterers and more likely to assault others. Based on the stories they tell about their lives, it appears that many are afflicted with unmanageable rage, have recurring difficulties with alcohol and drugs, and face educational deficits. These are not the only people who batter, but they are the ones who end up in batterer intervention programs.

ATV attempts to teach men that violence breaks social connections rather than strengthening them. The legal system is a central actor in reconstituting connection and violence in its threat that if the violence recurs, the man will go to jail, which is

---

[7]   Comparing the ATV population to the census designation of educational levels of people 25 years of age and above reveals that the ATV population lacks both extremes: while 11 percent of the general population has less than an eighth grade education, only 1 percent of the ATV population falls into this category.

the ultimate separation. One exercise, repeated in various forms throughout the training session, is to ask a man to describe a violent experience and break it down into the feelings, the actions, the underlying beliefs, and the consequences to him, to his partner, and to their children of his actions. The man presents the situation and the group collectively analyzes it. The conclusion drawn from the exercise is that the violence won power and control in the short run at the price of fear and suspicion from partners and children in the long run. Many of the men discuss how they use violence to hang on to their women. They prevent them from leaving by puncturing their tires, opposing their getting a job or visiting friends, and beating them if they go out without permission. Many constantly feared that their partners would abandon them for other men. Jealousy and suspicion foment violence and isolation of the woman. Thus, the men use violence to maintain their connections with women. ATV reverses the link, arguing that violence breaks the connection and that only by living without violence will the men be able to hold on to the women they desire. This discussion takes place in a therapeutic group situation in which each man is surrounded by other men in like circumstances, thus demonstrating the kinds of community that are possible without violence.

On the other hand, women in the support group are encouraged to break their connections with violent men in order to protect themselves. But this is not always possible or even what women desire, at least at the early stages of violence. For many women, the violent partner is someone who occasionally offers love and sexual pleasure and on whom they depend for economic support for themselves and their children. Men are typically penitent after incidents of violence and promise not to do it again, begging forgiveness. Women want to believe these promises. The women want connection, but without the violence. As one woman put it, "There is an emotional side to this situation that the courts don't understand." One woman talking in the support group bewailed the "hormones" which pulled her back to her abusive man, and regretted that there was no way she could see him just for her sexual needs.

The pressure to separate from the man in order to receive the protection of the legal system poses financial difficulties as well. Since they are typically poor, young, relatively uneducated, and caring for small children, these women are often dependent on their husbands as well as on welfare for support. One woman who is local, Hawaiian, in her forties, with teenaged children, complained in the women's support group:

> I didn't ask for a no-contact TRO, my dumb lawyer did. I'm angry at him. Now I can't ask for money for bills. Now I got to go to the kids for money, and they ask him. The kids are getting in the middle. He comes by everyday, but he is not supposed to. This is an order that lasts until November [meeting is in July]. There is no chance of my marriage getting back together now since I can't see him until then. He's living with another girl now, I've lost him. Jane [pseudonym for one of the women advocates at ATV] forgot about that appointment in court, so I had to handle it the best I could alone. I said in court I wanted contact, but the judge told me to be quiet. I didn't know what else to do. I don't know if he's coming to ATV because I can't talk to him. So I can't keep him.

This statement encapsulates the dilemma for women: protection requires ending a relationship that may involve some caring and financial support as well as violence. Moreover, it involves turning to a possibly alien system outside the boundaries of the social relationships she has constructed for herself. On the other hand, the legal system recognizes that violent men very often hit their wives again and that returning women to the same situation poses a very substantial risk of further violence.

There is a further twist to the connection/violence relationship. Women who are violent, or even who remain in violent homes, risk having their children removed by the child protective services. This is a constant source of discussion among the women in the support group. One woman, for example, stabbed her husband as he attacked her and is contemplating pleading guilty. Other women warned her to be careful, telling her about others who were railroaded into pleading guilty to such charges in the past who then lost their children. Thus, acknowledging the violence by asking the legal system for help or by fighting back risks another loss of connection, that with their children. Maintaining the connection with children may require not complaining about violence to oneself.

Thus, the courts and ATV convey messages about violence and connection which are quite different for men and for women. Men are told that violence earns them separation. They are encouraged to maintain connection through negotiation and compromise rather than asserting power and control over their partners. The women are encouraged in the support group to form connections with women in similar circumstances and to see that it is possible to separate from violent men. One of the new connections proffered is with the legal system. The law expects women to leave the violent partner in order to earn its full support. If a woman repeatedly calls the police and presses charges, then withdraws and refuses to prosecute, the courts and police become frustrated and ignore her complaints. In other words, if the woman is to mobilize the help offered by the legal system, she must be willing to go through with the process of penalizing the husband, of sending him to jail or to ATV, and consequently with severing her relationship with him. She is offered, instead of subordination to patriarchal authority in a violent relationship, the promise of liberal legalism: a self protected by legal rights, able to make autonomous decisions, as long as she is willing to sever the relationship with the man or, at the least, risk making him very angry by filing charges against him or testifying against him. Not only is this a difficult decision, but it is also a dangerous one. Men are most likely to be violent to women after the women have left them. The men rely on the old strategy of achieving connection through violence, putting the woman in considerable danger which the law can do little to mitigate. Indeed, the staff of the violence control program told me that after a highly publicized event of male violence occurs, women quietly slip back to the violent men they may have left out of fear that something like that will happen to them. There are frequent stories about rejected men hanging around the shelter, setting it on fire, going to their partner's houses, and other forms of harassment.

Women are encouraged to reconstitute themselves not as selves defined by relationships but as selves connected to the law, with rights defined by the legal system.

As women activate the legal system for help, they are expected to press forward with prosecution in a way that they often hesitate to do out of fear or conflicting concerns. The result is a withdrawal from the process, a failure to prosecute criminal cases, a request for contact rather than no-contact restraining orders, a reluctance to insist that the man attend the violence control program, which frustrates the best-intentioned legal personnel. Women enter the court as reluctant plaintiffs, welcoming the redefinition of violence as a crime and their right not to experience it, yet often afraid or unwilling to make the break with the men which is the main solution the legal system can provide.

This reluctance increases the possibility that these problems will be reframed as "garbage" cases. They have all the hallmarks of cases which are typically defined as garbage by the courts: difficulty in determining what happened, victims who refuse to prosecute, mutual battles with no unambiguously innocent victim or guilty villain, and a tendency to be ongoing, repeated, messy, and resistant to simple solutions (Merry 1990; Yngvesson 1988; 1993). The struggle to keep such cases defined as crimes rather than "garbage" by the court is a continuing challenge for feminist activists. But the larger struggle is to move toward a broader understanding of violence against women which takes into account their class subordination as well as their gender subordination. Women need not simply a choice-making self but also the means to make choices.

## Performing masculinity

Instead of changing behavior through deterrence, these new mechanisms seek to reshape the habits of everyday life, to encourage offenders to think through the consequences of their actions and choose to change. Feminist batterer intervention programs teach new models of masculinity in which sexual prowess and violence against women are displaced as the indicia of manhood with self-control of feelings, respect, and gender equality. Batterers are presented with new images of masculinity that celebrate negotiation and gender equality rather than physical domination and sexual control over women. Women are offered a new sense of self as endowed with rights not to be hit while men are encouraged to abandon a highly muscled and sexualized version of masculinity founded on the control of their women partners' activities and sexual lives. This self-regulatory discipline is supplemented by new security mechanisms such as temporary restraining orders which bypass the problem of reforming offenders altogether by requiring them to stay away. Courts no longer insist on the indissoluble family.

The major focus of the batterer intervention program is the reconstruction of masculinity and the critique of male privilege. In many cultural contexts, battering behavior lies at the heart of masculinity since masculine identities are defined in relation to women, particularly in the extent and nature of control which their gender allows them to exercise over women. Batterer intervention programs are engaged in contesting the degree and kind of power that men are entitled to hold

over women. That this is central to men's identities is underscored by the humiliation and shame they report when their wives fail to obey them or fight back in any
kind of public setting, including the legal system. When women do this, they spoil
the performance of masculinity. At the same time, men sometimes report shame at
their own battering behavior and acknowledge the loss of relationships with their
partners and children.

The group provides a tense and fraught setting for these men's performances of
masculinity since the audience includes their peers, a group of other men also
accused of battering, and a male and a female facilitator, who stand in for the law.
The men are required to attend, under penalty of criminal sanctions, because the
court has declared their actions illegal. In order to complete the program, they are
required to participate and to take oral tests on each segment of the class. Thus, they
remain under the authority of the program and its facilitators during the six- to
eight-month program. Under these circumstances, men appear to redefine their
masculinity, at least in the way they talk about it. At the same time, they also exhibit
a substantial resistance to change through argument and humor. Many fail to return
and face criminal sanctions. There are also variations in masculinity performances
based on race, class, or indigenous identity which emerge in particular as men seek
to justify or deny their violence in group discussions. The program emphasizes
self-management of anger, non-violent strategies for dealing with conflict, and
rethinking relations to women.

What is at stake in these classes is the definition of masculinity. The facilitators
present a new image of masculinity while the participants endeavor to adapt these
new ideas to their own visions or to resist them. The program asserts that violence is
learned behavior rather than psychopathology, thus focusing on the social and cultural determinants of the behavior rather than the pathology of the individual (see
Ptacek 1988). The curriculum does not differentiate among kinds of masculinity but
presents a theory of power and control strategies, male privilege, violence as learned
behavior, and techniques for changing beliefs about violence and about the way men
should treat women. Although it was designed for a very different part of the country, it was not significantly changed to adapt to the local social, class, or cultural
situation of this town in Hawai'i. By and large, the curriculum refuses to see male
battering as a phenomenon of particular racial, class, or religious groups but locates
it within an analysis of gender inequality and power.

Nor is a non-essentialized analysis of gender applied to battered women. Radical
feminism in the 1970s and 1980s emphasized the similarity in women's vulnerability
to violence as a strategic move to forestall identifying the problem as only characteristic of a particular category of women. Whether gender violence should be interpreted primarily through the lens of gender, and thus as a problem for all women, or
through a far more differentiated prism that joins gender with the ways structures
such as class, racism, citizenship, or nationality structure gender positions and performances, is a major debate in the field. From a political, activist perspective, seeing
all women as vulnerable to violence is enormously powerful and has motivated the
considerable advances in the movement. Moreover, it underscores the way that

women do experience violence in similar ways. However, defining the problem as one faced by "women" in a generic sense tends to ignore the other positions that render women vulnerable to violence and limit their capacities for exit. In particular, this approach has obscured the particular situation of battered black women who face double marginalization on the basis of race as well as gender (Crenshaw 1994; Connell 1995; hooks 1997). Such women may have difficulty turning to predominantly white women's shelters and face discrimination in court, for example. As Sarah Hautzinger's (2007) ethnography of a poor Afro-Brazilian community in Brazil indicates, violence in intimate relationships is inseparable from the violence of poverty and overwork, insufficient food, heavy-handed policing, and the impacts of racism.

The same dilemma about whether to acknowledge difference or not confronts work with male batterers. ATV offers a uniform image of desirable masculine behavior: negotiated decisions between partners, respect, equality, respectful language, and equality in major decisions. Men are taught to recognize the physical signals of anger in their bodies, to use cool-downs, to walk away from fights, and to practice "positive self-talk," meaning self-affirmation, willingness to accept criticism, and acceptance of not being in control all the time. Rather than probing into past injuries or experience with violence, the focus of this program is talking about better strategies for handling violence and treating women now. Little attention was given to men's childhood experiences with violence or the situations they grew up in, following the feminist position that battering is a product of the gender constructs rather than individual psychopathology.

Although the program is explicitly directed toward changing beliefs, it does not frame its project as re-educating men about masculinity. There is little discussion about the ways masculinity is defined in different ethnic/class groupings or between locals and mainlanders. The program is inspired by a radical feminist commitment to an understanding of battering as a social and cultural phenomenon related to patriarchy rather than the ethnic, racial, and class contexts of this violence (see Rodriquez 1988). Yet the group is highly culturally diverse and largely working class and poor, with many on welfare. Despite continuous efforts to have local people and non-whites as group leaders, most of the male and female facilitators during the 1990s were white, originally from the mainland although usually long resident in Hawai'i. Most speak a mainland dialect rather than the local pidgin common among participants. Looking at the way men in a batterer treatment program talk about their violence and justify or deny it provides a window into their continual construction and reconstruction of masculine selves performed for the audiences in the room and outside. Many of these examples are from the early 1990s, when the idea that gender violence was an offense was still quite new to the participants.

References to masculinity are a common aspect of group discussions, and play strongly in the excuses and justifications that men offer for their violence. For example, a male facilitator suggested that the purpose of battering is to intimidate and punish, and a local part-Hawaiian man who works as a carpenter replied, "What do you do when you got no control? You gotta have control over your wife. Look, we gotta all pay taxes to the government. The wife and kids they gotta pay you too, gotta have respect, right?" (November 14, 1991). Here the inescapable duty of paying taxes is equated to the duty of the wife to her husband. This man says that the cause of battering is weakness. Later he observes that, for him, male privilege is based on the Bible: "Woman made as a helper. She help you. God created man first and woman after. It's God's will. This is why we screwed up today – women are the king. When you go against God's will it gets screwed up" (November 14, 1991).

There are several recurring modes of justification for the violence which the men present to the group. First, they deny that their violence was extreme, excessive, or repeated: "I only did it once, just a little. This is the first time I hit her." These statements do not attempt to justify the violence nor do they display pride in the violence as a form of discipline and control. Instead, they serve to distance the speaker from the realm of "extreme" batterers. Some men differentiate themselves from the other men on the basis of their lesser violence. One man told me that he was not like most of the other men: for example, another participant tied his wife to a chair and beat her for several hours: "Now, *he* was violent." Another man said that he did not really belong here and should be in a different group without so many extreme people. He was angry that the police treated him just like every other person, putting him in handcuffs and having the lights going near his house. He was just sleeping on the couch, he maintained, and his wife called the cops. He never intended to hurt his wife, and now she is scared of him and he can hardly see his kids. Despite his denial of his violence, this man started the program three times because his partners kept filing TROs against him.

Some men assert that violence is natural to men, even a source of pride and respect, and that women like it. The men talked about being a tough guy and having to keep the toughness up, not backing down, not being different from others (August 1994). Some men describe their past battering in these terms. For example, one man, a Native Hawaiian in his twenties, speaking the local pidgin, said that in the past his idea was: "Be an asshole, be a jerk, bully – one of those macho guys, nobody can push you, act on impulse, be cruel – like I was to my nieces and nephews, make them afraid of me, my look. I don't want to do that anymore" (January 13, 1992; based on my notes, not tape recordings). Another man said, "Most men, when they're young, learn to be macho. Go into the service, learn to kill. It is hard to learn different" (January 13, 1992). These comments suggest the existence of constructions of masculinity which underlie their violence, although they may also feel shame and regret at the extent or nature of particular incidents. They also express some satisfaction at the effects of new techniques they are learning. For example, a Native Hawaiian man said that he was having better communication with his partner: "After she asking me things come better. I feel proud like that" (November 21, 1991). Another man said, "Do you let your old lady go anywhere she wants? If so, you will be shamed" (July 20, 1992).

One man claimed that "Men in certain countries think they have the right to batter women, that they are their property. There is a shred of this among all men" (July 8, 1992). A man described his violence this way: "She seemed too scared to leave – I go to her mother's house, go to her father's house – I am a hunter, I got guns" (January 16, 1992). Another man said, "She asked for it. She likes it. I need to prove I am a man" (January 7, 1992). A young man said that his partner liked it when he gets angry and she asks for it. "I need to prove I am a man. Maybe she try to make me mad so she can tell you guys [directed to the facilitators]" (January 7, 1992). He said his partner got mad because he was looking at girls, and she just slammed the door. If she hadn't slammed the door, he said, he wouldn't have hit her but he did it to show her who was boss (January 7, 1992). One young man told a group that he thought women found macho men attractive (November 12, 1991). On the other hand, going to the program undermines this masculinity: "They say you are pussy-whipped" (January 17, 1992). When told that the purpose of the program is to change beliefs, one man said, "We'll come home and say 'yes, dear.' And our wives will come here and say, What did you do to my husband?" (January 17, 1992).

Men often present themselves as entitled to power because of their economic roles: "Women should stay home and take care of the house. Men are the breadwinners" (January 7, 1992). Men talk a lot about the importance of having women at home when they come home from work, expecting them to have a dinner cooked and feeling frustrated and neglected if they don't, especially if they saw their mothers doing this for their fathers (July 26, 1993). Yet the intake information from the program reveals that many of the women are supporting themselves by working or welfare and the men do not have significantly greater income. The men are often dependent on women for support. These images of legitimate violence reflect cultural ideals rather than practices.

For many men, violence is a justified reaction to women's provocation and resistance to their control. A woman's failure to obey insults and humiliates the man so that he must assert his authority over her. Violent behavior is redefined as a reaction and is therefore justified. Men did not talk about their violence as discipline, but often described it as a reaction to women's misbehavior. A middle-class white man said, "When I don't get angry like my father did, I feel I'm not doing right" (July 8, 1992). Another said he beat his wife to show her he was angry and that "I'm the man"; she had no right to get mad but he did: "I never do nothing wrong" (January 7, 1992). One group produced the following list of reasons for violence:

she always picks on me
she hit me first
she's always flying off the handle
drugs/booze
she doesn't trust me
mouthing off
nagging
yelling
being made an ass in front of friends
treated my kids differently than hers
she complained

The language of masculinity was used to justify violence in these situations. "If women want equal rights as men, they have to take it like men" (July 8, 1992). "Women are violent, women provoke fights, it takes two to have a fight" (July 8, 1992). One man (married three times) said: "Men want their house in order, and see her as a fixture there. And if she makes trouble, she disturbs it. This is natural, that's the way things are" (July 8, 1992). A relatively educated white man presents a similar perspective: "Men are emotionally dependent on women, but they don't like to admit it. I get upset when she is moody and pregnant." He notes that when her attention shifts to the unborn child it is hard for emotionally dependent men (July 8, 1992).

Some of the group participants deny responsibility for their actions, claiming that "it just came over me. I can't control my feelings, it just comes on me, don't know why. I do impulse things, snap fast" (January 14, 1992). Another man said, "Before we learn this we never know nothing where all these things come from – actions, feelings – we just act, hit first" (January 23, 1992). Some naturalize violence, drawing connections between physiological states (high blood pressure) and violence as a release of that pressure. One 50-year-old man with a local accent said:

> I lived a violent life. It is a natural thing for me. I just go into a situation and it happens. My philosophy is, you mess with me, I warn you. Next time, I just do it. She knew this in Honolulu. I was as surprised as she was that I kicked her. [The woman he kicked in the head died 10 hours later of a blood clot in the brain.]

One of the other men in the group objects to this account, saying:

> In every person I ever hit, I choose where I hit 'em. I do little punches. People pick their shots.

The other man continues:

> But it just happened. Neither of us realized how serious it was. The lawyer said I had a good chance to get off. My son says, "I want to be just like you when I grow up, only thing is, *I don't want to kill my wife. I sure miss my mom.*"

Violence against women is also linked to images of masculinity and power which are rooted in distinctive ethnic and class cultures. An older man links his violence to sexual attractiveness and his proudly asserted identity as a Native Hawaiian man (July 21, 1992). He has eight children aged 10 to 22 years. The *haole* (white) wife is his second wife. The family lives on ancestral Hawaiian lands on a beach in a make-shift shelter. A significant number of families live this way on land which is designated as Hawaiian Homelands. After commenting that a slap is "Hawaiian love" (a common phrase), he said:

> Who's not afraid of one Hawaiian who act like an asshole? I'm born here, raised here, on my own land. I'm kama'aina.[8]

---

[8]   This term means native, person born in Hawai'i.

The female facilitator queries, "What about her rights?" He replies,

> She doesn't have any. She's a haole, I took her away from a haole husband, so she likes me better. That's why they call us Hawaiians. We don't steal wives, they come to us. Don't even have to play slack key.[9]

The facilitators constantly battle the resistant talk, trying to tame and control it while the men assert their own images of masculinity.

## Laughter and resistance

In the conversation about masculinity, some men resist the model presented by program staff, instead making jokes and saying things they know will be provocative to the facilitators, delighting and amusing the group. There is a good deal of joking and laughter in most group meetings. The joking among the men refers obliquely to another cultural world in which this behavior is acceptable, or at least is a way men bond together against women. The undercurrent of humor implies a different set of cultural assumptions about masculinity, not accepted in this sphere but still resonant in others. Sometimes one person becomes the center of these joking resistances, saying things the program leaders disapprove of but eliciting laughter from the group.

Laughter often follows remarks about domineering masculinity addressed to the female facilitator. For example, when a female facilitator asks what kind of tactic it is when a man asks his partner to do something, a participant replies "male privilege." When she asks what he could have done better, he replies, "Slap her face" and laughs (November 5, 1991). Later in the session, when he is reporting what happened to him that week, a young man says, "I slapped my old lady and punch her face," and laughs. When the discussion turns to the way some men use the Bible to justify male privilege, one man says that God made man and man was there first; it was woman who made the first mistake. The group agrees and laughs at this (November 5, 1991). A Portuguese man says he was drinking tequila and his wife didn't want him to drive, but he insisted and was weaving a little bit, at which all laughed (July 21, 1992). The female facilitator says, "This is dangerous, laughing minimizes it." He replies: "The next day she said cars were getting off the road around me. I was just driving with my head out the window. I don't remember much. I had experience driving cane trucks in the past, so I had experience. Now I see I should have let her drive." When the female facilitator uses the term "lickins" they laugh. The male facilitator talked about a man who was now comfortable hanging the laundry outside to dry, and the men laughed a lot at the image (August 1994). One man was quite vocal about his beliefs that men are men because they have "the balls" and that

---

9   This refers to a style of music played on the guitar that is unique to Hawai'i.

women were made to obey their men. "I have my opinion," he says, "you have yours, for one year I have been hearing yours and you can't make me believe yours." The female facilitator agrees that she can't make anyone believe something else, but that she wants him to be honest about why he believes what he does. The other guys laugh a lot at his comments (August 23, 1994). He keeps bringing up the fact that his partner kicked him in the balls: "what was I gonna do, just stand there?" Yet this man also admitted raping her, breaking her bones, and using degrading verbal abuse to her (August 25, 1994).

But, some of those who stay to the end of the group talk about change, again in terms of masculinity. One Hawaiian man, who lives in a camp on the beach, and claims to be very tough, says, "I let this fucker live because of this class." He had a very violent past, but now thinks that the tough thing to do is to walk away from fights. "Before, I slap anyone who come in my face. Now I walk away, got the knowledge to walk away when I feel the tensions. I like that part." Another commented, "I never thought about all of this before – I never took it down. I just did things. And it is a matter of beliefs" (January 14, 1992).

Masculinity is far more complicated than the vision which the program is trying to teach. In the face of its essentialized, uniform image, these men act out a subversive counterpoint of other ideas of masculinity, ideas which require obedience and respect from women, and tolerate violence or yelling when these are not forthcoming. At the same time, they endeavor to locate themselves within a legitimate masculine space within the program by presenting themselves as engaging in only minor violence, a necessary response to a woman's lack of obedience or respect. They claim to do this only rarely and when the woman makes it necessary. When such an image jars too sharply with other facts known to the group, the men say they don't understand their feelings and can't control them.

Excessive violence is a matter of cultural meaning and interpretation, of course. In bars or beach parties, some violence against partners is culturally approved, but not in court or the ATV program. Thus, the men must navigate a world in which they simultaneously seek to justify violence in terms of their partner's behavior and deny that they are often or excessively violent. Oddly, they both claim their violence was justified and that it is only an occasional and chance event and not really a basic characteristic of their personalities. Some present themselves as unable to stop themselves.

The stories they tell about their violence are clearly performative events, directed to the audience of the facilitators running a court-mandated program and to the other men in the program. The group leaders provide a distinctive image of masculinity based on ideas of gender equality and respect, yet the participants counter with their own, subversive, notions that women respect men who assert control over them through violence, that the violence is simply their response to women's provocations, and that they are in any case powerless to control their rage. There is a class dimension to this change: the image of masculinity being advocated is more characteristic of the educated middle class in this town than the working class and the poor. Humor and silence represent two potent modes of resistance to this reconstruction of masculinity, building on the history of class and ethnic resistance to *haole* authority and control. Despite the obvious resistance of the participants, however, for some the discussions in this program provide an appealing vision of negotiated gender equality.[10]

## Changing Forms of Control

By the end of the twentieth century, the feminist batterer intervention programs which labeled batterers as criminals and confronted them with their violence were being displaced by more therapeutic programs which focused on improving self-esteem, understanding feelings, and making choices. This transformation was fostered by the closer connections between violence programs and the state. These changes in modes of managing gender violence are characteristic of more general changes taking place in the transition from an industrial to a post-industrial society. In the last few decades, new forms of regulation based on self-management have widely displaced older systems of discipline based on punishment. While courts in the nineteenth century punished offenders by imposing fines, those of the late twentieth serve as conduits for a wide array of therapeutic interventions, all of which strive in various ways to induce the defendant to participate in transforming himself and promise him greater autonomy and control over his or her life (see Rose 1999).

Post-industrial society relies on an extensive apparatus of traditional forms of incarceration and punishment as well, but prison is largely reserved for offenses which threaten strangers (see Ewick 1997). For men who batter women, the prison is held at a distance, replaced by psychotherapeutic encouragement to learn about one's feelings and to take control over one's life, with the reward of having better love and better sex in intimate relationships.

The new disciplinary techniques work on persons rather than actions, seeking to reform them through rehabilitation and repentance. Disciplinary systems incorporate a broad range of therapeutic and group discussion techniques ranging from batterer intervention programs to alcoholics-anonymous-style self-help meetings (see Rose 1989; Valverde 1998). Some are designed to reform by forcing the body to follow an orderly sequence of activities in work and everyday life while others reform through introspection and insight, requiring consent from the subject of transformation. As Simon points out, prison reform models from the early nineteenth century already incorporated these two approaches to discipline: one was based on habituation of the body and coordination with the machinery of production while the other developed skills of self-management and self-control and promoted autonomy and integrity (Simon 1993b: 29). These two forms continued to provide alternative models of discipline throughout the nineteenth and early twentieth

---

[10]   For a careful and thoughtful analysis of Hawaiian masculinity, see Tengan (2008).

centuries, but the latter came to predominate. In the late twentieth century, the criminal justice system in the USA has increasingly turned to introspective forms of discipline and self-management (Simon 1993b).

# Conclusions

Although Hilo is one small town, its changing practices of managing wife battering parallel those of big cities and exemplify shifting forms of governance in contemporary industrialized cities in the USA. In Hilo, as in many larger cities, responsibility for control of violence against women has shifted from kin and neighbors to the state. It is the law rather than the family to which these battered women turn. Such a decision is not easy and is often discouraged by kin and friends. Yet the skyrocketing number of complaints shows that the turn to the law is happening in many parts of the United States. It took a protracted struggle led by a powerful social movement to increase the severity of punishments and to develop and implement civil protective orders. Many judges still question their validity as a legal procedure and police are often lax in enforcing them. Overworked prosecutors ignore TRO violations. Yet the trilogy of punishment, safety, and reform mechanisms provide survivors of violence more opportunities for support from the state.

In Hilo, as well as in large industrial cities, governance of everyday behavior by the law is shaped by inequalities linked to class and ethnicity. Those who end up with TROs or in batterer treatment programs are typically the poorest and least educated segments of the male population, disproportionately members of colonized and disadvantaged communities. These mechanisms increase the safety of women but also increase control over the poor. Protecting women from battering enhances discipline over men who are already the target of state systems of control. Wealthier men in Hilo also beat their wives (although this is hard to find out in any systematic way), but they very rarely appear in criminal court or batterer intervention programs and only slightly more often in Family Court. It is largely poor men who are sanctioned by the law. Privileged batterers usually escape.

The mechanisms of punishment, safety, and reform are interlocking. Each operates only in conjunction with the others and can be understood only within the matrix created by the whole system. None could function as well on its own. Men would not attend ATV unless required to; two days in jail have little impact on helping men to rethink masculinity; requiring a batterer to stay away from one victim leaves him/her free to hit the next one. Spatial separation without criminal penalties for violating it has little effect. The modes of intervention are not simply shifting from punishment to safety to therapy, but there is a pattern of growth and layering. The new is added to the old which then redefines the meanings and operation of both. Punishment forms the bedrock for the newer technologies of reform and safety. This is not an evolutionary relationship but an intersecting one.

And to some extent, this pattern is global. The invention of the TRO for gender violence was quickly followed by its rapid spread through the USA and globally. It is the cornerstone of the 2006 law to control domestic violence in India discussed in Chapter 2. There is now a global diffusion of batterer intervention programs, no-drop policies, and restraining orders. These new technologies of controlling gender violence circulate transnationally within cities large and small. They have recently been joined by a newer approach: the identification of gender violence as a human rights violation. The next chapter shows how this happened and its implications for understanding and preventing gender violence.

## Questions for Further Discussion

1   Compare the following three interventions in domestic violence: punishment, safety, and reform. What are the goals of each strategy? How are they different, and how are they connected? Which groups are most affected by these interventions? Do they address interpersonal or structural violence (see Chapter 1)? Explain.
2   Play the role of a court judge, one who batters, and one who has been battered. How do these actors conceptualize violence? How does each player view the role of the law in the management of domestic violence? Do women and others who have been battered gain or lose control of their lives by turning to the law? Explain.
3   How is masculinity performed in the Hilo example, and how is it related to gender violence? Is its performance unchanging over time and across race, ethnicity, class, and age? Explain.

## Video Suggestions

*Macho*, by Lucinda Broadbent (Scotland/Nicaragua, 2000), 26 minutes

Filmed in the context of political scandal in Nicaragua – when in 1998 Sandinista revolutionary hero and President Daniel Ortega was charged for the rape and battery of his stepdaughter, Soilamerica Narvacz – *Macho* gives voice not only to the victims of gender violence. Through the internationally acclaimed organization, Men against Violence, we meet male victimizers who unlearn the rules of male chauvinism (machismo) in support groups and through local activism. From the streets of Managua to workshops in San Francisco, California, men challenge the sentiment that sexual, physical, and mental abuse is part of the repertoire of male power.

*Sentenced to Marriage*, by Anat Zuria (Israel, 2004), 65 minutes

Divorce in Israel is granted not according to secular law, but by religious courts. This film gains rare access to the divorce hearings of three women who have been denied divorce by rabbinical courts for as many as five years despite their many attempts to end their marriages sooner. While in legal limbo, women are forbidden contact with other men, but husbands are allowed to live with other women, withhold child support, and begin new families. Out of desperation, some of these independent, well-educated, working women buy a divorce from their husbands for large sums. The law, for them, becomes an instrument of their disempowerment.

*Sisters in Law*, by Kim Longinotto, co-directed by Florence Ayisi
(Cameroon/UK, 2005), 104 minutes

In the town of Kumba, Cameroon, domestic violence is common. There has not been a conviction for spousal abuse for 17 years. But two women – State Prosecutor Vera Ngassa and Court President Beatrice Ntuba – encourage survivors of domestic violence to fight the pattern of abuse, despite pressure from their families and communities to remain silent. With compassion and wit, these two lively progressives impart wisdom, justice, and stiff sentences to those convicted of perpetrating all forms of violence in the home, including rape, spousal abuse, and child abuse.

# 4

# Gender Violence as a Human Rights Violation

Defining gender violence as a violation of human rights is a relatively new approach to the problem. In the late 1980s and early 1990s, the global feminist social movement worked to introduce this idea to the human rights community and, by the early years of the twenty-first century, succeeded in establishing the right to protection from gender violence as a core dimension of women's human rights. This is another example of the process described in Chapter 2, in which a social movement defines a problem and generates support from legal institutions and states. After describing how gender violence became a human rights violation articulated in formal documents of international law, this chapter discusses one of the most important new issues in the gender violence and human rights field, that of the trafficking of sex workers.

In the early 1990s, a transnational movement coalesced around the idea that violence against women was a human rights violation. It built on the work of activists around the world who set up shelters, counseling centers, and batterer treatment programs, often borrowing from each other and adapting ideas from one context to another. Anti-rape movements began in Hong Kong and Fiji in the late 1980s and early 1990s, for example, and concern about rape in police custody galvanized activists in India in the mid 1980s. American activists developed anti-rape movements at the same time. The defense of women who killed their batterers also became a rallying cry in the USA and in other parts of the world. In the late 1980s and early 1990s, feminist movements in Europe, the United States, Australia (Silard 1994), Argentina (Oller 1994), Brazil (Thomas 1994), India (Bush 1992), the Virgin Islands (Morrow 1994), and many other parts of the world developed strategies to protect women from violence in the home through shelters, support groups for victims, and criminalization of battering. The need for intervention was widely recognized in the nations of the global south as well as the north (e.g. Ofei-Aboagye 1994).

During this period, strategies, programs, and information circulated globally. One of the most widespread approaches was embodied in the "power and control wheel," a graphic representation of the theory that violence takes many forms such as intimidation, minimizing the significance of the violence, denying responsibility for the violence, isolating the victim, exercising male privilege, and using emotional forms of abuse (see Pence and Paymar 1993). The wheel was developed by the Domestic Abuse Intervention Project (DAIP) in Duluth, Minnesota in the early 1980s and widely used in batterer intervention programs such as the one I studied in Hilo and in women's support groups. It is used in many places around the world, including New Zealand, Germany, Scotland, Canada, Israel, St. Croix in the Virgin Islands, Fiji, and in the USA in such culturally distinct locations as the Pine Ridge Indian Reservation and Marine Corps bases. Information about programs and approaches are widely disseminated through the Internet. For example, in 1999–2000 a virtual working group under the auspices of UNIFEM conducted an email exchange about approaches to violence against women which included 2,300 participants in 120 countries.

After two decades of work at the national and local level, in the early 1990s some activists turned to a more global strategy, working through transnational NGOs and UN agencies. In fact, the campaign against violence against women is one of the few successful examples of a transnational collective action network, as women in various parts of the world tried out and adopted similar techniques (see Keck and Sikkink 1998). The emergence of a transnational movement opposing violence against women was facilitated by an extraordinary series of global conferences on women sponsored by the UN between 1975 and 1995. The first meeting, held in Mexico City in 1975, focused on equality, development, and peace. However, attention gradually shifted from peace to human rights, with a growing interest in defining violence against women as a human rights offense expressed in the 1980 Copenhagen and 1985 Nairobi meetings. It was not a major issue in the 1975 and 1980 global women's conferences, although it was mentioned in the 1980 Copenhagen document (Thomas 1999: 244–245; Stephenson 1995). The Nairobi Forward-Looking Strategies developed in 1985 identified reducing violence against women as a basic strategy for addressing the issue of peace (United Nations 1995b: 125).

In 1990 the UN's Economic and Social Council adopted a resolution recommended by the Commission on the Status of Women stating that violence against women in the family and society derives from their unequal status in society and recommending that governments take immediate measures to establish appropriate penalties for violence against women as well as to develop policies to prevent and control violence against women in the family, workplace, and society (United Nations 1995b: 131–132). This recommendation suggests developing correctional, educational, and social services including shelters and training programs for law enforcement officers, judiciary, health, and social service personnel. The major UN convention on women's rights, the 1979 Convention on the Elimination of All Forms of Discrimination against Women (CEDAW) does not mention violence against women explicitly, but the committee monitoring the Convention developed an initial recommendation against violence in 1989 and formulated a broader recommendation which defined gender-based violence as a form of discrimination in 1992.

The 1992 statement placed violence against women squarely within the rubric of human rights and fundamental freedoms and made clear that states are obliged to eliminate violence perpetrated by public authorities and by private persons (United Nations 1995b: 131–132; Cook 1994b: 165).

At the 1993 UN Conference on Human Rights in Vienna, sponsored by the High Commission on Human Rights, this issue became even more important (see Schuler 1992). Global activism by women's NGOs drew attention to the issue of violence against women. A worldwide petition campaign gathered over 300,000 signatures from 123 countries, putting the issue of violence against women at the center of the conference (Friedman 1995: 27–31). The concluding document, the Vienna Declaration and Programme of Action, formally recognized the human rights of women as "an inalienable integral and indivisible part of human rights" (Connors 1996: 27). In addition to working to eliminate violence against women in public and private life, this document advocated "the elimination of gender bias in the administration of justice and the eradication of any conflicts which may arise between the rights of women and the harmful effects of certain traditional or customary practices" (sec. II, B, para. 38, UN Doc. A/Conf.157/24, October 1993, quoted in Thomas 1999: 249). The Vienna Declaration specifically called for the appointment of a special rapporteur on violence against women and the drafting of a declaration eliminating violence against women.

In 1994 the UN Commission on Human Rights condemned gender-based violence and appointed the requested rapporteur (United Nations 1992b: 132). The Special Rapporteur on Violence against Women is mandated to collect information relating to violence against women, to recommend measures to remedy it, and to work with other members of the Commission on Human Rights (CHR), the human rights body that predated the recently created Human Rights Council. The Special Rapporteur on Violence against Women appointed by the CHR chairman in 1994, Radhika Coomaraswamy, was very effective in bringing more attention to the issue. During her tenure as Special Rapporteur from 1994 until 2003, she prepared several substantial reports defining violence against women and investigating its various manifestations around the world. These reports helped to define violence against women as a human rights violation along with the duty of states to exercise "due diligence" in preventing violence against women in the family, the community, and the public space.

Also in the early 1990s, the UN's Commission on the Status of Women recommended the formulation of an international instrument on violence against women and developed the Declaration on the Elimination of Violence against Women in 1993, working with meetings of groups of experts. In 1994 the General Assembly of the United Nations adopted the Declaration on the Elimination of Violence against Women unanimously (Van Bueren 1995: 753). Although it has no binding force, this Declaration does have the moral strength of world consensus (Coomaraswamy and Kois 1999: 182). It is a comprehensive document which defines violence against women broadly to include physical, sexual, and psychological harm or threats of harm in public or private life (Article 1). It names gender-based violence as a violation of human rights and as an instance of sex discrimination and inequality (Connors 1996: 27–28). The Declaration attributes the roots of gender violence to historically unequal power relations between men and women, arguing that it is socially constructed and historically justified rather than natural (Coomaraswamy and Kois 1999: 183). It prohibits invoking custom, tradition, or religious consider-ations to avoid its obligations and urges states to exercise "due diligence" to prevent, investigate, and punish acts of violence against women whether perpetrated by the state or private persons (Article 4; Van Bueren 1995: 753).

Scholars and nongovernmental organizations contributed in very significant ways to this redefinition of gender violence. In 1994 Rhonda Copelon (1994), a professor of law at the City University of New York Law School, labeled domestic violence a form of torture, a position supported by Amnesty International (2001). Dorothy Thomas, head of the Women's Rights Division of Human Rights Watch in the early 1990s, worked hard to define gender violence as a human rights violation. As her colleague at the Bunting Institute at Radcliffe in 1994, I listened to her talk about getting Human Rights Watch, one of the largest human rights organizations, to take women's rights and gender violence seriously.

The Fourth World Conference on Women in Beijing in 1995, often called the Beijing Conference, clearly named violence against women as a violation of human rights and fundamental freedoms. Its final policy document, the Platform for Action, defined violence against women broadly as "any act of gender-based violence that results in, or is likely to result in, physical, sexual or psychological harm or suffering to women, including threats of such acts, coercion or arbitrary deprivation of lib-erty, whether occurring in public or private life" (sec. D, 113). It includes gender-based violence in the family, the community, or perpetrated by the state, including acts of violence and sexual abuse during armed conflict, forced sterilization and abortion, and female infanticide. By declaring protection from violence for women and girl children as a universal human right, the conference articulated a dramatic expansion of human rights. The Platform declares that:

> Violence against women both violates and impairs or nullifies the enjoyment by women of their human rights and fundamental freedoms. The long-standing failure to protect and promote those rights and freedoms in the case of violence against women is a matter of concern to all States and should be addressed. (Platform for Action, sec. D, 112)

In 2002 the Special Rapporteur on Violence against Women, Radhika Coomaraswamy, produced a report on cultural practices in the family that are vio-lent to women. She described these practices as "an important issue that would define the international human rights debate over the next decade" (HR/CN/02/32, April 10, 2002, UN Press Release). This report moved the critique of gender violence into a new domain of behavior, that of sexuality and its regulation, and challenged cultural practices considered acceptable by at least some members of many societies. The report discussed a variety of practices in the family that are violent toward women and harmful to their health such as female genital mutilation, honor killings, pledging of daughters to temples at an early age to be sex workers or handmaidens of gods (the *devadasi* system in India and similar systems in Nepal, Benin, Nigeria, Togo, and Ghana), witch hunting (found mainly in Asia and Africa), caste-based discrimination and violence, early and forced marriage, marital rape, discriminatory laws, son preference, restrictive practices such as foot-binding and veiling, and images of beauty that emphasize thinness (a widespread problem in the West). The report argues that these cultural practices harmful to women's human rights to bodily integrity and expression have avoided national and international scrutiny "because they are seen as cultural practices that deserve tolerance and respect." "Cultural relativism," she asserts,

is often used as an excuse to permit inhumane and discriminatory practices against women in the community despite clear provisions in many human rights instruments, including the Convention on the Elimination of all Forms of Discrimination against Women, in accordance with which States parties shall take all appropriate measures to modify the social and cultural patterns of conduct of men and women, with a view to achieving the elimination of prejudices and customary and all other practices which are based on the idea of the inferiority or the superiority of either of the sexes or on stereotyped roles for men and women. (Article 5, E/CN.4/2002/83, p. 3)

Coomaraswamy asserted that all cultures have such practices and that many focus on the regulation of female sexuality. Some of these practices are discussed in Chapter 6.

In 2003 the US division of Amnesty International, one of the oldest and most established human rights organizations, initiated a major global campaign against violence against women, using a human rights framework (www.amnestyusa.org/stopviolence/about.html). As anthropologist Sheila Dauer, Director of Amnesty International USA's Women's Program says, "By providing the global human rights framework for the struggle, Amnesty International will show how international human rights standards cut across national boundaries, cultures and religions and how we can hold governments accountable to meet their obligations to protect women and girls from violence regardless of who commits it or where it is committed" (http://takeaction.amnestyusa.org/Newsletter/?nlid=20&nlaid=81). For an organization that had focused on political prisoners, this was a big change.

In 2003 the General Assembly of the UN asked the Secretary-General to prepare an in-depth study of global violence against women, which was presented to the General Assembly in 2006. This was the first time that the General Assembly had ever discussed the issue. The report asserts that violence against women is a pressing human rights issue and highlights the ongoing persistence of the problem, ways for governments to respond more effectively, and approaches to increase governmental and international accountability. While asserting the widespread prevalence of the problem, it argues that its particular manifestations are shaped by factors such as ethnicity, class, age, sexual orientation, disability, nationality, and religion. It argues that the roots of violence against women are gender inequality, discrimination against women in public and private spheres, patriarchal disparities of power, and economic inequalities. "Violence against women is one of the key means through which male control over women's agency and sexuality is maintained" (Executive Summary, p. 1). Its authors include many of the leading scholars who have worked to promote a human rights approach to gender violence, including the Americans Charlotte Bunch and Elizabeth Schneider (www.un.org/womenwatch/daw/vaw; see Schneider 2000; 2004; Bunch 1990; 1997). Like this book, the report grounds the problem in larger social structures of inequality rather than the dynamics of inter-personal relationships.

Thus the 1990s and 2000s saw a dramatic expansion of the international move-ment against gender violence. Through international conferences, UN declarations, and international NGO activism, violence against women was defined as a human rights violation. The original meaning of violence against women – male violence against their partners in the form of rape, assault, and murder – has expanded to include female genital mutilation/cutting/excision, gender-based violence by police and military forces in armed conflict as well as everyday life, violence against refugee women and asylum seekers, trafficking in sex workers, sexual harassment, forced pregnancy, forced abortion, forced sterilization, female feticide and infanticide, early and forced marriage, honor killings, and widowhood violations (see Cook 1994a: 20; Keck and Sikkink 1998). The conjoining of these disparate issues is the product of sustained activism among a transnational network of NGOs over the last 20 years (Keck and Sikkink 1998). It has been facilitated by the emergence of the human rights system and the structure formed by the UN and its declarations and conven-tions. These formal mechanisms operate in parallel with an energetic and imagina-tive NGO community which pressures governments to develop global regulatory instruments that control violence against women and then to abide by them (see further Merry 2006).

## The Human Rights Framework

In order to appreciate the implications of defining gender violence as a human rights violation, it is important to understand what human rights law can do. Human rights is, in effect, a system of quasi-law. It has many features that are lawlike, but it lacks an enforcement mechanism parallel to that of state law. Like state law systems, human rights operates through statutes which are produced through quasi-legislative processes of commission meetings and deliberations with the assistance of experts under the auspices of UN organizations. The precise texts of the declarations and conventions are produced through a painstaking process of examining words and meanings in a variety of preliminary and working group meetings which are then presented to the General Assembly for approval (see Riles 1999; Merry 2006). Once approved, conventions must be submitted to the member nations of the UN for ratification. They are established internationally only when a sufficient number of nations ratify the agreement. Human rights conventions become part of national legal systems only when a country ratifies them, passes laws to implement them, and enforces them domestically. Declarations, on the other hand, are simply passed by the General Assembly (Kim 1991: 119). They are statements of principle that gradually become part of customary international law but do not require nations to ratify them. The Universal Declaration of Human Rights of 1948 has achieved that status, but other declarations remain more aspirational. Because the UN system is grounded in a network of sovereign nations, it has no binding power beyond the consent of these constituent nations.

However, a range of civil society organizations and actors, including NGOs, support compliance with human rights conventions and declarations as well as providing expertise in the drafting of documents (Stephenson 1995; Keck and Sikkink 1998). The major weapon of human rights compliance is communication: exposing points of violation of human rights documents and using international public opinion to condemn violating states. Such a mechanism is clearly dependent on the international system of power and the interests of powerful nations in pressing for human rights compliance. It also relies on the information gathering and dissemination work of NGOs. Inevitably, rights promoted by the most powerful nations will be more effectively urged on non-compliant nations. As violence against women became a more important issue in the United States and Europe, for example, its prominence within the human rights system grew. However, if an issue loses importance for the activists of politically powerful nations, it is likely to drop off the international agenda. Keck and Sikkink (1998) propose a boomerang model to describe this form of human rights pressure: local groups facing neglect of a human rights violation in their own country appeal to international NGOs, who in turn mobilize political support within a dominant country and induce it to put pressure on the weaker country. Thus, the enforcement of human rights depends greatly on the international balance of power and the agendas of the economically and politically powerful nations, in effect the nations of the north rather than the south.

Despite these difficulties in enforcement, human rights declarations and conventions contribute to cultural change. They articulate new norms legitimated by the fact that they were produced through a process of international deliberation that resulted in consensus. Communications systems such as the Internet disseminate these documents and bring global attention to behavior that is defined as a human rights violation. Although these networks of communication and the consequent mobilization of public opinion cannot be called law, they can serve as powerful motivators for local actors concerned about their public image on the international stage. Mobilizing transnational public opinion through reports, information exchange, and the media and the arts contributes in important ways to strengthening the quasi-legal system of human rights.

Although the idea of human rights grows out of a 200-year-old tradition rooted in the European Enlightenment, the expansion of the contemporary human rights system is a product of the last 60 years. The contemporary human rights system was inspired by the particular historical circumstance of the Holocaust. In the wake of this event, many argued that the protection of citizens could no longer be left to states alone. Individuals needed protection from abusive states. The international regime of human rights argued that, by virtue of their humanity, all individuals are entitled to a basic modicum of human dignity. Moreover, certain human rights are universal, fundamental, and inalienable and thus cannot and should not be overridden by cultural and religious traditions. The accident of birth in a particular social group or culture should have no bearing on individuals' intrinsic worth or right to be treated as a human being (Zechenter 1997: 319–320). The decolonization movement of the 1950s and 1960s also shaped human rights discourse. As colonized peoples began to press for decolonization, self-determination emerged as an important human rights concept (see Merry 2000; Rajagopal 2003).

In response to such historical and social processes, the UN human rights framework has continued to evolve and change. Although human rights originally referred to civil and political rights rooted in liberal theory, the concept has expanded to include social and economic rights, collective rights, and cultural rights. Guarantees to employment and fair working conditions, health, food, and social security, education, and participation in the cultural life of the community were promoted by socialist and social welfare states which emphasized economic, social, and cultural rights as well as political rights, based in part on the experiences of the industrial revolution. The USA accepts civil and political rights more enthusiastically than economic, social, and cultural ones but African states emphasize social, economic, and cultural rights over civil rights.

Collective rights are among the most recent rights, but they build on twentieth-century concerns with minority rights, language rights, and rights to self-determination (e.g. Asch 1984; Wilmsen 1989; Trask 1993; Coulter 1994; Tennant 1994; Sierra 1995; Anaya 1996; Cowan 2003). Indigenous peoples in particular have sought rights which are collective and whose beneficiaries are historically formed communities rather than individuals or states (Anaya 1996: 48). As Anaya notes, these rights not only conflict with the dominant individual/state dichotomy which underlies the creation of international standards, but they also challenge state sovereignty. Claims to cultural rights are also collective. The authentic and culturally distinct self-representations which collective rights sometimes require leads to constructed misrepresentations of histories and ways of life (Friedman 1996; Rogers 1996; Povinelli 2002). In other words, making claims to cultural rights often requires framing these claims in terms of an essentialized, homogeneous, "traditional" culture (see Jackson 1995; Merry 1997). This requirement contradicts the flexible and changing nature of the cultural life of indigenous communities and often requires them to present claims in tragically inappropriate terms (Povinelli 1998). Women's rights are also collective rights, and are similarly dependent on an essentialized understanding of gender.

Despite its Western Enlightenment origins, the human rights system is not fixed but changes in response to new global circumstances. This is a pluralized, flexible, and responsive system which develops over time (Messer 1997: 295). It is the product of negotiation and discussion rather than imposition. As the concept has expanded from its initial meaning within liberalism – the protection of the individual from the state – to a series of obligations by states to their members such as rights to food, housing, self-determination, and other collective rights, the content, diversity, and nature of rights has changed. Nevertheless, women's rights are not only newcomers to the human rights field but also rather uneasily adapted to its core categories. For example, Jack Donnelly (2003), a prominent human rights legal scholar, objects to using a collective rights approach for women since he argues that individual rights adequately cover the issues that women are concerned with. The assertion that "women's rights are human rights" is an important rallying cry, but not a universally accepted principle.

## Using the human rights framework for gender violence

Violence against women is not easily defined as a human rights violation. Human rights violations are typically actions of states, yet many forms of domestic violence and sexual assault are perpetrated by private citizens. Beginning in 1990, activists argued that a state's failure to protect women from violence is itself a human rights violation (Bunch 1990; Thomas and Beasley 1993). Governments are not required to prevent all criminal activity against their populations, but if they fail to prosecute crime against one part of the population as energetically as a similar crime against another part, they are guilty of discrimination. Given the historically lax treatment of gender violence and rape, governments were clearly acting in a discriminatory way in their failure to prosecute and punish sexual and physical assaults against women as energetically as assaults against men. States that fail to protect their members from violence in a discriminatory way violate their responsibilities toward these members (Bunch 1990; Thomas and Beasley 1993; Romany 1994). They have not exercised sufficient effort – due diligence – in protecting them. If assault or murder is prosecuted less avidly when it occurs against women in intimate relationships than under other circumstances, a state has discriminated on the basis of gender. This constitutes a human rights violation. In its general recommendation on this topic the CEDAW Committee asserted that violence against women is a form of discrimination, defining gender-based violence as "a form of discrimination which seriously inhibits women's ability to enjoy rights and freedoms on a basis of equality with men" (CEDAW General Recommendation 19, note 3, 1992).

The 1992 recommendation of the CEDAW Committee that defined gender-based violence as a form of discrimination made clear that states are obliged to eliminate violence perpetrated by public authorities and by private persons (Cook 1994b: 165). The doctrine asserts state responsibility for failures to protect women from violence (Bunch 1990; Thomas and Beasely 1993; Cook 1994b). Although individual perpetrators are not legally liable under international human rights law, states are responsible for their failure to meet international obligations, even for acts by private persons, if they fail to make an effort to eliminate or mitigate the acts (Cook 1994b: 151). Within national legal systems, assault and murder are universally considered as crimes (United Nations 1995b: 137), but wife beating is shielded by its location in a legally and culturally constructed private sphere. Historically, in the USA as well as in many other parts of the world, it has been regarded as less serious than other kinds of assault. Thus the emergence of violence against women as a distinct human rights violation depends on redefining the family so that it is no longer a shelter from legal scrutiny and highlighting the discriminatory effects of regarding it in these terms. It requires an assertion that women are a special category of persons entitled to rights because they are women, and demands recognition for these collective rights.

The Commission on the Status of Women considered violence against women in connection with racism and HIV/AIDS in 2001 and poverty and natural disasters in 2002. In 2003 it was again a central focus. The Commission on Human Rights has passed a unanimous resolution against violence against women and another against trafficking in women every year since the mid 1990s. Several regional documents and agreements also condemn violence against women, directly or implicitly, such as the 1969 American Convention on Human Rights and its Additional Protocol in the Area of Economic, Social and Cultural Rights; the 1994 Inter-American Convention on the Prevention, Punishment and Eradication of Violence against Women (Convention of Belem do Para); the 1981 African Charter on Human and Peoples' Rights; and the 1999 Grand Baie Declaration and Plan of Action on Human Rights.

In the last few years, US activists have started using the human rights framework at home. Although the USA has not ratified CEDAW and there is considerable resistance to applying human rights domestically, a group of scholars and activists argue that a human rights framework redefines gender violence in productive ways. By the late 1990s domestic violence in the USA was increasingly treated as an individual problem amenable to therapy rather than as a structural problem requiring social change. In contrast, the international human rights framework emphasizes the links between gender violence and inequality (Schneider 2000: 56; 2004). Human rights offer a broader perspective on gender violence, one that considers not just the victim's right to protection from assault but also her right to health care, housing, education, and employment (Thomas 2000: 1122). This approach emphasizes the links between gender violence and social justice issues such as workplace discrimination, pay equity, reproductive choice, and child care and health care (Schneider 2000: 28; 2004). It incorporates the framework of intersectionality that combines gender with race, language, religion, national origin, and a variety of other factors in the analysis of identity.

Dorothy Thomas (2000: 1122), the founding director of the Women's Rights Project of Human Rights Watch from 1989 to 1998, thinks that the surprising fissure between US women's rights activists and the international movement comes from historic American resistance to scrutiny under international standards that might expose and challenge domestic abuse. Moreover, many Americans think that civil rights applies to "us" and human rights to "them" (Thomas 2000: 1123). But there is a growing turn to human rights, which Schneider attributes to frustration with litigating women's rights cases in the USA and the internationalization of domestic organizations. She anticipates greater use of human rights arguments in domestic women's rights litigation and greater attention to the USA's ratification of CEDAW (Schneider 2004: 707).

Indeed, there has been greater collaboration between civil rights and human rights approaches in the last few years. Three of the largest US-based human rights organizations – Amnesty International, Human Rights Watch, and International Human Rights Law Group – have increased their work on the USA while a few women-focused US human rights groups, such as the Center for Human Rights Education in Atlanta and the Women's Rights Network in Boston emerged in the late 1990s (Thomas 2000: 1124). But focusing on women's rights in the USA is still a minor part of the work of US human rights groups. A 1996 report of the Women's Rights Project of Human Rights Watch chronicled patterns of sexual abuse of women in US prisons in five states, noting that this violated the Convention against Torture and the International Covenant of Civil and Political Rights, both documents signed by the USA (Human Rights Watch, Women's Rights Project 1996). However, according to the website of the Women's Rights Division of Human Rights Watch, only 6 percent of almost 100 reports published between 1991 and 2004 deal with US issues (www.hrw.org/doc/?t=women_pub).

In the early 2000s the Battered Mothers' Testimony Project of the Women's Rights Network at the Wellesley Centers for Women used human rights reporting to document battered women and children's experiences with the law in the Massachusetts Family Court System (Cuthbert et al. 2002). The co-directors of the project, Carrie Cuthbert and Kim Slote, were international human rights lawyers who had already organized several international meetings of domestic violence advocates. They used international human rights reporting techniques, including the staging of a tribunal, to address at home the situation of battered mothers in court.

Another indication of this new interest in human rights is the appeal to international law for US problems (Schneider 2004: 706–707). For example, in March 2007 Jessica Lenahan (Gonzales) filed a suit in the Inter-American Commission on Human Rights, an entity of the Organization of American States, concerning the failure of a Colorado police department to enforce a restraining order (Gardella 2007). This is the first time US attorneys have used international human rights law to protect domestic violence victims and their children. In 1999 Jessica Lenahan, then Gonzales, had a restraining order against her husband in the town of Castle Rock, Colorado, which allowed him some visitation rights. When Lenahan discovered that her daughters, aged 10, 8, and 7, were missing, she called the police for help. She continued to call the police from 6 p.m. until 3.20 a.m., when her husband drove to the local police department, opened fire on the building, and was killed by the police. The daughters were found dead in the car, killed hours earlier. In 2000 she filed a $30 million lawsuit against the police department and three of its members, alleging that they had violated her right to due process by failing to enforce the restraining order. The district court dismissed the case. On appeal, the Tenth Circuit gave her a property right to police enforcement of the order. The police department appealed this decision to the US Supreme Court. In 2005 the Supreme Court said that Lenahan's due process rights had not been violated since she had no personal entitlement to police enforcement of her restraining order.

Lawyers from Columbia Law School's Human Rights Institute and Human Rights Clinic and from the American Civil Liberties Union took the case to the Inter-American Court in 2007. Since the USA has not signed the American Convention on Human Rights, its decision will not be binding, but the USA has submitted a thorough response to the claims and is likely to take the court's findings seriously. The attorneys and Lenahan see this as a way to build consensus on domestic violence as a human rights issue and submit this case to the court of public opinion.

Other US lawyers working on domestic violence are also contemplating bringing cases to this court in the future (Gardella 2007). For example, in May 2007 several national and state organizations, including the Leadership Council on Child Abuse and Interpersonal Violence and the NOW Foundation, filed a petition in the Inter-American Commission on Human Rights charging that the USA has failed to protect the life, liberties, security, and other human rights of abused mothers and their children by frequently awarding child custody to abusers and child molesters. The complaint describes several cases where there was clear medical evidence of child sexual abuse yet the abusing father was given full custody of the children he had abused. The petitioners say the problem is endemic in the family law courts across the country (www.stopfamilyviolence.org).

Thus there are indications that human rights are becoming a more important resource for gender violence activism in the USA as well as in other countries, but the American separation of domestic advocacy based on a civil rights framework and international advocacy using a human rights perspective is a longstanding one. The new rapprochement is taking place among the intellectual leaders of the US domestic violence and sexual assault movements and some more internationally focused NGOs, but is not characteristic of local US programs focused on service delivery. These programs generally have an exclusively civil rights-based focus, as does most of the social science scholarship on domestic violence and sexual assault in the USA.

## Universal Human Rights and the Question of Culture

The definition of violence against women as a human rights violation, framed in universalistic terms and applicable everywhere around the world, raises difficult questions of culture and rights. Even though violence exists in a culture-free zone of injury and death, its meanings are deeply shaped by social contexts. The substrate of violence against women is a universal space of pain and suffering which can be understood across cultural differences, but gender-based violence is embedded in cultural understandings of gender and sexuality as well as in the institutions of marriage, community, and state legal regulations of marriage, divorce, inheritance, and child custody. Yet the cultural resistance to women's human rights assumes a view of culture as homogeneous, consensual, and relatively static. However, many of the practices of gender violence are contested both within local communities and through influences from other societies. Ideas about appropriate and illegitimate violence are changing, and with them ideas about recourse for help in these situations. Those who defend culture against rights construct an unrealistic image of culture in an effort to avoid the rights critiques leveled by insiders as well as outsiders to a social group. The human rights project against violence against women is seeking to change ideas of what forms of violence are legitimate. Many religious and political leaders resist this change, invoking the need to protect culture. Since defenses of culture become the basis for defending male control over women, feminist activists often lose patience with cultural defenses despite their commitment to cultural diversity.

Conceptualizing violence against women as a human rights violation typically means demanding changes in local cultural practices concerning sexuality, marriage, and the family. Women's vulnerability to violence depends on entrenched sociocultural practices involving marriage, work, and religious and secular ideologies of masculinity and femininity (see Schuler 1992; Kerr 1993; Cook 1994b; Bunch 1997). Conventions on the rights of women typically require states which ratify them to change cultural practices which subordinate women. The 1992 Declaration on the Elimination of Violence against Women issued by the CEDAW Committee says that "States should condemn violence against women, and should not invoke any custom, tradition, or religion or other consideration to avoid their obligation with respect to its elimination" (Cook 1994b: 167, citing CEDAW General Recommendation 19 at 1, UN Doc., CEDAW/C/1992/L.1/Add.15 (1992)). However, some states claim that UN documents on women's rights such as CEDAW violate their own cultural practices and have ratified the treaty only with extensive reservations. According to the National Committee on UN/CEDAW, by 2006, 183 countries had ratified CEDAW, but it has more substantive reservations against it than any other international treaty (Bunch 1997: 44). One-third of the ratifying states have substantive reservations to parts of CEDAW (United Nations 1997: 49).

Thus women's rights to protection from violence seem diametrically opposed to the protection of culture. But this new category of human rights violation merges a wide variety of behaviors such as rape in wartime, wife battering, and female genital mutilation (Keck and Sikkink 1998). These activities vary significantly in their local cultural support. Some are clearly illegal, such as rape in wartime; others are tolerated within the private space of the family, such as wife battering; while others are local cultural practices supported within local communities, as discussed in Chapter 6. Of this last group, many are currently being contested and some have been outlawed, such as female genital cutting which is now illegal in several African states. To regard violence against women as an opposition between culture and rights is to fail to acknowledge the contested and variable cultural support these acts receive in different social groups. Such a view assumes that all of these actions are part of "culture" and that there are no debates within a society about their acceptability.

It is possible to find a space that respects cultural differences and at the same time protects women from violence. These often appear as opposite goals. Cultural beliefs and institutions often permit and encourage violence against women, and protecting women requires substantial shifts in beliefs about gender as well as changes in the institutions that govern women's lives such as marriage, divorce, education, and work opportunities. Human rights activists, social service reformers, and government policy-makers constantly tack between the goals of respecting cultural difference and protecting women's safety. They use pragmatic compromise and situationally determined decision-making.

The major international documents concerning violence against women are less negotiative. They condemn the use of cultural justifications for harming women. The 1993 Vienna Declaration stressed the importance of "the eradication of any conflicts which may arise between the rights of women and the harmful effects of certain traditional or customary practices, cultural prejudices and religious extremism" (Vienna Declaration and Platform for Action (A/conf.157/24/Part I: 19, para. 38)).[1] This paragraph does not, however, explicitly condemn such customs and practices. The 1995 Platform for Action from the Beijing Fourth World Conference on Women takes a stronger stand. It states: "Violence against women throughout the life cycle derives essentially from cultural patterns, in particular the harmful effects of certain traditional or customary practices and all acts of extremism linked to race, sex, language or religion that perpetuate the lower status accorded to women in the family, the workplace, the community and society" (United Nations 1995a: sec. D, 118, p. 75). According to Strategic Objective D.1, governments should "Condemn violence against women and refrain from invoking any custom, tradition or religious consideration to avoid their obligations with respect to its elimination as set out in the Declaration on the Elimination of Violence against Women" (United Nations 1995b: D.1, 124(a), p. 76). By urging governments to refrain from invoking culture as a defense, the Platform goes beyond the 1993 document that asks governments to reconcile conflicts between rights and culture. The Women's Convention (CEDAW) uses similar language in requiring ratifying states to change cultural practices that subordinate women. According to General Recommendation 19 issued by the CEDAW Committee: "States should condemn violence against women, and should not invoke any custom, tradition, or religion or other consideration to avoid their obligation with respect to its elimination" (Cook 1994b: 167, citing CEDAW General Recommendation 19 at 1, UN Doc., CEDAW/C/1992/L.1/Add.15 (1992)).

---

[1]   The Declaration by the General Assembly of 1993 is similarly clear in its condemnation of culture as a justification for violence against women. It explicitly rejects that any notion of cultural relativism should permit violence against women and prohibits states from using tradition to skirt compliance while holding individual states accountable for their inaction in protecting its female citizens from violence (Ulrich 2000: 652). Ulrich (2000: 653) thinks this declaration makes progress toward the view that it is essential to demolish social, economic, and cultural power structures that have kept women dominated for centuries.

A prominent NGO based in Asia that helps NGOs develop shadow reports and attend CEDAW hearings concurs with this view that culture is often used as a justification for oppressing women. In a posting on the electronic listserve "Endviolence," managed by UNIFEM, Beng Hui, the Information and Communications Officer for International Women's Rights Action Watch, Asia/Pacific (IWRAW-AP), writes from Kuala Lumpur in response to the question, What about situations where some women in a society consider a practice to be legitimate and others consider it violence?

> In the view of IWRAW Asia Pacific, [ending] any belief, practice or policy that results in harm cannot be seen as violating the cultural right of any community/society. Thus, even if there are women within a community/society who accept cultural practices that result in the violation of fundamental human rights, we should speak out against this since we need to adhere to certain standards. This is especially necessary when persons who are being violated may not necessarily have the power to object …
>
> Given that 169 states (governments) have ratified the CEDAW Convention, women should utilise this treaty to demand that cultural practices which limit women's rights be eliminated. The recent amendments to the inheritance laws in Nepal is a good example of how governments can intervene to challenge and change negative cultural values and practices. Prior to the amendments, women had limited inheritance rights i.e. linked to their marital status, because culture viewed that they should be dependent on their husbands for economic resources. While it is too early to know if this legal reform will result in changing cultural values, it is still useful to remember that governments *can* – and under CEDAW, *are obligated to* – take action to eliminate all forms of discrimination against women, including those which have cultural origins. (end violence@mail.edc.org, June 21, 2002).

One of the basic conceptions in discussions of women's rights to protection from violence is that of "harmful traditional practices." Originally developed to describe female genital cutting, this term describes practices that have some cultural legitimacy yet are harmful to women. In their discussion of traditional practices harmful to women, Coomaraswamy and Kois refer to cultural and traditional practices interchangeably. They note, for example, that violence against women is inherent in patriarchal traditions and culture (Coomaraswamy and Kois 1999: 190). Customs criticized as harmful traditional practices include widow immolation, prenatal sex selection, and female infanticide as a result of son preference, child marriage, arranged or forced marriage, polygamy, seclusion and veiling, and food taboos for women, as discussed in more detail in Chapter 6. Female genital cutting is the central issue around which the conception of harmful cultural practices or harmful traditional practices has coalesced.[2] This practice has inspired Western critiques

---

[2] For example, in the 1998 version of the Commission on Human Rights resolution on violence against women, it was the only "traditional or customary practice" listed (para. 11), while resolutions in subsequent years expanded the list. Female genital cutting, as it is less pejoratively called (see Boyle 2002), is a form of genital surgery that is widely seen as having harmful health consequences such as infections, painful urination and menstruation, difficulties in childbirth, and other complications.

since the 1930s, initially focusing on health hazards but more recently on the gender oppression inherent in the practice (Boyle 2002).[3] Thus genital cutting became the prototype of a practice justified by custom and culture and redefined as an act of violence and a breach of women's human rights (Bernard 1996: 79). Yet in the USA, domestic violence, rape in wartime, and stalking are not labeled as harmful cultural practices nor are forms of violence against women's bodies such as cosmetic surgery, dieting, and the wearing of high heels.

Theorizing culture as an open and flexible system radically changes the debate about human rights and their localization. It offers a far more accurate model for thinking about the intersections between global reform movements and local cultural practices. Moreover, a conception of culture as contentious practice provides a more accurate framework for human rights activism. This conception of culture does not eliminate tensions between rights concepts and cultural beliefs. Nor does it resolve the gap between general principles and the complexities of local contexts. Given its global reach, the human rights system must articulate general principles and cannot treat each local situation as distinct. When transnational reformers confront the incredible local complexity around the world, there is an inevitable tendency to simplify, to miss the nuances and the specific ways power is allocated in each situation. But adopting this concept of culture does focus attention on the strengths of local social arrangements in promoting human rights ideals and the importance of framing universalistic reforms in local cultural terms.

## Trafficking in Women

One of the hottest current issues in the human rights approach to violence against women is sex trafficking, the global circulation of women to serve in the sex trade. Trafficking in women for sex work is an old problem, but the end of communism, the advent of governmental strategies of market autonomy and deregulation called neoliberalism, and the increasing inequality in wealth around the world has fueled a rapid growth in sex trafficking since the 1990s. More women than ever are being drawn into the most coercive segments of prostitution, and many more are crossing national borders in order to do so. The increasing global inequality in wealth is

---

[3]  A Working Group on Traditional Practices was formed by the Human Rights Commission in 1986 (Bernard 1996: 78). In 1989, in response to NGO activism, the Sub-Commission on the Prevention of Discrimination and Protection of Minorities of the Human Rights Commission created a Special Rapporteur on Traditional Practices Affecting the Health of Women and Children (Report of the Special Rapporteur on Traditional Practices affecting the Health of Women and Children, UN Doc. E/CN.4/ Sub.2/1990/44). In 1990 the CEDAW Committee, being gravely concerned "that there are continuing cultural, traditional and economic pressures which help to perpetuate harmful practices, such as female circumcision," adopted a general recommendation (no. 14) that suggested that states parties should take measures to eradicate the practice of female circumcision (Bernard 1996: 78).

driving this process, while ever tighter border regulations condemn more and more of these women to moving illegally. Undocumented sex workers are even more vulnerable to exploitative working conditions, reinforced by violence and threats of blackmail, so that their illegal status makes them more readily coerced and less able to resist abuse and violence.

Trafficking is driven by increasing demand, fueled both by income disparities within and among countries, and by customers who seek relationships with women in which their dominance is unambiguous and compliance greater. As Paola Monzini notes, women generally move from patriarchal societies or those where women's political and economic position has recently declined to more gender-egalitarian ones and from poorer to richer ones (Monzini 2005: 52). According to the UN Office on Drugs and Crime, the countries of origin, in diminishing order of frequency, are Ukraine, Russia, Nigeria, Albania, Moldova, Bulgaria, China, Thailand, the Czech Republic, Lithuania, and Poland while the most often cited destination countries are Italy, the USA, and Germany (Kangaspunta 2003, quoted in Monzini 2005: 52). The US State Department estimates that 800,000 to 900,000 people are trafficked each year, while other US official agencies place the figure at 600,000 to 800,000 a year, of whom 70 percent are women and 50 percent under age. Moreover, a far larger number, perhaps 2 to 4 million, are thought to be trafficked inside their country, although it is hard to be sure. It is clear, however, that this is a highly lucrative trade, with estimates of the earnings from trafficking of young women and girls for the global sex market as high as $7 billion, out of a total $52 billion for the sex industry as a whole (Monzini 2005: 50; see also Peach 2008).

During the late nineteenth and early twentieth centuries, an earlier wave of trafficking of women for sex work was named the "white slave trade." While much of the movement took place within Europe, there were also substantial movements of women from China to Chinese overseas communities. This pattern, then as now, was largely under the control of organized crime. Another great expansion of sex trafficking began in the 1980s and 1990s, although precise numbers are hard to determine. This more recent move is greatly facilitated by the Internet and its capacity to market pornography and sex workers on a global scale. Trafficking expanded greatly in Japan beginning in the 1980s and in eastern Europe in the 1990s in the post-communist period. In Russia, the burgeoning market in sex workers and pornography is controlled by organized crime networks. In some countries, such as the former Soviet Union, Vietnam, Cambodia, and China, women move internally from poor rural areas to wealthier urban centers. War and political crisis, such as in Cambodia, Kosovo, and parts of Africa, also promote sex trafficking, again under the control of local racketeers. The Vietnam war contributed to global sex trafficking by opening up parts of southeast Asia, such as Thailand, to the sex trade as American soldiers used these regions for recreation and relaxation. At the end of the war, these regions became part of a pattern of international tourism which included sexual services. Similarly, the US military bases in the Philippines spawned a large prostitution market which has facilitated substantial movements of Filipino women into sex work and being trafficked (Monzini 2005: 3–26).

Sex workers experience a wide range of working situations and levels of exploitation, ranging from those who are independent, chose their hours and working conditions, and keep all of their earnings, to women who have no control over their work or their income. Women who are coercively moved, or trafficked, tend to be the most exploited. Victims of trafficking often live in semi-imprisonment, isolated from the rest of society and constantly subjected to physical and mental violence. They may work 10 to 15 hours a day for days at a time, yet get little money. They often agree to unprotected sex or do dangerous or humiliating acts in order to increase their income or because they have no choice. They are charged large fees for their living expenses, propelling them into a situation of permanent debt. In many cases, their trip to the place of work is also charged to them, increasing their level of debt. They are intensively supervised, and have great difficulty escaping. Typically, they are under the control of criminal gangs which use violence, debt, and threats to reveal their activities to their families to keep them under control. They may take their passports and other documents, so that the women are unable to travel and fear the police (Monzini 2005: 41–48).

There are two separate components to trafficking carried out by different networks: those who arrange travel for the women and prepare forged documents, paying off government officials and border guards, and those who arrange the conditions of work such as housing, access to customers, and surveillance of the women. The criminal gangs that engage in trafficking typically specialize in one of these two activities, so that the networks can spread to new areas of supply and to new destination areas.

Trafficked women come from areas of increasing inequality, such as the Ukraine and Nigeria. In formerly socialist countries, the shift from government-owned property and business to private ownership, called privatization, destroyed many jobs and left new groups in poverty. Large movements of trafficked women began in the late 1980s alongside an economic restructuring program (called structural adjustment) that cuts back on government services, and the liberalization of the international market (Monzini 2005: 64). As border controls increased, intermediaries and traffickers had to be bought off, raising the cost of trafficking. Europol estimates that 400,000 people enter Europe illegally each year, in a business worth €1 billion (Monzini 2005: 67). Trafficked women are often induced to make substantial payments or incur large debts, but may be tricked as to what their final destination or manner of work will be. For example, the International Organization for Migration reports that charges for travel from China to Europe are between $10,000 and $15,000 (Monzini 2005: 68).

Thus, trafficking involves both recruitment and exploitation, but the fundamental element of both is coercion. The definition of trafficking incorporates both. The most widely used international definition, given in the 2000 UN Protocol to Prevent, Suppress, and Punish Trafficking in Persons, especially Women and Children attached to the 2000 UN Convention against Transnational Organized Crime, stresses recruitment and travel, but also incorporates exploitation (Monzini 2005: 50 n. 11; 56–57; see Warren 2007). It defines "trafficking in persons" as the recruitment, transportation, transfer, harbouring or receipt of persons, by means of the threat or use of force, or other forms of coercion, or abduction, or fraud, or deception, or the abuse of power or of a position of vulnerability or of the giving or receiving of payments or benefits to achieve the consent of a person having control over another person, for the purpose of exploitation. Exploitation shall include, at a minimum, the exploitation of the prostitution of others, or other forms of sexual exploitation, forced labour or services, slavery or practices similar to slavery, servitude, or the removal of organs. (United Nations 2000: Article 3(a))

The statement says that the consent of the victim of trafficking is irrelevant where forms of coercion listed in Article 3 have been employed (Monzini 2005: 56–57). Moreover, children under the age of 18 cannot consent to trafficking (Warren 2007: 6). As Kay Warren (2007) notes in her analysis of the full text of the protocol, it continually stresses the vulnerability of the victims of trafficking, portrayed repeatedly as "women and girls," and denying the possibility of consent or agency. As we shall see below, this reflects a particular ideological position toward sex trafficking, but it is not the only one.

Clearly, trafficking is both secretive and very profitable, greased by bribes and payoffs. There are enormous difficulties in the prevention of trafficking. The global inequalities in wealth that drive trafficking are growing, even as efforts to control borders are increasing. Demand remains strong. It is not only poverty that initiates such flows of people, of course, but also armed conflict, now a rampant problem in many parts of the developing world. There are many NGOs and governments working on the problem, who have succeeded in raising awareness of its extent and severity (see Warren 2007). Although activists agree that transnational prostitution is a reflection of sharp inequalities in class, gender, race, and between nations, there are fundamental differences in how they see the problem and its solution. There is a contentious debate between those who see prostitution itself as a form of violence against women and those who see providing sex as a form of work and want to improve the conditions of labor. These groups form two different alliances and take different approaches to the problem (see Peach 2008).

The first group, the "abolitionists," begins from a critique of prostitution itself as inherently degrading to a woman's sense of dignity and as a form of oppression of women embedded in unequal gender relations. It sees no social legitimacy to prostitution, and argues that prostitution can never be freely chosen but is always a form of abuse that causes physical and psychological harm. Women who become prostitutes make up an underclass and typically come from abused families and have little education or economic opportunity. Thus prostitution is seen as being incompatible with human dignity and should be abolished.

The first anti-trafficking nongovernmental organization established in the current era is the Coalition against Trafficking in Women (CATW), formed in 1988. Its mission statement asserts that "It is a fundamental human right to be free of sexual exploitation in all its forms. Women and girls have the right to sexual integrity and autonomy" (www.catwinternational.org). This organization takes the position that

"Prostitution is itself violence against women" (Coalition against Trafficking in Women 2003, quoted in Peach 2008: 11). In alliance with the International Abolitionist Federation, these groups focus on government failure to enforce laws against prostitution and advocate penalizing customers and dissuading them from participating (Monzini 2005: 52–54). They argue that all prostitution exploits women, regardless of their consent, and that the existence of prostitution affects all women since it justifies the sale of women, reduces women to their sexual function, and eroticizes women's inequality. "Sexual exploitation is a vehicle for racism and 'first world' domination, disproportionately victimizing minority and 'third world' women" (www.catwinternational.org/about/index.php). CATW argues that prostitution should remain illegal and governments should more actively enforce anti-prostitution laws. Legalization would only encourage sex trafficking and prostitution. They oppose the term "sex work" as legitimizing the commercial sex industry and campaign against both prostitution and sex trafficking. The 2000 UN Trafficking Protocol similarly makes consent by the trafficked person irrelevant to prostitution when it is in any way coerced.

The second approach, that of the "reformists," views prostitution which is coerced as wrong but seeks to define voluntary forms of prostitution as work. They argue that women and men who provide sexual services should be viewed as workers, without moral judgment. Sex work is not inherently lacking in dignity if it is performed in a reputable way on the basis of free choice. The sex worker must be able to negotiate the terms of the exchange freely with the right to refuse any client or act, in suitable surroundings, and the price must reflect market rates. Some argue that sex work should be decriminalized or even legalized. This approach claims that, under these conditions, the prostitute is not selling herself but a service. She is in an occupation that offers considerable freedom and autonomy. Selling sexual services is not inherently a problem, but becomes so only when society condemns it and does not offer its workers adequate protection such as work and safety regulations and health services. Reformists advocate giving sex workers the same rights and protections as other workers, especially against HIV/AIDS.

One of the leading organizations, the Global Alliance against Trafficking in Women (GAATW), opposes trafficking but not prostitution. In alliance with Save the Children, Amnesty International, and Anti-Slavery International, it developed ten points to be presented at the November 2007 International Convention against Human Trafficking in Vienna, Austria. These points advocate a human rights approach that recognizes the root causes of trafficking in poverty and lack of education and seeks a participatory approach in responding to the needs of all affected people, including children (www.gaatw.net). This focuses on preventing and minimizing exploitation, holding traffickers accountable, and developing coordinated national and international approaches, along with collecting data on and providing analysis of the problem. The group advocates devoting special attention to trafficked children (www.gaatw.net/publications/NGO%20Submission_GIFT_goals.pdf). Many in this group argue that the majority of trafficked women are aware that they are traveling to become sex workers and enter the business for pragmatic reasons

(Peach 2008: 14). For example, a study of women trafficked from Thailand to Japan found that 74 percent had already worked in the sex trade in Thailand and knew they were being trafficked for sex work (Peach 2008: 18). Of course, what does it mean to enter sex work voluntarily if the alternative is to starve or watch one's children starve?

The reformist approach argues that focusing on prostitution itself distracts from considering the abuses of worker rights that prostitutes experience (Peach 2008: 15). Moreover, they argue that the sex trade cannot be eliminated, and that efforts to do so drive women into secrecy which denies them any state protection and makes them more vulnerable to marginalization, exploitation, and abuse (Peach 2008: 15). They criticize "rescue missions," often funded by Christian NGOs, that seek to "save" trafficked women from brothels and other establishments. Women often do not wish to be rescued, and if sent home may soon return to sex work (Peach 2008: 16).

However, this perspective fails to take account of the extent to which prostitution is grounded in male dominance over women, and that it remains a far more stigmatized form of labor than other forms of gendered low-wage work and one that is subject to far more acute and pervasive forms of violence. An International Labor Organization survey of sex workers in Asia finds that prostitution is one of the most alienating forms of labor and is often experienced as immoral despite offering a good option for earning money (Peach 2008: 20).

Although this movement is widespread in countries such as India and Thailand where there are strong traditions of prostitution, it has barely begun to develop in places such as the post-socialist world where trafficking is growing rapidly and is a relatively new development (Monzini 2005: 54–55). It is acquiring a larger international presence, however, and is active in international conventions.

To a large extent, these two anti-trafficking alliances focus on different dimensions of the sex trade. The abolitionists foreground the most coerced and exploited workers, focusing on child trafficking, and condemn the coercive conditions of the semi-enslaved trafficked woman, while the reformists imagine a world in which prostitutes work with considerable autonomy to protect themselves and retain their earnings.

Both abolitionists and reformists advocate a human rights approach. Yet much of the global approach to sex trafficking views it as a problem of organized crime. The major protocols and conventions condemning trafficking in the UN system focus on organized crime networks and many of the control efforts work to identify networks of traffickers and apprehend them. The most common definition of trafficking comes from a protocol attached to the UN Convention against Transnational Organized Crime (2000) and discussions of trafficking take place in Vienna surrounding debates about organized crime rather than in Geneva, the center of UN human rights activities, or New York, where the Commission on the Status of Women and the committee that monitors CEDAW, the Women's Convention, regularly meet. A human rights approach would place greater emphasis on the life circumstances of the trafficked women and their children, seeking to find ways to reintegrate them into society or provide them pathways to pursue an autonomous and freely chosen life of sex work, rather than on techniques of tracking and apprehending traffickers. However, even the human rights approach fails to recognize the forms of subjectivity of trafficked women engaged in various degrees of coerced prostitution, in which there is no bright line between consenting workers and coerced ones (Warren 2007). Human rights approaches assume that solutions can be achieved through law, but the law has clearly already failed to prevent this activity.

Despite differences in approach, all these groups see the origins of trafficking in poverty and lack of education and opportunity as well as gender inequality. They recognize that trafficking cannot be separated from global inequality. Moreover, these various approaches focus on different sectors of the prostitution continuum. Trafficked women occupy the most coerced and least autonomous end of the spectrum. This is also the domain of the greatest violence, since women's lack of funds, illegal status, and dependence on organized crime networks subject them to mechanisms of violence and control they cannot escape. These women are also most vulnerable to sexually transmitted diseases and least able to insist on protected sex. Those who advocate for sex worker rights concentrate on the other end of the spectrum, occupied by relatively affluent, stable, and autonomous persons who live legally in their own country. The spectrum of prostitution is shaped by poverty, racism, and migration, and women at the coerced end are disproportionately exposed to violence in their homes, their workplaces, and their neighborhood. At the same time, their customers, pimps, traffickers, and managers act with wide margins of impunity.

## Conclusions

This analysis of human rights as a developing and changing system enforced by transnational civil society and public opinion reveals the importance of ongoing social movements in support of particular human rights. Such rights emerge out of political movements, such as the women's liberation movement of the 1970s and the indigenous people's movements of the 1970s and 1980s. As these groups frame their issues in terms of human rights and put them on the agenda of the major human rights institutions of the UN, they reshape the human rights system. At the same time, the strength and effectiveness of any human rights issue depends on continuing mobilization by these groups and sustained political activism in maintaining their visibility. In many ways, human rights represents a political resource, a way of framing problems, rather than a system of law for preventing them. As a discourse, it can be used by local actors around the world who seek to define their problems in these terms. Sex trafficking is an example of an issue newly defined as a human rights violation. On the other hand, as a quasi-law system, the power of human rights is deeply dependent on continued activism by local groups as well as by transnational NGOs, governments, and UN bodies. As Chapter 2 and this chapter indicate, local movements have defined gender violence as a human rights problem and promoted conferences, declarations, conventions, and investigative efforts by the international community. These developments are the result of local agents mobilizing national and global law in the face of local resistance rather than the global imposition of a new moral order.

The violence against women movement, along with the larger women's rights movement in which it is embedded, includes demands for changes in cultural practices surrounding marriage and women's unequal legal, educational, and social status. Such demands for cultural change have been resisted by many countries, particularly those with a religious basis to conceptions of marriage and family. As international declarations and platforms condemning violence against women as a human rights violation are disseminated, they confront important contradictions. Women's rights to protection from violence often conflict with communities' rights to self-determination. If the dominant cultural value in a community is an enduring marriage with extensive husbandly authority and control in the family, controlling violence against women means reshaping the institutions of marriage and family. International lawyers and activists must negotiate the contradiction between protecting rights to culture and protecting women from violence.

As we have seen, the law serves simultaneously to support existing systems of authority, such as those rooted in the family, and to provide a language for and institutional access to a system of power which challenges that authority. Feminists have criticized the capacity of the law to change inequalities of power, arguing that it is a patriarchal institution rooted in male power. Nevertheless, they rely on the law to contest patriarchy. Navigating this space is a challenge, but it offers a powerful social justice framework and the possibility of international political pressure.

## Questions for Further Discussion

1 Does the conceptualization of women's rights as human rights advance protections against acts of gender violence? Using the USA as an example, reflect on what is lost and what is gained by using this frame. What conditions allow for human rights to emerge and become recognized by various actors at the local, national, regional, and international levels? Consider what constitutes a human rights violation, and how international consensus about violations is formed.

2 Why is culture seen by many actors as an impediment to the realization of women's rights? Who uses arguments that favor "traditional" practices, and how does power factor into their arguments? Do you think it is possible to negotiate a middle ground that respects culture and protects women against violence at the same time?

3 Activists who seek protection for sex workers are characterized as either "abolitionists" or "reformists." How does each group understand the problem of sex trafficking, and how in turn does it shape the goals of their activism? What

tensions arise between these groups as a result? Consider the role of male privilege, organized crime, exploitative working conditions, and inequalities of wealth. Finally, how does human rights factor into the activism they promote?

## Video Suggestions

*Beyond Beijing*, by Shirini Heerah and Enrique Berrios
(England, 1996), 42 minutes

In a personal document of the 1995 United Nations Fourth World Conference on Women in Beijing, this film captures through one participant's eyes the intensity of spirit at the largest gathering of women ever assembled in history. But rather than just trumpet the moment, the narrator balances her account by acknowledging the logistical problems and political controversies surrounding the event. What emerges is a comprehensive portrayal of official meetings and the parallel NGO Forum convened by grass-roots activists to commemorate women's art and achievements both north and south.

*Remote Sensing*, by Ursula Biemann (Switzerland, 2001), 53 minutes

This video essay traces the circuitous routes that reorganize women geographically for work in the global sex trade. From the Philippines to Nigeria, from Bulgaria to Germany, from Nicaragua to the United States, women move like cargo as transnational capital creates the landscape for the sexualization of labor and the recruitment of poor minority women and girls in prostitution, adoption, and forced marriage. Incorporating satellite imagery and computerized text, the film captures not only the conditions that contribute to the global trade in women, but the technologies that make their displacement possible in a post-socialist, militarized world.

*Trading Women*, by David Feingold
(USA/Thailand/China/Burma/Laos, 2003), 77 minutes

Based on interviews with major UN officials, US politicians, brothel owners, activists, sex workers, trafficked girls and their parents, this documentary film dispels many myths about the global sex trade in southeast Asia. It questions the boundary between consent and coercion, examines the implications of citizenship in countries that have long denied groups participation in the political state, and explores the roots of trafficking in poverty, sustained internal conflict, military dictatorship, a growing tourist industry, state corruption, and discriminatory migration policies.

*The Vienna Tribunal*, by Gerry Rogers (Canada, 1994), 48 minutes

*The Vienna Tribunal* mingles moving personal testimonies of gender violence with footage of the Global Tribunal on Violations of Women's Rights, held in conjunction with the UN World Conference on Human Rights in Vienna in 1993. Made with support from the Center for Women's Global Leadership at Rutgers University, the film documents the growing sentiment among activists who first claimed that women's rights are human rights. It provides not only a glimpse into the history of the movement, but also the sense of solidarity galvanized among women who participated in the Tribunal.

# 5

# Poverty, Racism, and Migration

Social groups that confront structural violence are particularly vulnerable to interpersonal gender violence. Poverty, hunger, social exclusion, and humiliation are forms of structural violence derived from social processes such as colonialism, racism, and illegal migration. These processes create conditions of structural violence that increase individuals' vulnerability to interpersonal violence. Both men and women in relatively powerless positions such as the poor, illegal migrants, and subordinated caste or racial groups are likely to experience disproportionate forms of interpersonal violence. They are more likely than others to encounter violence in the family, among neighbors, from strangers, and from the wider society. Women in these positions are even more vulnerable than men. This chapter discusses the evidence that there is a relationship between these processes, forms of structural violence, and interpersonal gender violence.

## Poverty and Racism

While many people assume that gender violence is characteristic of the poor, the relationship between income and the experience of violence is far more complex. In the years before the battered women's movement, domestic violence was generally attributed to the lifestyle of the poor or, in the words of temperance activists, to the evils of the "drunken brute" (Field and Field 1973; Pleck 1987; Gordon 2002 [1988]). However, the social movement of the 1970s in the USA insisted that battering happens in all social classes and is based on gender inequality more than class differences. Ethnographic and statistical data indicate that poverty increases vulnerability to interpersonal violence. Of course, poor men and women also resist interpersonal violence. Indeed, battering often occurs when women are challenging their partners and resisting their control. Hautzinger's (2007) study of Brazil discussed in Chapter 1, as well as several other case studies in this book, show clearly that violence often follows women's efforts to resist male control and develop strategies for coping with violence.

Nevertheless, research shows that the ability of poor women to cope with violence is undermined by their tendency to work in precarious, part-time, low-wage, and often no-benefit jobs (Adelman 2004: 66). Madelaine Adelman advocates seeing domestic violence within a political economy framework which reveals the intersections among domestic violence and economic, political, and historical conditions and dominant family ideologies. Instead of seeing domestic violence as part of the value system of the poor, this approach considers how poverty increases vulnerability to violence and how battering itself exacerbates poverty. Women of color typically face even greater difficulties in the job market as they encounter discrimination in education, work, and housing, thus rendering them even more vulnerable to domestic violence.

There are clear economic consequences to gender violence. A woman experiencing violence is likely to become poorer (Adelman 2004: 65). Her batterer may prevent her from working, obstruct her access to welfare, and withhold his wages or seize hers. He may prevent her acquiring further education or training as he seeks to control her activities and isolate her. Poverty then limits a woman's ability to leave a battering situation. She may be dependent on her batterer's income or assistance with child care and child support. Moving to a shelter leads to loss of employment and abandoning of her home. Injuries may prevent her working. Thus poverty tends to entrap women in battering relationships, while these relationships block her access to work and education.

Racism also shapes women's vulnerability to violence. Racialized communities typically receive less effective criminal justice responses to gender violence. Often, men in these communities are not forced to take responsibility for their violence. Shelters and other services for battered women are usually less adequate for women of color and partners in lesbian and gay relationships (see, e.g., Crenshaw 1994; Ristock 2002). A New York advocacy organization for formerly battered women, Voices of Women, is working to improve the way courts handle custody disputes that involve battering, since they find that battered women, particularly if they are poor and minority, tend to face more difficulties in court. Battered women in communities whose members are disproportionately incarcerated, such as African Americans, Native Americans, or Native Hawaiians, must choose between protecting their communities or defending themselves and their children by turning to a suspect and racialized police force and judiciary.

Many communities of color already experience disproportionate violence from the governments where they live, which makes them skeptical of the police and courts. For example, Andrea Smith (2005) documents the range of forms of violence endured by Native Americans from dispossession of land, to forced attendance at boarding schools dedicated to eliminating native language and culture, to medical interventions to limit reproduction (see also Incite! 2006). In the USA, racial and ethnic minorities and the poor typically experience a lack of attention to protection from crime, neighborhood destruction and displacement, toxic wastes, air pollution, and poor schools. McGillivray and Comaskey (1999) describe the ambivalence battered Aboriginal Canadian women feel about turning to the courts for help.

This pattern is found in other countries as well as the USA and Canada. Nadera Shalhoub-Kevorkian analyzes the reluctance of Israeli police to help battered Israeli Palestinian women, interpreted through the lens of culture and religion. The police officers put national security concerns first, viewing domestic violence as a less important problem for which they do not have time. Moreover, Israeli Palestinians were portrayed as the "other," with "primitive" ideas about women. Police assumed that violence was part of their "culture" and tended to see the Israeli Palestinians as belonging to a violent society among whom at least some were terrorists (2004: 178–182). Mindie Lazarus-Black (2007) shows how the bureaucratic procedures of courts in Trinidad produce delayed interventions and pressure to reconcile in ways that undermine women's ability to get help in situations of battering even when new legislation provides for help.

Violence against women is a common strategy for maintaining unequal relationships among social groups. In some contexts, men of dominant groups, including police officers, use rape to assert control over subordinate groups. For example, Indian castes are social groups based on descent in which caste membership defines where people eat and live, and who they marry. Castes are clearly ranked, with different social status and power allocated on the basis of caste status. It is common for upper-caste men to use violence against lower-caste people, including women, in order to reinforce the hierarchy. Those of lowest caste status, called Dalits, are particularly vulnerable. A recent human rights report by the Center for Human Rights and Global Justice of the New York University Law School documents the extent of violence against Dalit women, sometimes by landlords who use sexual abuse and other forms of violence and humiliation against Dalit women to inflict "lessons" and crush movements for political empowerment or labor movements within Dalit communities. In one case, a labor activist whose daughter was gang-raped in 2002 defied the threats of his landlord and upper-caste leaders in seeking prosecution against the perpetrators. He was attacked by the landlords and beaten so badly that both his arms and one of his legs had to be amputated and his remaining leg was permanently disabled (Center for Human Rights and Global Justice and Human Rights Watch 2007: 60–62). Yet the government fails to punish the perpetrators in most cases and sometimes even participates in these actions. In most cases, police fail to investigate or prosecute the incidents and the actors escape punishment (CHRGJ and Human Rights Watch 2007: 62; see also Kapadia 2002). Indeed, as Chapter 2 indicated, movements against police rape were critically important in initiating the Indian women's movement (see Kumar 1993).

## Statistical Evidence

Although data from both police and court reports and victimization surveys indicate differences by class and race, to what extent this reflects actual behavior rather than reported behavior is hard to determine. In the USA, the National Crime

Victimization Survey (NCVS) from 1987 to 1991 found that women were victims of violence by lone offenders who were intimates at the rate of 5 per 1,000 population (Bureau of Justice Statistics 1994: 2). Black and white women had similar rates of victimization, 5 per 1,000, but less educated and poorer women were more often victimized. Three per 1,000 college graduates were battered, while high school graduates and people with some college had a rate of 6 per 1,000, and less than high school 5 per 1,000. Women with family incomes under $10,000 had the highest rate at 11 per 1,000, and those with family incomes over $30,000 had the lowest rate at 2 per 1,000 (BJS 1994: 2). The statistics confirm that violence is more common after separation: divorced or separated women had higher rates of violence by intimates (16 per 1,000) than never married (7 per 1,000) or married women (1.5 per 1,000) (BJS 1994: 2).

Victimization survey data from 1992–1996 did report differences in women's victimization by race/ethnicity, with the rate of victimization for black women at 12 per 1,000 compared to 8 per 1,000 for white women and 6 per 1,000 for Asians and Pacific Islanders. Men's rate of victimization from intimate violence was only one-fifth that of women and did not show any significant ethnic differences (Greenfield et al. 1998: 13). Strikingly, women's income had a major impact on their rates of victimization, but rates for men did not vary with income much at all (Greenfield et al. 1998: 14). In 1992–1993, the rate of violent victimizations for women by intimates varied significantly by income, from 19.9 for those with incomes under $10,000 to 4.5 for those with annual family incomes over $50,000 (Bachman and Saltzman 1995: 4). There were also no statistically significant differences by race/ethnicity for victimization by lone offenders who are intimates (Bachman and Saltzman 1995: 4). It is notable that income has a much greater impact on rate of victimization than education or ethnicity.

More recent data indicate a similar situation, although it still offers a very partial picture of the distribution of rape and domestic violence in the American population. FBI data published online in 2007 document the frequency of offenses, where they occur demographically, and what arrestees – not victims – look like based on age, race, and sex alone. The FBI's Uniform Crime Reporting (UCR) Program collects data on and separates offenses according to the following categories: murder, forcible rape, robbery, aggravated assault, burglary, larceny-theft, motor vehicle theft, and arson. The first four are considered violent offenses. The FBI defines forcible rape as "the carnal knowledge of a female forcibly [assaulted] against her will. Assaults and attempts to commit rape by force or threat of force are also included; however, statutory rape (without force) and other sex offenses are excluded" (www.fbi.gov/ucr/05cius/offenses/violent_crime/forcible_rape.html).

The FBI does not explicitly gather information on gender violence; rather, it is subsumed in and diffused among other categories. FBI data are *not* disaggregated according to the victims who experience violence. Therefore the FBI does not account for the populations disproportionately affected by violence. Data *are* disaggregated by geography based on the proportion of crime that happens in cities (including suburban and non-suburban cities), metropolitan counties, non-metropolitan counties, and suburbs. Data on forcible rape are also compiled for colleges and universities. The rate of forcible rapes in 2005 was estimated at 62.5 offenses per 100,000 US female inhabitants. Based on rape offenses actually reported to the UCR Program in 2005, rapes by force comprised 91.8 percent of reported rape offenses, and assaults to rape attempts accounted for 8.2 percent. The FBI does demarcate the race, age, and sex (but not income or education levels) of those arrested for forcible rapes. Of the 18,405 arrests made in 2005 for forcible rapes, 65.1 percent of arrestees were white, 32.7 percent black, 1.2 percent Native American or Alaskan native, and 1.0 percent Asian or Pacific Islander. Data are not disaggregated according to Latino populations. By age, 44.5 percent were under the age of 25 while 98.5 percent of offenders for forcible rape were male and 1.5 percent female.

The invisibility of gender violence in the records of official criminal justice agencies reflects its lack of importance to those engaged in record-keeping and knowledge creation. If gender violence is not considered important, it is not counted. Records are kept of forms of behavior or persons deemed important or threatening. For example, although assault is a fundamental violation in most legal systems, only recently has gender violence been statistically separated from the total pool of assault cases. Before the creation of a separate criminal offense of spouse abuse in Hawai'i, for example, gender violence cases were classified along with all other assault cases. In the Hilo Family Court, civil restraining orders were not given a special designation until 1990 but were recorded simply as civil protective orders.

Earlier records were even more indifferent to this issue. Police statistics from the 1940s and 1950s report "offenses against the family" and assaults (County of Hawai'i, Police Department 1947: 17), but it is not clear whether an offense against the family is gender violence or how many assaults were within the family. The pattern of silence continues through the 1980s. By 1988, the annual report of the Hawai'i County Police Department still failed to separate gender violence from other assault arrests. Only since 1990 have the record-keeping procedures of the courts distinguished gender violence from other violence. Similarly, the Bureau of Justice Statistics victimization data discussed below refer to "family violence" to describe rape and domestic assaults, even though they include boyfriends/girlfriends, same-sex partners, divorcees, and children under that heading. Thus, they use a narrower term to describe a broader range of relationships in their data.[1] Only since 1992 have family violence statistics been kept separately.

Even the presentation of data shows that this offense was viewed as relatively trivial in the past. For example, the County of Hawai'i Police Department has counted calls for help in domestic cases since the 1970s, but they are recorded as "domestic trouble cases" and buried in the back pages of police reports in a long list of "Miscellaneous Public Complaints" or "Miscellaneous Services and Reports" which includes finding lost pets and responding to false alarms. As late as 1988, the annual police report lists domestic trouble along with other miscellaneous services while

---

[1]  I am grateful to Jennifer Telesca for this observation.

thefts of property, arrests for drunk driving, and numbers of marijuana plants eradicated receive high visibility.

Official records are cultural documents. They count whatever is considered important and ignore the rest. Problems considered unimportant, such as gender violence, are buried within larger categories so that it is impossible to determine how many cases there are. Statistics create a sense of truthfulness, but they are themselves the product of dominant political concerns. What gets enumerated is a product of cultural processes of classification and ordering that respond to political pressures. These processes of counting then produce their own truths of behavior. The categories which are used and those which are not are powerfully productive of social knowledge.

Victimization studies are intended to provide a different kind of information. Unlike the FBI, the Bureau of Justice Statistics (BJS) profiles victims. BJS bases its data on the National Crime Victimization Survey (NCVS), the nation's primary source of information on criminal victimization. Knowledge about victimhood is collected each year and is "obtained from a nationally representative sample of 77,200 households comprising nearly 134,000 persons on the frequency, characteristics and consequences of criminal victimization in the United States" (www.ojp. usdoj.gov/bjs/cvict.htm#ncvs). The NCVS is a 28-page survey that estimates the likelihood of victimization according to such offenses as rape, sexual assault, robbery, assault, theft, household burglary, and motor vehicle theft. According to BJS, the NCVS is "the largest national forum for victims to describe the impact of crime and characteristics of violent offenders" (www.ojp.usdoj.gov/bjs/cvict.htm#ncvs).[2] The survey began in 1973, and was redesigned in 1992. The redesign was prompted by the need for better data on sexual assaults and domestic violence.

NCVS uses the heading "family violence" – not domestic or gender violence – to designate victims of personal crimes. Offense categories include aggravated assault, assault, rape/sexual assault, robbery, and simple assault. The NCVS defines rape more expansively than the FBI as "forced sexual intercourse including both psychological coercion as well as physical force. Forced sexual intercourse means penetration by the offender(s) [and] includes attempted rapes, male as well as female victims, and both heterosexual and homosexual rape. Attempted rape includes verbal threats of rape" (www.ojp.usdoj.gov/bjs/intimate/definitions.htm). Psychological and verbal assaults regardless of sex and gender are therefore included should a victim deem them offensive and criminal. Intimate partners are defined as current or former spouses, and boyfriends or girlfriends in both heterosexual and same-sex relationships. Other relatives (parent, child, sibling, grandparent, in-law, cousin), acquaintances (friend, coworker, neighbor, schoolmate, someone known), and strangers are not included in the figures on intimate partner victimization.

In 2004 the non-fatal violent victimization rate among women over the age of 12 was 3.8 per 1,000 among intimates, 1.4 among other relatives, 5.5 among friends or

---

[2] For a copy of the survey see www.ojp.usdoj.gov/bjs/pub/pdf/ncvs104.pdf.

acquaintances, and 6.3 among strangers. Females are more likely than males to experience both fatal and non-fatal intimate partner violence. For the period 1993 through 2004, intimate partners account for 30 percent of all female homicides, and 5 percent of all male homicides. Most intimate homicides involved spouses and ex-spouses, although the number of deaths by boyfriends and girlfriends approximates the same level. Females aged 20–34 were at the greatest risk of non-fatal intimate partner violence, especially those aged 20–24. Females who were separated from their partners reported higher rates than females of other marital statuses. Those married reported the lowest rates of non-fatal intimate partner violence. The non-fatal intimate partner victimization rate per 1,000 females aged 12 and over in 2004 was 1.0 among the married, 9.3 among the divorced, 41.8 among the separated, and 5.0 among the non-married.

In addition to age, marital status, and victim–offender relationships, statistics on "family violence" are disaggregated according to sex, race, family income, and home-ownership. For those experiencing non-fatal violent victimization in 2004, 3.4 per 1,000 were white females, 6.6 black females, and 1.1 white males. On average in the period 1993–2004, the annual rate of non-fatal intimate violence was highest among American Indian females at 18.2 per 1,000, while black females averaged 8.2, white females 6.3, American Indian males 5.0, Asian females 1.5, black males 1.5, white males 1.1, and Asian males 0.1. Curiously, separate statistical charts document victimization according to "Hispanic origin" in the years between 1993 and 2004. The rate of non-fatal intimate victimization was 6.0 per 1,000 among Hispanic females and 6.5 among non-Hispanic females, and 0.9 among Hispanic males and 1.2 among non-Hispanic males.

From 1993 to 2004, the persons living in households with lower annual incomes experienced the highest average annual rates of non-fatal intimate partner victimization. Persons living in households that earned higher incomes had lower average annual rates than those with less income. Females remained at greater risk than males regardless of income level. The average annual non-fatal intimate partner victimization rates per 1,000 by income and gender in the period 1993–2004 were as follows: for persons annually earning less than $7,500, the victimization rate was highest at 18.4 per 1,000; for income levels between $7,500 and $24,999, the victimization rate was 9.5 per 1,000; for income levels between $25,000 and $49,999, the victimization rate was 5.9 per 1,000; and for wage earners over $50,000, the victimization rate was lowest at 2.8 per 1,000. Similarly, non-fatal intimate partner violence rates between 1993 and 2004 were considerably higher for persons living in rental housing than other types of housing regardless of the victim's sex. Females residing in rental housing were victimized at an average annual rate of more than three times that of females living in housing that they owned. In almost half (43 percent) of the households with intimate partner violence in this period, children lived in the household.[3] Statistics on educational levels were not available online.

---

[3]   For a good overview of the statistics, see www.ojp.usdoj.gov/bjs/intimate/victims.htm.

This information indicates that there is a rough relationship between victimization and poverty nationwide that has persisted for at least two decades. But it also shows the very limited nature of this data and its inability to account for the complex relationships among gender violence and gender, race, class, ethnicity, religion, education, and income in particular social contexts.

## The Difficulty of Measuring Gender Violence

As these data indicate, there are two ways to determine the frequency and distribution of gender violence: reports from criminal justice agencies and victimization surveys. Both of these indicate that poorer people and racial minorities are more likely to be perpetrators or victims of gender violence than richer ones or those of dominant racial groups. However, a closer look at the way these data are collected shows that neither is able to provide a clear answer about how gender violence differs between class and racial groups.

A common approach to understanding gender violence is to examine how often people call the police or go to court to petition for civil protective orders or to lodge a criminal complaint. In other words, how often do victims of gender violence seek help from the state? Legal intervention takes place only when a victim has a legal consciousness which defines the law as relevant to her everyday life and possesses a sense of entitlement to use it. She must understand herself as a rights-bearing legal subject who can turn to the government for help. There is no way of knowing how many people are battered who fail to complain. Criminal justice statistics on gender violence are primarily measures of the public's willingness to consider the state an appropriate and useful place to turn with respect to violence and police willingness to arrest. Some cases are also counted because the injuries are serious enough to come to the attention of hospital emergency workers. As mandatory arrest policies have become more widespread in the USA, arrest has become more common even when the victim has not complained (on this debate see Sherman and Berk 1984). However, in the large majority of cases, data on who uses the legal system reflect the view that violence in the home is a crime.

Data on help-seeking leave out wealthier victims who turn to counseling or other private means of redress and/or are financially able to leave the battering situation. They also exclude those who are so alienated from the criminal justice system that they would rather endure violence than invite police attention to the family. As the founders of the organization Incite! argue, it is difficult for women of color to summon the police to their homes to arrest and possibly imprison the already over-incarcerated men of their communities. They ask why the battered women's movement had to turn so extensively toward criminal justice interventions (Davis 2000; 2001; Smith 2005). Others are unable to participate because they are illegal immigrants or because the forms of redress are ill suited to their identities and concerns, such as lesbian, gay, bisexual, transgendered, and queer (LGBTQ) partners in same-sex relationships (Adelman 2004: 58). bell hooks describes the reluctance of some women to acknowledge to themselves that they are battered, particularly after they encounter the dismissive attitudes of medical people toward their injuries (hooks 1997).

The second form of measurement is the victimization survey. Surveys of the frequency of victimization also indicate some variation on the basis of social class, but again these data need to be interpreted carefully. One of the difficulties with the survey approach is that gender violence is ultimately a matter of interpretation. A person may experience violence but see it as discipline or normal rather than as abuse or victimization. For example, a study of battering in a Chinese village reports that battered women interpret their experience as "fighting" rather than abuse (Liu and Chan 1999). Roger Lancaster's (1992) study of violence in Nicaragua shows how these acts are naturalized and taken for granted. As we shall see below, communities in the USA have their own ways of conceptualizing what domestic violence is, and these ideas change over time.

Identifying gender violence depends on cultural interpretation and meaning-making that changes over time and between cultures. The absence of documentation of gender violence may mean that it does not happen or that it is ignored. In order for it to be counted it must be noticed. The light of public attention has to shine into the previously dark and unnoticed corners of family life to reveal what had seemed natural. There is ample evidence that gender violence was both very common and largely unremarked in the past. That we now hear more about it does not mean it is increasing, but it does suggest that it is more visible to others besides the victims.

Recognizing the importance of data collection to addressing this problem, the 2006 report to the UN Secretary-General on violence against women (discussed in Chapter 4) notes that although 71 countries have done at least one survey on violence against women, there is a lack of reliable data in many countries. The report argues that it is essential to have such information to track changes over time and to provide data disaggregated by age and ethnicity as well as other factors. It advocates creating a set of international indicators on violence against women using comparable methods to define and measure violence (www.un.org/womenwatch/daw/vaw, Executive Summary, p. 2). As we have seen, this is a difficult project even nationally, but one that is essential to developing effective modes of intervention.

## A Case Study of Hilo, Hawai'i

In order to develop a more fine-grained portrait of the social and economic characteristics of batterers and those they injure, it is necessary to look at far smaller social units than the nation. The data from intake forms used at the women's center in Hilo, Hawai'i provide a particularly detailed picture of the social identities of people who end up in court with domestic violence problems. The questionnaires are unusual in the extent of demographic data they collected and the picture they provide of batterers and their victims. As we saw in Chapter 3, the clientele of the Alternatives to Violence (ATV) program, as reported in 1,574 intake questionnaires of clients between 1990 and 1998 is poorer, less educated, and younger than the rest of the town.[4] Almost all came through the courts: at least three-quarters of the people in this program were required to attend by the civil or criminal legal system. Wealthier defendants who can pay for private counseling or alternative treatment can usually avoid ATV. Few defendants hired lawyers, but those who did were more likely to have other choices of programs or to avoid them altogether. Men living with their partners and children are more likely to be sent to ATV than those who have no children and plan to separate. Poorer victims who are financially dependent on their partners are less able to move out.

The respondents are two-thirds men and one-third women.[5] This was a youthful population, with one-third in their twenties and almost a quarter in their thirties. The group is ethnically highly varied, although it does not represent a cross-section of the ethnic makeup of the town. These people are more likely to be Hawaiian, white, or Portuguese than the larger population and less likely to be Japanese. A comparison of the ethnic breakdown of the ATV population, divided by gender, and that of the 1990 census (also based on self-report data on ethnicity) indicates that Hawaiians are over-represented in comparison to the total population, especially Hawaiian men, as are white women. Hawaiians form about 20 percent of the Hilo population but 39 percent of the ATV clientele.

Although one-third (35 percent) of the town's residents are of Japanese ancestry, Japanese men and women are only 5 percent of the total ATV clientele, with Japanese men appearing more rarely than Japanese women. It is hard to know how to interpret this disparity. The common view among Hilo Japanese Americans is that shame and fear of public exposure deter Japanese women from calling the police or going to court when they are battered. It is possible that the movement of the Japanese into middle-class occupations and housing has somewhat diminished the pressures that contribute to gender violence. It is also possible that Japanese batterers and their victims are less likely to be referred to ATV than members of other groups who conform more closely to the cultural group referred to as "local," whose members make up the bulk of the ATV program. Perhaps ATV seems a particularly appropriate referral for Hawaiian and Portuguese ancestry people, those who are at the core of "local" culture. People in these groups are more likely to be in the criminal justice

---

[4] These questionnaires were filled in during an intake interview with the staff member who asked the client the questions.

[5] The questionnaire and its categories of ethnicity, religion, and ways of defining abuse, were designed by program staff in the late 1980s. Occasionally, a person was required to attend ATV more than once, and would therefore fill out a new intake form. Thus they represent separate intakes, although not necessarily different people, but, because intake forms are not associated with names in order to preserve anonymity, it is impossible to know how many individuals are represented by these 1,574 intake interviews. Although there were some repeats, the large majority of the clients were not.

system for other offenses as well. Indeed, almost half the men in the feminist batterer program had been arrested for something else besides battering.

As described in Chapter 3, the educational level of the ATV population is lower than that of the town and is relatively poor.[6] Over half earn under $8,000 a year, a low income even in a place where housing costs are relatively low for substandard housing and subsistence activities of hunting and fishing routinely supplement incomes. Only 6 percent earn above $25,000 a year.[7] In sum, the group of people which ends up in court and is referred to ATV is a relatively narrow slice of the town's population in terms of age, education, ethnicity, and income: it is a young, working-class, local population which has developed a shared culture composed of elements from many of the groups which settled in the area. These characteristics of ATV participants were relatively stable over this period, despite a dramatic rise in recourse to the courts for help. During the 1980s and 1990s, recourse to courts increased far faster than population growth, yet the composition of the ATV population remained the same in terms of the age, ethnicity, education, income, and religion. The new consciousness that gender violence is a crime did not bring a different ethnic, class, or age group into the courts but simply a higher proportion of the same group.

The Hawai'i research also shows how culturally embedded understandings of violence determine how a person responds to a survey question. Ways of thinking and talking about violence in the family are expressed locally by the terms "lickins," "dirty lickins," and "stink eye." The term "lickins" appears in the court records as early as the late nineteenth century, suggesting that it is a long established local category for understanding violence. Today, "lickins" generally refers to hitting by parents of their children or husbands of their wives, generally understood as discipline. Administering lickins is part of the responsibility of a parent or husband to his or her wayward dependants. A second term, "dirty lickins," seems to refer to a more severe degree of violence which has far less cultural support or authorization. It is often used as a threat, in that the person who does not behave will receive dirty lickins. The boundary between the two categories is blurred, but the existence of the two suggests a fundamental distinction between violence administered by a socially endowed authority whose purpose is fundamentally corrective and that administered by a person, perhaps lacking such authority, which results in serious injury. The latter has far less cultural support. Thus the distinction between lickins and dirty lickins represents the cultural boundary between legitimate disciplinary violence and illegitimate and excessive violence. The law does not recognize this distinction, however. Responses to a survey question will differ depending on how an injured person defines her experience.

---

[6]  It is not clear whether this information refers to family income or individual income, since the question simply asks the person to specify his/her income. Since about half of the respondents are not currently living with their partners, it is probable that their response refers to their individual income. Yet the large majority of these people say that they have children, whether or not they are living with them at the moment, so they may well be supporting more than themselves on this income.

[7]  Although fees for the program were based on income, clients did not know this at the time of the interview, so they had no reason to conceal their income.

Both "lickins" and "dirty lickins" are used to describe violence against children and wives. Mary, a 41-year-old woman with four children and four grandchildren, who grew up in the plantations and was beaten by her husband, said that lickins are like a spanking – they are beatings that a parent uses to discipline a child. Dirty lickins are bad beatings. A punch in the face, one punch, is a lickin, while beatings, punches, and pulling hair are dirty lickins. She remembers that when she was growing up, if she was bad she got a lickin. Her mother used to slap her or hit her with a belt, and for her that was a lickin, even if her mother didn't think so. When a woman got lickins, people thought it was natural. When Mary was growing up, men of the household thought lickins was discipline. They also thought women should cook, serve them, get up, and serve them again. I asked if there was a line beyond which the violence was considered too severe and she said no: for men, there is nothing that is too much. But women were very rarely killed. Dirty lickins, she said, was as bad as it got.

Lickins are more severe than slaps, but what is a lickin to one person may not be to another. For example, in a family court hearing a man said, "I don't lick my baby. Sometimes I give her a slap, but I never beat her up." Here, lickins is differentiated from a slap which is a less serious blow. Which of these forms of violence comes to be defined as gender violence in a victimization survey clearly depends on the cultural categories the respondent uses.

Another common phrase, "stink eye," means to look at a person "really mean," showing that you do not like them and that there is a beating coming. This is a kind of discipline which says "Get back in your place." Insults are referred to as "talking stink." Many battered women say the talk hurts more than the blows, and they would take the physical abuse any time over the insults. As one woman put it, the insults get inside you and make you feel bad about everything. Emotional abuse is the worst. But for many, "stink eye" and other threats and insults are defined as commonplace and inevitable rather than as lickins or abuse. For example, one young woman interviewed in 1992 said that her husband used to punch the wall and hold her up against the wall so that he left bruises on her arm and talked right up in her face, but she didn't know that was abuse. She was just glad that he did not hit her. I asked her if she had any word for it, and she said no, it just seemed like the thing people do, that this is the way it was when she was a child and that it seemed like the way things are – you just have to accept it. However, when she talked to a counselor, she persuaded her that it was abuse and she did not have to accept it. This encouraged her to come to the support group at ATV.

In the past, it was common for women to think of violence as discipline which must be endured. For example, in 1992 I interviewed a woman I will call Elizabeth who was born in 1926 and raised in a plantation camp. Elizabeth's grandparents came from Portugal in the 1890s to work on the plantations and her parents and her husband continued to work on the plantation. She still lives in a plantation settlement, but none of her children do. Elizabeth described violence as commonplace but largely ignored. When she was young, nobody talked about men hitting women, although it happened often. Mothers said, as did hers, "You made your bed, now you lie on it." Her mother was raised that way too. Nobody stopped anyone for hitting his wife, even though in the dense plantation camps, people overheard the fights and blows. They did not get involved and no one ever called the police about it. Elizabeth thought that about half the families had violent fights, but there were distinct ethnic patterns. It was, she said, especially common in the Puerto Rican families. The Filipinos would slash their wives, but the Japanese were more quiet. They would fight in whispers. They hit as much as the rest, but just more privately. The Portuguese were mostly "mouth," she thought, not so much engaged in hitting. When I asked about the Hawaiians, she said "They used to pound them out too," but there were few Hawaiians on the plantation.

Another woman I interviewed in 1992, whom I will call Ruth, was born in 1935 and raised in a remote Hawaiian community of perhaps ten families in the Puna region. Her mother was pure Hawaiian and spoke Hawaiian and her mother's father was a Protestant minister. Ruth described frequent parties and fights in this village. About once a week, people would make "swipe" out of fermented pineapple juice and have parties with lots of drinking. Fights were common, but the next day, everybody would make up. In the tape-recorded interview, Ruth described women's vulnerability to violence and the lack of intervention by police from the outside. When I asked her if women ever got hit, she said:

> Oh yes, but we were young, we just watched, we couldn't do anything about it. Women never used to hit back. But every time they used to get hit. This was pretty common. Hawaiians used to fight with their wives. I don't know why, maybe custom, cultural things, I don't know. I decided when I was young I didn't want to marry a Hawaiian, they just beat up so much.

I asked whether anyone did anything when men started to hit women.

> Oh, they would try to stop the fight, but when you get high, it is hard to stop the fists. It happened at Hawaiian parties, but usually after the party. Maybe a person has said something and the other person can't take it. Or Hawaiians get jealous, maybe someone has talked to their wives. Or they flirt with the next man, and problems come. Hawaiians are the same as others, not different. When Hawaiians hit, they do it with all their might. Now it would be called abuse.

I asked, did anyone call the police? She replied that when she was growing up, they never called the police. She didn't even know that the police existed and in any case her family did not have a telephone. At the time, the predominant view was that you have to take care of your own problems. I asked if the older people got involved in these problems, and she said no. The person doing the violence, even if he were younger, would say keep quiet, keep out of this, this isn't your problem. Not all men were violent – some were more sensible than those who were drunk. Ruth concluded, "This was just fighting. But you could walk to school with no fear of someone watching you." In the same area, there were often cockfights which the police would break up, maybe once a month.

Ruth married a Japanese man and raised her children in a predominantly Japanese plantation camp in the same area. Here she did not see so much violence. In the camp during the 1950s

> I didn't notice punching, hitting. I don't remember seeing anything. There weren't Hawaiian parties like when I was a child. I didn't see women hit by husbands. Wasn't da kine. Maybe they have some fights, just like everyday life, but not like when I was a child. I liked camp life. I really enjoyed it. The kids all grew up together. We would sit around together, talk story, it was nice.

These stories, along with many others, suggest that violence within camps and villages in the first three-quarters of the twentieth century was common and accepted, even regarded as natural and an inevitable part of marital life. There was a reluctance to intervene in violent behavior that was considered discipline and another family's private business. Police reports indicate few calls for help. Clearly, people who hold such views of domestic violence are unlikely to respond to a victimization survey in the same way as those who have come to see it as a crime.

Over the last 20 years, there has been a sea change in Hilo as activists have insisted that police, prosecutors, and judges take domestic violence more seriously and battered women began to ask the legal system for help. Clearly, victims of violence that used to put up with violence from intimates are now calling the police and going to court.[8] The increase in civil temporary restraining orders (TROs) suggests that women are more inclined to turn to the legal system for help. The even greater increase in criminal cases indicates that police are more energetic in making arrests and prosecutors in pressing charges. Thus these changes reflect both significant alterations in police and legal practices and changes in patterns of complaining about wife battering. They measure a changing legal consciousness of rights not to be battered as well as increases in battering. Wife battering has a long history in this area (see Merry 2002), but it led only to calls to the police and courts for help from the mid 1980s. The fact that calls to the police for help have increased more slowly than criminal prosecutions suggests that the change is the result of victims' greater willingness to turn to the law for help. Restraining order requests in Massachusetts also increased dramatically between 1981 and 1993, from 15,000 a year to 56,000 (Ptacek 1999: 62).

---

[8] During the 20-year period from 1974 to 1998, the population of the County of Hawai'i doubled, but the number of calls to the police for domestic trouble cases more than quadrupled (County of Hawai'i 1997). The number of requests for civil protective orders, commonly called temporary restraining orders or TROs, also increased dramatically from the early 1970s. Between 1971 and 1978, there were seven TROs issued in Hilo for domestic violence situations. There were 250 in 1985, 320 in 1991, and 412 in 1998. The number of criminal cases of domestic violence in East Hawai'i, the Hilo side of the island, has increased even more, from 31 in 1979 and 9 in 1980, to 538 in 1998. On the island as a whole, during the 16 years between 1979 and 1995, the number of criminal cases of wife battering increased 25 times from a very small initial number to almost 800 out of a population of 135,000. In 1993 there was one call to the police for every 58 residents and one charge of Abuse of a Household Member for every 183 residents in the county. In 1994 domestic violence cases were about 30 percent of the active probation caseload of the criminal court. The numbers have continued to escalate through 2000.

Thus women's willingness to complain and to seek help from the legal system shifted rapidly from the early 1990s. In the late 1970s and early 1980s, many women reported that the police would simply tell an abusive husband to calm down and take a walk. Now more women think the abuse is not acceptable. Older participants in the ATV program contrast the present understanding with that of their childhoods, when violence was simply ignored. While the mothers of older women said, "Just put up with it, that is the way it is," younger women's mothers now support them and tell them they should complain. Instead of "lickins" and "stink eye," women now talk about "battering," "abuse," and "assault." These new terms are located within the legal and professional domain rather than the everyday world of gender relations. Since these words are also those generated by elite whites, this is simultaneously a change from "local" working-class terms to more professionalized, mainland categories. The advocates who help women file applications for restraining orders and who run the groups encourage the women to see themselves as endowed by rights. Although they take on this idea only slowly and reluctantly, they are clearly more willing to call the police and file applications for restraining orders in the family court than in the past.

Thus, when people are interviewed about their experiences of violence, the answer is more subtle and interpretive than it might seem. There are clearly historical changes in how violence is defined in the family and how it is given meaning. There is a shift from discipline to abuse and the gradual incorporation of forms of harassment and humiliation that injure the spirit without harming the body into the category of domestic violence. The decision to call an official agency for help is an interpretive moment that depends on these categorizations. People call for help when they feel that they were wronged and are entitled to help. They identify themselves in surveys as victims of gender violence when these actions seem like abuse rather than normal. Despite these limitations to criminal justice statistics and victimization survey data, they do show that there is a connection between gender violence and poverty, racial discrimination, and other forms of social marginalization.

## Migration and the Law in the USA

Immigrant women are particularly vulnerable to violence, particularly illegal immigrant women. Immigration itself poses significant and jarring stressors that could lead to the escalation of violence. When immigrant women leave their abusers, they risk the condemnation of their community, on which they are particularly dependent. Immigrant woman can be quite isolated and dependent on their linguistic and national communities for social supports such as interest-free loans, clothing, shelter, food, babysitting services, contacts to navigate immigration laws, access to family in the native country through informal messaging systems, and on occasion physical protection. Abusers often maintain control over their victims by limiting access to outside work and language skills, increasing dependence on this community.

For the burgeoning population of illegal immigrants in both the USA and Europe, abuse poses special problems because of women's dependence on their spouses and partners for residency authorization. Women are particularly vulnerable to men on whom they depend to acquire legal status. As immigration regulations in the USA have tightened, particularly in the post 9/11 period, women who come without documents to join partners who are documented or citizens are even more dependent on them. Abused undocumented women fear discovery by immigration police and deportation (see Mendelson 2004). Salcido and Adelman (2004: 163) describe the dilemmas of a woman who immigrated illegally into Arizona from Mexico, married a man with residence papers, had a child, then found that he was isolating her, preventing her from working, and beating her. She now faces a legal limbo, unable to work legally and facing deportation and contestation over custody of her US-born daughter. In another example, a Mexican woman married a US citizen, but he followed and beat her, seeking to prevent her acquiring legal permanent residence by strategies such as hiding her mail from the Immigration and Naturalization Service (INS) and using her illegal status to control and contain her (Salcido and Adelman 2004: 166–167).

The threat of deportation is a powerful weapon for an abuser.[9] Women often discover, too late, that their documentation was falsified or that their abuser has withdrawn sponsorship of their citizenship (Zenobia Lai (Managing Attorney, Asian Outreach Unit, Greater Boston Legal Services), interview by Hao Nguyen, November 17, 2004). At other times, the abuser gives out false information and horror stories to maintain his victim's obedience. Out of fear, they remain with the abuser. Recent laws in the USA have somewhat ameliorated undocumented women's vulnerability to this form of violence. The 2000 Victims of Trafficking and Violence Protection Act offered protections to trafficked women (Mendelson 2004: 211). The 1994 Violence against Women Act (VAWA) enabled battered immigrants to petition for permanent status themselves if they had married in "good faith" (in other words, not simply in order to immigrate), lived with their spouse in the USA for at least three years, were victims of battery or extreme cruelty, would suffer extreme hardship if they were deported, and were of good moral character (Salcido and Adelman 2004: 164). Despite its efforts to help battered immigrants, the law poses significant obstacles to providing protection for battered undocumented women. These women face the current anti-immigration climate in the USA and laws such as the 1996 Illegal Immigration Reform and Immigrant Responsibility Act (IIRIRA). The 1996 law increased the grounds for deportation and limited judicial review of deportation cases (Wood 2004: 141). For immigrant women attempting to leave their abusive partners, Acts like the IIRIRA put both them and their partners at greater risk of deportation, either of which may spell disaster for a financially dependent partner.

VAWA 2000 attempted to enhance immigrant women's access to protective orders and added additional protections against deportation. The threshold for petition

---

[9]   I am grateful to Hao Nguyen for her ethnographic and documentary work on the section on immigration.

approval was also decreased, so that a woman no longer had to produce evidence that deportation would cause her and her children "extreme hardship" in their native country, a claim that was often difficult if not impossible to prove. Under VAWA, she could self-petition for a green card or permanent residence instead of relying on the abuser to sponsor her, as long as she was: (1) legally married to the US citizen or permanent resident abusive spouse; (2) battered during the marriage in the USA; and (3) a person of good moral character. Unmarried women or those married to a non-citizen are excluded; the law helps only women who are married to US citizens or permanent residents. Thus, despite these efforts to give undocumented women victims of violence some protection to complain, only a fraction of abused women are eligible for help. Women migrants are usually very dependent on the men who are sponsoring their entrance into the USA and thus reluctant to complain to the criminal justice system (see also Bhattacharjee 1997). However, in interviews with nine undocumented California women who were battered, Mendelson (2004: 215) found that they were deeply grateful for the VAWA legalization process and found it liberating for their relationships, consciousness, and possibilities.

A case in Boston provides another example of the success of the VAWA process. Hao Nguyen, my research assistant, reported a 2003 case in which a woman's immigration status was manipulated by her abuser as a form of punishment and control. Lin was an elderly Chinese woman who married a widower with US citizenship. Over time, he became very violent and controlling. The work visa that allowed her to enter the United States expired during their marriage. In 2003 her husband filed a petition for permanent residency as her sponsor. In the subsequent immigration interview, however, he claimed he had been forced into marriage with Lin, in an attempt to have his petition for her residency rejected. Lin later fled from her husband upon discovery of the deception, but was then undocumented. Her husband filed a missing persons report. When she had not reappeared after 90 days, the United States Citizenship and Immigration Service (USCIS) began deportation proceedings. She sought help from Greater Boston Legal Services, which assisted her with her VAWA self-petition. The deportation was ultimately stayed by a sympathetic judge. It took one year for her petition to be accepted and for her status to change from undocumented to documented. During this time, Lin, as an undocumented "illegal" alien, was ineligible for a work visa and was dependent on various organizations and shelters for her survival (interview with Zenobia Lai).

Lin used the immigration benefits of VAWA to stabilize her residency status and avoid deportation. Her case is a VAWA success story. However, her interactions with immigration are the exception. Massachusetts, and the immigration courts in Boston in particular, are considered liberal and sympathetic to immigrants. But there have been cases in Boston and elsewhere where judges have ruled against a battered woman based on technicalities or erroneous assumptions about the nature of domestic violence (Anon. 2004; Ptacek 1999: 172–175). Other court systems in the United States take a harder stance on undocumented immigrants (Deborah Weissman (University of North Carolina, School of Law), interview by Hao Nguyen, December 9, 2004).

Immigration law changed rapidly post-9/11 – 69 immigration regulations with 49 specific anti-terrorism regulations were enacted between September 11 2001 and September 2003 (Murthy 2004). The intense pressure for reform resulted in the former Immigration and Naturalization Service (INS)'s absorption into the Department of Homeland Security in March 2003. The former INS was divided into the US Citizenship and Immigration Services (USCIS) and Immigration and Customs Enforcement (ICE), the enforcement arm of the agency. With the placement of INS in the Department of Homeland Security, ICE and USCIS were primarily focused on security.

The grounds for deportation have increased markedly since the inception of ICE due to the support of the Bush administration and former Attorney General John Ashcroft. The increasing strength of ICE is worrisome for immigrant rights activists. ICE, as the enforcement arm, has received far more funding than USCIS (Murthy 2004: 4). The department has enthusiastically embraced its role, declaring on its home page, "ICE removals of criminal and other illegal aliens hit a new record in the latest fiscal year" (http://www.ice.gov). The quickness with which Lin's deportation proceedings occurred is an example of a frightening new, but undiscerning, efficiency.

For abused immigrant women and their advocates, post-9/11 immigration enforcement is intimidating. The acronym for enforcement, ICE, is purposely cold and unyielding. Similarly, the department refers to deportation as "illegal alien removal." All three words enforce a sense of otherness that a semantically equivalent term like "undocumented immigrant deportation" does not. Creating a sense of the "other" is key to the department's sense of righteousness – a righteousness reflected in almost all areas of foreign and domestic security policy. There are VAWA cases and naturalization hearings where women have been held in detention or deported (Deborah Weissman). Lin's sympathetic judge, by staying the deportation hearings, enabled her to complete her VAWA application. Less understanding judges could have interpreted Lin's request for a stay as a manipulation and denied it, thereby subjecting her to deportation (Deborah Weissman).

Post-9/11 immigration anxiety has also slowed down the process. Petitions that had taken 2–3 months in 1997 were taking 2–3 years by 2003 (Zenobia Lai). While women wait for their petition to be approved, they are ineligible for work permits, child support, and most federal, state, and local non-emergency services. The waiting period causes economic hardship as well as taking a severe emotional toll. Usually, deportation hearings have already begun and advocates work to delay the hearings until the petition is approved or denied. More petitions are also being denied based on a stricter interpretation of the "good moral character" criterion for approval. Women who admit to using a false social security number to receive a work permit, a common practice among undocumented women, are now considered of "poor moral character" and ineligible for a green card (Deborah Weissman). The official precedent, written in a memo, had been to preclude the use of false social security numbers in determining "moral character." The understanding had been that the action was done by undocumented women only to attain a work permit to maintain economic stability.

Post-9/11 trauma and anger has opened the door to opportunistic anti-immigrant sentiments that have impacted the behavior of police and at times compromised their ability to serve immigrant communities. Senators and Congressmen have responded to the growing clamor for police to assume the enforcement powers of ICE officials by introducing two national bills that would fund training for police. Police would need to ask about the immigration status of the individuals they have been called to help. An undocumented woman calling for help from an abusive husband, for example, would be subject to immigration status questions that could lead to her deportation. Most police precincts have a domestic violence unit that receives grants from VAWA. Part of the requirements for the funds is that the department assist domestic violence victims in all matters concerning their safety, including immigration. By taking on the mantle of enforcers, the police whom battered women summon for help become the people they avoid in order to not be detained because of their immigration status. De facto discrimination against immigrants would occur, further isolating a vulnerable group from support and help. The demand for security and stringency in immigration enforcement has meant a sharp increase in deportation and the increasing pressure of ICE and others to continue with the same pace of arrests. VAWA is vulnerable to pressures placed on immigration agents and local level anti-immigrant sentiments. In this way, VAWA cannot extend too far beyond contemporary biases and animosities, but is at least an attempt, however imperfect, at offering some legal protection for battered immigrant women.

## Vulnerability and Impunity: A Case Study of Ciudad Juárez

The vulnerability of poor migrant women to violence has become particularly visible in the case of the city of Ciudad Juárez, a town just south of the US border with Mexico.[10] It has received national attention recently because of the extraordinary number of young women who have been killed there. According to the Mexican government, there have been 379 murders of women between 1993 and 2005 and 34 missing women, although activists argue that there are many more. According to Amnesty International (2003), the Juárez-Chihuahua *feminicidio* (femicide, or the killing of women and girls) accounts for over 400 deaths of poor women and girls, some of whom were sexually assaulted at the time of murder, some fitting a pattern of serial killings. Bodies are discarded on the outskirts of town or in empty city lots, construction sites, and dumpsters. Some murders stem from domestic violence (Washington Office on Latin America (WOLA) 2006a). The nongovernmental organization, Bring Our Daughters Home (Nuestras Hijas de Regreso a Casa) estimates that as of 2003 an additional 600 women have disappeared (Camacho 2005: 259), their bodies never recovered. More than half of the female victims were aged between

---

[10]   Jennifer Telesca did most of the research and writing for this section, for which I am very appreciative.

13 and 22. Some had children and were heads of household (Amnesty International 2003). Although there are no simple explanations for this high murder rate, it is connected to the emergence of factories (*maquila*) along the border, a pattern of labor migration of poor single women as low-paid labor to these factories, the narcotics trade, and widespread impunity for perpetrators.

Here again, statistics are very sketchy and inconsistent. It is not clear why counting began in 1993, for example, or why only women's deaths are included and not men's. Nor is it clear which deaths count as *feminicidio* murders. The statistics are a political football. For the social movement that has developed focusing on Ciudad Juárez, high numbers justify a sense of crisis so that activists develop their own, higher, counts, while government officials eager to downplay the problem probably minimize the number of femicides.

Separated from El Paso, Texas by the Río Grande, Ciudad Juárez is located in the Mexican state of Chihuahua. It is a major artery for movements north and south, where people, goods, and capital traverse the US/Mexico border. In 1993, a year before the North American Free Trade Agreement (NAFTA) came into effect, reports began to appear about *feminicidio*. Ten years later, Amnesty International published its report, *Mexico: Intolerable Killings: 10 Years of Abductions and Murders in Ciudad Juárez and Chihuahua*. It opens with the following passage:

> It is 10.15 on the night of 19 February 2001. People living near waste ground close to a *maquila* (an assembly plant) in Ciudad Juárez dial 060, the number of the municipal police emergency services, to inform them that an apparently naked young woman is being beaten and raped by two men in a car. No patrol car is dispatched in response to the first call. Following a second call, a police unit is sent out but does not arrive until 11.25 pm, too late to intervene … On 21 February the body of a young woman was found on the waste ground near to where the emergency call had been made. It was wrapped in a blanket and showed signs of physical and sexual violence. The cause of death was found to be asphyxia resulting from strangulation. The body of the young woman was identified by the parents as being that of Lilia Alejandra. (AI 2003)

The police never investigated the lack of response to the first emergency phone call. The waste ground near the *maquila* where Lilia Alejandra's body was found remains dark, without municipal lighting from which to see at night the small cross that commemorates her death (AI 2003). It is a reminder of how women in Ciudad Juárez and Chihuahua City, the state capital, remain vulnerable and unprotected.

On the US/Mexico border, transnational corporations that benefit from free trade coexist with powerful narco-traffickers. Beginning in the 1960s border industrialization transformed the landscape of Ciudad Juárez. It has since tripled in size and now supports approximately 1.5 million people. Nearly 50,000 people migrate to Ciudad Juárez annually from Mexico and Central America (Wright 2001: 93) looking for income on either side of the border. The 2000 census indicates that some 40 percent of Juárez residents have lived in the city for less than five years (Camacho 2005: 261). The rapid growth has produced fragile public services, environmental degradation, and overcrowded schools (Wright 2001: 98).

After the passage of NAFTA (Nathan 2003), the Juárez *maquilas* mushroomed, employing many of these migrants. About eighty Fortune 500 companies, including Alcoa, General Electric, DuPont, Ford, Honeywell, and 3M (AI 2003), account for the nearly 300 *maquilas* in Ciudad Juárez (Wright 2001: 93). All enjoy low or non-existent taxes and little to no regulation (AI 2003). Some *maquilas* make products for export 24 hours a day and pay workers as little as $0.35 per hour (Wright 2001: 111). Others pay workers about $55 for a 45-hour working week (Nathan 2003). The *maquilas* hire mostly women and girls because their hands are said to be nimble and their labor docile (Nathan 2003). Women and girls are less likely to complain and organize their labor (Hise 2006).

Human Rights Watch reports that *maquilas* routinely discriminate against women by forcing them to undergo pregnancy tests as a term of employment. If women are found to be pregnant, their employment is terminated (Human Rights Watch 1996). In a country like Mexico, where gender roles once held women in the domestic sphere, the fact that women are now out of the home earning and spending their own wages while men, the former breadwinners, struggle to find jobs creates great tension (Nathan 2003; Hise 2006). *Maquila* workers comprise nearly one-third of the victims (AI 2003). Some *maquila* workers travel long distances alone to get to work, some to start a shift in the middle of the night (Hise 2006). At least one woman was turned away by her employer when she arrived late and was victimized when she returned home (Hise 2006). Waitresses, students, and workers in the informal economy are also victims of this violence (AI 2003).

Amnesty International reporter Debbie Nathan (2003) describes the range of violence: "Wives are shot at home, execution style, and then burned by husbands; a female drug trafficker dissolved in a vat of acid ... A 19-year-old molested his 10-year niece, killed her so she wouldn't tell, and dumped her corpse in the desert." It is what the police call "situational," routine violence. The attorney general's office in Chihuahua blamed parents for neglect and scolded them for raising their daughters without morals (Nathan 2003). Police and other authorities frequently blame victims for their murder, denouncing them as prostitutes or drug addicts upon arriving at a crime scene (Hise 2006). As in other situations of gender violence, responsibility is transferred to the victim for somehow instigating or provoking the violence. This is another example of the process of "responsibilization," in which those who fail to fit into patterns defined as normal are held responsible for their suffering.

In this frontier region, police and government officials grant impunity to perpetrators. Gross discrimination, negligence, and corruption are rampant. Inquiries by international, national, and state human rights organizations and women's groups have criticized the Mexican government for its inefficient and incompetent investigation of these murders (Equality Now 2006). All victims and their families share a common experience of flagrant state negligence. In the words of Evangelina Arce, mother of Silvia Arce who went missing in March 1998:

> We went to her workplace, we went to see her friends, we went to see her clients ...
> I went to the Special Prosecutor's office and they couldn't find the report I'd lodged ...
> We went to the Special Prosecutor's office, then to the Office for the Care of Victims

and all those places … We went there time and time again … They said there were no lines of enquiry, it went from one prosecutor to another, but no investigation was carried out and they didn't do a search for her either … We went to Chihuahua, we asked for copies of the file, there we saw that there had been no movement in the proceedings for four and a half years and that they had not searched for Silvia … We went to see the governor … he told me don't worry, we're going to get them, we're going to see that justice is done. Next time we went to see him, he asked us why we were asking him for justice and said we should be asking the previous governor. (AI 2003)

Years of frustration begin at the moment in which a daughter, sister, mother, or girlfriend go missing. State law prohibits families from filing missing person reports until 72 hours have passed (WOLA 2005). Mishandling, falsifying, and destroying evidence is common (AI 2003) as is the incorrect identification of victims (WOLA 2005). Victims' mothers routinely experience loss of work, collapse of their marriage, and exclusion from communities (Camacho 2005: 272). Their voices are said to defame the city and discourage tourism (Hise 2006). Police commonly tell mothers "that if they wish to see their daughters alive again they should refrain from 'creating scandal in the streets'" (Camacho 2005: 273).

Homicide falls under the jurisdiction of the state police of Chihuahua, not under municipal or federal authorities (WOLA 2005). Only when crimes are directly linked to weapon or drug trafficking are federal authorities called in (WOLA 2005). Torture is a common method of investigation (Hise 2006). For example, two days after eight women's bodies were found in an empty lot in 2001, the police rounded up two bus drivers and tortured them into confessing. No physical evidence linked them to the murders. One of them died in prison. Meanwhile, his lawyer was shot dead by police who claimed that they had mistaken him for a fugitive. Even the victims' families believe that they are scapegoats (WOLA 2004). But once a conviction is made, a case is closed (Hise 2006). Amnesty International (2003) concluded: "The authorities have failed in their duty to exercise due diligence in four areas: the investigation of the crimes, punishment of those responsible, the provision of reparations to the victims and crime prevention." Other international bodies such as the Inter-American Commission on Human Rights (IACHR), part of the Organization of American States (OAS), and the United Nations Committee on the Elimination of Discrimination against Women (the CEDAW Committee) have launched similar condemnations. All suggest that impunity significantly contributes to the perpetuation of violence against women.

As early as 1998, the Mexican government under the National Human Rights Commission (Comisión Nacional de Derechos Humanos) carried out its own investigation of the Juárez-Chihuahua *feminicidio*. It issued Recommendation 48/98, concluding that judicial, state, and municipal authorities were guilty of negligence and dereliction of duty (AI 2003). The recommendation was rejected by the local and state authorities, who claimed that the Commission was trying to damage the ruling party (PAN) at the time of an election. However, when the historically dominant political party PRI won the elections, the recommendations were still not implemented. Also in 1998, the Special Prosecutor's Office for the Investigation of the Murder of Women (Fiscalía Especial para la Investigación de Homocidios de Mujeres (FEIHM) ) was set up (AI 2003). In an unprecedented move in 2004, a special federal prosecutor,

María López Urbina, named 131 state officials who she believed were responsible for negligence and abuse of authority. Nonetheless, judges have failed to issue arrest warrants for those officials who are otherwise fit for prosecution (WOLA 2005). In 2005 she was replaced without explanation. The newly appointed Special Prosecutor, Alicia Perez Duarte, criticized local and state police for their acquiescence to drug mafia and organized crime. Her comments contradicted denials by the Chihuahua Office of the State Attorney General, for she draws links between the murders and the rise of the Carrillo Fuentes drug cartel and does not discount possible links to the rings of international money laundering, prostitution, and pedophilia that use Internet cafes, modeling agencies, and computer education schools as guises for their operation (Paterson 2006: 4). Indeed, upon the arrest of one narco-trafficker, a necklace adorned by a woman's nipple was found hanging from his neck (Hise 2006). In 2006 the position of special prosecutor was eliminated with a final report. That report implicated 177 public servants, including judicial, police, and prosecutorial staff, involved in 120 cases in administrative or criminal negligence (Equality Now 2006). Meanwhile, the murders continue. In July 2006, 23-year-old Elsa Anglae Jurado Torres was doused with gasoline and set on fire by an unidentified man in Ciudad Juárez. She died five days later (Equality Now 2006).

In 1998 the United Nations Special Rapporteur on Extrajudicial, Summary, or Arbitrary Executions, Asma Jahangir, became the first authority of the international community to draw attention to the gender-based murders (AI 2003). Other international bodies such as IACHR have called for women to be free from violence and discrimination (Inter-American Court of Human Rights (IACHR) 2003). In 2002 the IACHR granted "precautionary measures on behalf of the wives of two men detained in connection with the murders who have allegedly been tortured" and on behalf of the defense lawyer and local human rights defender who were subjected to threats and intimidation (AI 2003). In 2006 the IACHR published two cases as admissible related to the Juárez-Chihuahua murders, one of which was filed by Evangelina Arce (see above). As Marisela Ortiz, co-founder of Bring Our Daughters Home, suggests: "I believe the only hope that the mothers have left is for justice to come from outside. Until now our organization has brought petitions of denunciation to the IACHR and we believe that starting from there may cause some response" (Hise 2006).

Concern over the Juárez-Chihuahua *feminicidio* has also reached the halls of the US Congress. In March 2005 Congresswoman Hilda Solis (D-CA) and Senator Jeff Bingaman (D-NM) introduced House and Senate resolutions that condemned the murders, offered condolences to victims' families, and encouraged the State Department to become more involved in efforts to resolve the crimes. The resolution was approved both in the House and Senate by unanimous vote in May 2006 (WOLA 2006b). Among other efforts by the US government, the US Agency for International Development (USAID) has provided $5 million in assistance to enhance the transparency of the Chihuahua criminal justice system (WOLA 2006a).

The failure of the Mexican authorities to see the murders as a pattern of violence against women denies victims' families a "proper response and an effective judicial remedy" (AI 2003). The gender of the victim is a significant factor in crime: it influences the motive and context in which a crime occurs; it affects the type of violence endured by women and the ways authorities respond – or do not respond – to it (AI 2003). Recent years have also seen a spike in the murders of women and girls in other parts of Latin America, including Guatemala, Colombia, Peru, and Bolivia. Unfortunately, *feminicidio* is not isolated to US/Mexico border towns. As this case study demonstrates, poverty, isolation, and urbanization contribute to young women's vulnerability to violence, while state indifference to the problem allows it to flourish. Both violence within intimate relationships and among strangers mushroom under these conditions of opportunity and impunity for those who use violence against others.

## Conclusions

Income inequality, racism, and illegal migration create the conditions of structural violence that increase women and men's vulnerability to gendered forms of interpersonal violence. Undocumented women are especially vulnerable to violence and coercion from police, customs officials, and their sponsors on whom they must depend for legal documents. Governments considering immigration reform should take into account the impact of stringent border regulations on patterns of violence against those who cross illegally. Young women leaving the security of community and family for work are also vulnerable, particularly in the absence of an effective police presence, as is the case in Ciudad Juárez.

As this chapter has shown, women who live with violence tend to become poorer. They lose autonomy and control over their lives, whether they are home workers, low-paid wager earners, or undocumented migrants. Indigenous peoples and communities of color encounter structural violence such as exclusions from housing and jobs, state violence in the forms of unequal policing and interpersonal violence. Poor and minority women get less protection from the police and criminal justice system. Perpetrators are less likely to be caught and punished for beating poor women than for violating richer ones. This level of impunity encourages violence of many kinds against poor, marginalized, minority women. Despite the difficulties of statistically measuring the impact of poverty, race, and migration status on gender violence, qualitative data supports the statistical indications that the effects of poverty, racism, and illegal migration on gender violence are significant and widespread.

## Questions for Further Discussion

1   What do statistics tell us about the nature of gender violence in the USA? What do they hide? Are they neutral and objective? To what degree do statistics change if one takes into account how gender violence is defined and measured?

2  Discuss the role of poverty, race, and citizenship in the lives of women most affected by gender violence in the USA. Has their access to protections against gender violence expanded or contracted over time? How does the contemporary political climate contribute to the way safeguards are imagined and implemented?

3  Women who live with violence tend to become poorer or, worse, die because of it. Name some of the ways in which structural violence becomes interpersonal violence through the case studies of Hilo, Hawai'i and Ciudad Juárez, Mexico.

## Video Suggestions

*On the Edge: The Femicide in Ciudad Juárez*, by Steve Hise
(USA, 2006), 58 minutes

On the US/Mexico border, where goods, drugs, and people traverse, hundreds of murders of poor young women have been repeatedly ignored by the police since at least 1993, and left unresolved by the government, despite the persistence of family members and activists who seek justice and an end to impunity for the perpetrators of these crimes. This documentary film explores the range of social, political, and economic factors that contribute to the killings, and situates them in ways that help us understand Ciudad Juárez not as an isolated phenomenon but as a lens into the wider global political economy.

*Rosita*, by Barbara Attie and Janet Goldwater (USA/Nicaragua, 2005), 58 minutes

In January 2003, a 9-year-old girl from Nicaragua was raped on her way to school while her parents – illiterate and poor – worked the coffee fields in Costa Rica for a modicum of cash. Rosa (or Rosita) became pregnant before her first menstruation and contracted sexually transmitted diseases. This film traces the family's odyssey as they escape Costa Rica for Nicaragua in an attempt to save their only child's life through a "therapeutic abortion." What unfolds is a powerful story about their encounter with the law, government officials and agencies of state, the Roman Catholic Church, the medical establishment, and, not least, the press.

*Voices Heard Sisters Unseen*, by Grace Poore (USA, 1995), 75 minutes

In this film women in the USA tell first-hand their stories of gender violence, but because of their identity they remain largely outside of the state's protective services. Interviews, poetry, dance and music performances present another side to domestic violence not often told by the deaf, the disabled, prostitutes, lesbians, HIV-positive persons, and undocumented immigrants. Each voices the particular challenges faced as they become "re-victimized" in the courtroom, by police, and in social service provisioning. It is an important reminder for an integrated response to gender violence.

# 6

# Violent "Cultural" Practices
# in the Family

The international violence against women movement has defined several practices embedded in systems of kinship and marriage as instances of gender violence (see Coomaraswamy 2002). They are typically described as "cultural" practices, even though the anthropological understanding of culture sees *all* social practices as constituted by cultural understandings. These practices are normatively supported. They are seen as socially desirable acts that constitute moral and modest behavior for women. Most are designed to safeguard, restrict, and control women's sexuality. Although some individuals and groups fight against them or covertly resist them, these "cultural" practices are often energetically defended by political leaders who define them as central to their national or ethnic identity.

The family practices generally viewed as violence against women by international activists include: (1) early and forced marriage, although there is no agreement on the age at which a woman is too young to marry; (2) female genital cutting, also referred to as female genital mutilation (FGM) by the activists who first drew attention to the practice; (3) female feticide, or sex selection, which occurs in societies that value sons over daughters so that daughters are disproportionately killed as infants or aborted; (4) "honor" killings, murders of women who are thought to have dishonored their family through a lapse of sexual modesty; (5) widow immolation or burning, called *sati*, when a widow throws herself on her husband's funeral pyre, a practice in India now more or less defunct; (6) foot-binding, a practice in China now eliminated; (7) widowhood rituals that involve ritual humiliation of the widow or mandatory sexual intercourse with a relative or village head; (8) pledging of daughters to temples at an early age to be sex workers or handmaidens of gods (the *devadasi* system in India and similar systems in Nepal, Benin, Nigeria, Togo, and Ghana); (9) caste-based discrimination and violence; and (10) Western women's eating disorders and cosmetic plastic surgery intended to achieve hyper-thin bodies and particular facial configurations defined as beautiful. These so-called beauty practices are carried out by women who feel that they must redesign their bodies to conform to social expectations. Some international human rights activists have suggested that the requirement that women wear veils and other forms of extensive bodily covering is also a form of violence against women, but this idea is hotly contested.

Clearly, this is a highly diverse set of practices. All were considered desirable forms of behavior by at least some segments of the wider society at some historical moment. Each exists within the framework of a kinship system and an ideology of gender and sexuality. Most assume that chastity outside marriage is essential to being a virtuous, moral woman. For example, prohibiting widow remarriage or requiring the widow to kill herself on her husband's funeral pyre were both designed to guarantee chastity after the husband's death. Rape of lower-caste women by upper-caste men is effective as an assertion of caste hierarchy since it shames the woman's husband and kin as well as injuring the woman herself.

Forms of gender violence rooted in kinship structures are usually described as "harmful traditional practices," as if they were ancient holdovers from an unchanging past. However, what are regarded as "harmful traditional practices" are constantly changing in response to current conditions. For example, women leaders in Nigeria resist early marriage campaigns because they say that in the environment of chaos and economic insecurity they now face, it is safer and better for a girl to marry before puberty to guarantee that she will be a virgin and have a home and social position as a wife (Bunting and Merry 2007). In countries where female genital cutting is thought to express a higher social status or a nationalist identity, the incidence is increasing as the surgery comes to represent support for the nation. Women in the Darfur region of the Sudan, for example, have been increasing the practice of FGC in an effort to create a more Arab identity for themselves. Although *sati* was virtually eliminated in India decades ago, a new conservative Hindu political movement in India celebrates the few that still occur as expressions of a true Hindu identity and morality. Rather than seeing these cultural practices as remote in time and place, as the term "harmful traditional practice" implies, it would be better to regard them as reflecting contemporary concerns about women's sexuality and child-bearing. Veiling, chastity belts, female genital cutting, and purdah or seclusion are clearly intended to control women's sexual and reproductive lives.

Many of these practices are now being contested and are changing. Some have been made illegal. Many African societies have active movements against female genital cutting and rates are dropping in some countries. Countries have passed laws against FGC in Africa, North America, and Europe. China outlawed and eliminated foot-binding in the mid twentieth century. Indian feminists have virtually eliminated the practice of widow immolation and are energetically campaigning against sex selection and female feticide. Killing a fetus because it is female is illegal in India, although it is legal to have a test of a fetus's sex and legal to have an abortion. The disparity between the birth rate of boys and girls has been growing, however, suggesting that the kinship-based preference for sons remains strong and that parents are still choosing to abort female fetuses. Although the rate of domestic violence remains high, it is no longer simply understood as legitimate discipline by the male head of the family. National and international movements have targeted all of these practices and have had some effect on the normative support they receive as well as their legality.

This chapter will focus on two of the mostly widely discussed examples of such "cultural practices": honor killing and female genital cutting. Both of these occur within family systems organized by descent through males, in which women marry in from other families and are responsible for producing male heirs. This kinship pattern, called a patrilineal, patrilocal kinship system by anthropologists, tends to maximize male power over women and commonly creates a patriarchal family. Male control over women's sexuality assumes great importance as a way to ensure that the children women bear belong to their husbands. Guaranteeing that the offspring are genuinely descended from the males of the kin group requires substantial surveillance of a woman's sexual behavior. Marrying a girl before she reaches puberty means she is more likely to be a virgin, and secluding her in the house or requiring her to wear a full body covering when she ventures beyond her door restricts her access to other sexual partners. Surgical reconstruction of a woman's vagina to smooth its features and restrict the opening emphasizes her purity while making sexual encounters with her more difficult. It may diminish her sexual desire, and probably her sexual pleasure.

Where a woman's sexual behavior reflects on the honor of her husband and his family, strict control over the expression of her sexuality is particularly important. Threatening to kill her if she steps outside these strict boundaries serves to control her sexual behavior. Modest conduct is central to a woman's reputation and virtue and reflects positively on her family. Within this framework, a woman who sullies the honor of her family must be killed to protect the whole family's honor.

## "Honor" Killings

An honor killing is the murder of a woman by her father or brother for engaging in sex outside marriage or for being suspected of doing so. It is part of a larger category of crimes of honor that include assault, confinement, or interference with choice in marriage in situations where these acts are justified by the need to maintain male honor by controlling women's sexual conduct (Welchman and Hossain 2005: 4). Crimes of honor serve to regulate women's sexuality and are seen as legitimate means of maintaining a family's reputation or a community's borders by preventing transgression of its norms (Baxi et al. 2006: 1250). A woman accused of an honor violation is not necessarily killed immediately, but may live under a constant threat of death, a death-in-life that Shalhoub-Kevorkian (2002b: 581) argues is itself a form of woman-killing, or "femicide." Crimes of honor are another version of crimes of passion. In both cases, the violence against the woman is justified by a man's fury at the discovery or suspicion of a woman's sexual interaction with another man which he feels dishonors him. Garden-variety domestic violence is similar, in that it often erupts from sexual jealousy and anger if a partner is suspected or found to be sexually active with someone else, as we saw in Chapter 3. The batterer often feels shamed by his apparent lack of control over his partner's sexuality and responds with violence.

Honor killings are a form of gender violence rooted in conceptions of family honor and shame. Family honor depends on the bravery and courage of men and the sexual modesty of their women. Failures by either men or women can inflict damage on the whole family. Thus, when a woman fails to behave modestly or engages in sex outside of marriage, she brings humiliation and shame upon her entire family. Under some circumstances, family members react by killing her in order to preserve the honor of the family. Families that kill their daughters may find this painful and difficult, yet feel driven to do so in order to preserve their honor from the slurs and assaults of others. Killings occur not only when women chose to have sex outside marriage, but also when they are suspected of doing so, even when there is no basis for the suspicion. Women who are raped are also shamed, even though they were forced to have sex. Despite substantial campaigns against this practice, it still occurs in parts of the Middle East and south Asia and sometimes among diasporic populations from these regions living in Europe and North America.

The following example from the Amnesty International website in 2005 describes a typical honor killing. It is important to note that there was considerable opposition to the killing by both family members and government officials. The girl's father was opposed, as was the governor of the district, the village elders, and the local police. Moreover, the victim had a women's legal aid center to turn to for help. Clearly, controlling honor killing poses particular difficulties when the threat comes from a woman's own family. Desperate to recover the family's honor, family members carry out such killings even though they find the process painful. The only way to protect a woman in this situation is to put her, in effect, in prison.

In January 2003, Amira Aoud, a 43-year-old woman from the West Bank village of Abu Qash, murdered one of her nine children on grounds of "family honour," despite her husband's opposition. Her 17-year-old daughter Rufayda had been repeatedly raped by two of her brothers, aged 20 and 22. In November 2002 Rufayda broke her leg and was taken to hospital, where doctors discovered that she was eight months pregnant and informed her family. The Palestinian Health and Social Affairs Ministries, fearing that Rufayda was at risk of being killed by her family, moved her to a safe place in Bethlehem, where at the end of December she gave birth to a boy, who was subsequently adopted. Since Rufayda wanted to return home to her family, the Governor of Ramallah asked Rufayda's family and the village elders to pledge in writing that they would not harm her. The family promised not to harm her but the Mayor of the village expressed concern that it could not be guaranteed that she would be safe with her family. Eventually Rufayda returned home without notifying anyone but soon afterwards she contacted the Women's Centre for Legal Aid and Counseling (WCLAC) saying that she was in danger from her family. WCLAC asked the police in Ramallah to intervene but the police could not get to the village in time due to Israeli army checkpoints. In the meantime, while her husband was absent, Amira Qaoud killed her daughter by wrapping a bag around her head, slitting her wrists, and hitting her on the head. She reportedly took advantage of her husband's absence because he objected to her killing their daughter. She was arrested and detained for a few months but was then released pending her trial and remained at liberty at the time of writing, two years after the killing. In a media interview Rufayda's mother maintained that she had to kill her daughter to protect her family's honour and states that before killing her daughter she had tried to force her to commit suicide but the girl refused. Both Rufayda's brothers were sentenced to 10 years imprisonment for rape. There are conflicting reports as to whether the two brothers are still in prison or have been released. (Amnesty International 2005a: 27–28)

Although honor killings are perceived to be related to Islam, this practice is not supported in Islam, nor is its incidence restricted to Muslim-dominant countries. As Asma Jahangir, UN Special Rapporteur on Extrajudicial, Summary, or Arbitrary Executions said in her 2000 report:

> The practice of "honour killings" is more prevalent although not limited to countries where the majority of the population is Muslim. In this regard it should be noted that a number of renowned Islamic leaders and scholars have publicly condemned this practice and clarified that it has no religious basis. (Report of the Special Rapporteur on Extrajudicial, Summary, or Arbitrary Executions, UN Doc. E/CN.4/2000/3, January 25, 2000, para. 78, quoted in Welchman and Hossain 2005: 13)

Moreover, there is a wide diversity in social practices among Muslim societies. Even non-Muslim communities carry out "crimes of honor" in Muslim-majority societies (Welchman and Hossain 2005: 15). The UN Special Rapporteur on Violence against Women reported crimes of honor in Brazil, Denmark, Egypt, Iraq, Israel and the occupied territories, Jordan, Kuwait, Lebanon, Morocco, the Netherlands, Pakistan, Qatar, Sweden, Turkey, and Yemen (Coomaraswamy 2005: xii).

In India and Pakistan, caste or community members, as well as family members, commit "crimes of honor" when women's actions are seen as threatening to the honor of the caste or community. Marriage to a person of another caste or community or a person the family disapproves of are thought to dishonor the caste, community, or family. Such dishonor is typically handled by caste *panchayats* or *jirgahs*, informal community-based adjudicatory systems that have existed since medieval times, although not unchanged. Caste *panchayats* are all-male groups that see themselves as guardians of caste interests and "honor" and operate in parallel with elected state *panchayats*, often seeing themselves as endowed with a "divine right" to adjudicate marriages that cross caste lines. They rely on forms of public violence to regulate intercaste or interreligion marriage. The police, government officials, and local politicians refuse to get involved in their decisions (Baxi et al. 2006: 1243). These bodies make pronouncements about the honor of their caste and carry out actions designed to preserve it, including revenge rapes, burning down houses, lynchings and beatings. Because there are close links between caste *panchayats* and government-sponsored *panchayats*, the state makes few efforts to control the actions of caste *panchayats* even when their actions violate the constitution (Baxi et al. 2006: 1244). Moreover, there is a widespread belief that social issues should be left to caste leaders rather than handled under state law, which has different criteria for social justice.

In Pakistan, under the Hudood Ordinance passed in 1979, *zina*, or willful sexual intercourse between a man and a woman who are not married, is a crime. Pregnancy is treated as proof of adultery. Women who are unchaste are imprisoned without the possibility of bail or any legal assistance, possibly for years. However, appellate courts in Pakistan increasingly reject honor killings of women by their families, and in some cases refuse to excuse the offense because the killing was done on the grounds of honor. For example, in a case in 2002, *Muhammad Siddique* vs. *the State*, the court upheld the conviction of a father who had murdered his daughter, her husband, and their infant child to teach his daughter a lesson about the dangers of marrying according to her choice. These decisions opposing honor killings draw on Islamic law, Pakistan's constitution, and international human rights law. They reflect the significant impact of campaigns by women's groups and human rights activists against "crimes of honor" as well as a desire to challenge the idea that Islam legitimates violence against women (Baxi et al. 2006: 1245–1248).

Despite government opposition to honor killing in Palestine and South Asia, courts often find ways to avoid holding perpetrators responsible for such killings. In many countries, the courts are notoriously lenient toward those who kill in the name of honor. Punishments are often mitigated or eliminated. Until recently, crimes of honor committed in the heat of passion on discovering sexual misconduct received little or no punishment. The Jordanian Penal Code, applied in the West Bank, states in Article 340 that a man who surprises his wife or one of his women committing adultery and wounds or kills one or both of the parties is exempt from liability. Moreover, if a man finds his wife or one of his female relatives in an "unlawful bed" and kills or injures one or both of them, he is liable to a lesser penalty because of extenuating circumstances (Shalhoub-Kevorkian 2002a: 580). Article 340 comes from the Ottoman Penal Code of 1858 and the French Penal Code of 1810, underscoring the close linkage between European and Middle Eastern ideas of honor, violence, and sexual control. There is currently a movement in Jordan to repeal this article and to increase punishments for crimes of honor, but Article 340 itself is rarely used (Abu-Odeh 2000). In the case of a rape, if a rapist agrees to marry his victim, the court can cease legal action or suspend the sentence of the offender (Shalhoub-Kevorkian 2002a: 592).

Nadera Shalhoub-Kevorkian (2002a) documents a series of techniques used by Palestinian courts to mitigate or avoid prosecution of those who engage in honor killing. For example, many female deaths in court records are listed as caused by "fate and destiny," which prosecutors define as actions that are not premeditated or intentional but accidental, so that no party is liable (Shalhoub-Kevorkian 2002a: 586). Although Article 340 excuses killing at the moment of discovery, it is rarely used because it depends on finding the sexual act in progress. Instead, many cases were initially charged as intentional murder or premeditated murder, but sentences were mitigated if the perpetrator was provoked (Shalhoub-Kevorkian 2002a: 587). Shalhoub-Kevorkian describes several cases that were prosecuted as intentional murder but received reduced sentences. One was the case of Nawal:

> Nawal, age 24, was accused by her family of behaving dishonorably, as people in their village were gossiping about her. In fear, she asked for police protection. Consequently, her brothers were called to the local police station and were obliged to sign a pledge not to cause her any harm. Only three of her four brothers signed, and it was the fourth brother, 25-year-old Sa'alem, who killed her. He beat her repeatedly, pushing her against a wall, then tied a plastic wire around her neck, and strangled her until she died. Sa'alem was charged with premeditated murder (Article 328), which was later modified to intentional murder (Article 326). His sentence was reduced to six months owing to both mitigating excuse (Articles 97, 98) and extenuating circumstances (Article 100). (Shalhoub-Kevorkian 2002a: 589)

In this case, there was no evidence of misconduct beyond rumors. Shalhoub-Kevorkian found that prosecutors often spent little effort trying to collect evidence and were more sympathetic to the perpetrator than the victim. Given the widespread impunity for honor killing, Shalhoub-Kevorkian advocates hymen reconstruction surgery in order to preserve a woman's life. Fully mindful that this approach fails to challenge the claim that a woman who loses her virginity outside marriage dishonors her family, she feels that it is more important to save a woman's life than to challenge the principle.

There has been substantial criticism of honor killing in the international human rights community and activism by women's and human rights groups in many counties where this is practiced, particularly since the mid 1990s. The use of the term "honor" has been much debated, since it takes the perpetrator's perspective that these actions defend his honor. Some activists argue for the assertion of women's rights as individuals and condemn religious and kinship-based control, while others advocate working through kinship and community structures. There are, in fact, strong and growing movements against honor crimes in many countries, led by activists from those countries with the support of other countries and international laws and organizations. But simplistic efforts to point to Islam as the root cause of honor killings has generated resistance rather than reform. It is important not to adopt a stereotypical association of honor with the "East" and passion with the "West," or of "reason" with the global north and "irrational male violence and female passivity" with the global south (Welchman and Hossain 2005: 13). The use of violence to restrict women's sexuality has a long history in Europe as well as in the Middle East and South Asia, and in all of these regions, men's actions to control women's sexuality are more or less tolerated rather than punished. These practices are expressions of a patriarchal kinship system in which power and resources flow through males and women are an essential if fragile link between generations of men. A similar kinship structure and concern about controlling women's sexuality accounts for a second major issue, female genital cutting.

## Female Genital Cutting

One of the most widely debated and criticized practices of gender violence is female genital cutting. It is considered a core violation of women's human rights by some and a longstanding way of preserving women's virtue by others. Female genital cutting, also called female circumcision or female genital mutilation (FGM) by early reformers, refers to several different forms of surgery performed on young women's genitalia. The surgical alterations range from nicking or relatively minor excision of the clitoris to a substantial slicing away of the genital region and clitoris and a surgical closing of the opening to allow only a very small space for urine and menstrual blood. In 1995 the World Health Organization classified the practice into four types, ranging from various forms of pricking or incision of the clitoris to excision of the prepuce with or without excision of part or all of the clitoris to infibulation, the excision of part or all of the external genitalia and stitching together the vaginal opening (Toubia 1999: 16). The most extreme process, infibulation, is practiced in only 15–20 percent of cases of female genital cutting. Nahib Toubia (1999: 15), a Sudanese doctor who has worked tirelessly to eliminate female circumcision for many years, recommends using the standardized WHO classification in her manual for health professionals dealing with circumcised women.

This practice is similar to honor killing in that it is concerned with preserving women's virginity and sexual modesty, particularly in the dangerous years before marriage. The surgery is conceptualized as a way to maintain women's purity. It seeks to diminish pleasure in sex and therefore to reduce desire. Critics emphasize the health hazards of the surgery itself and its long-term consequences for a woman's reproductive and physical health such as bleeding, infection, and death (Toubia 1994a; 1994b). Some have challenged the evidence for negative health consequences, however, pointing out that much of the data is based on individual case studies or small and badly designed studies (Obermeyer 1999; Shell-Duncan 2001). Some studies (e.g. Wassef 2001) report that men support the practice because they think that circumcised women make better wives.

These surgeries are common in a broad region stretching from west Africa through the Middle East and South Asia. Although sometimes thought of as an Islamic religious practice, it is far older and may have originated in ancient Egypt. With contemporary migration, it occurs in Europe and North America as well. Perhaps 130 million girls and women have had some form of circumcision, most of whom live in Africa. There have been campaigns against the practice throughout the twentieth century, but they gained in strength during the feminist movement of the 1970s. The activists of that period used the term "female genital mutilation" instead of "female circumcision" to emphasize its violation. They mobilized an international reform campaign which is still going strong, with many international as well as national organizations seeking to end the practice. Activists in Africa prefer the term "female genital cutting."

European reformers tried to eliminate these practices early in the twentieth century. Missionaries from the Church of Scotland in Kenya waged a campaign against what they called clitoridectomy among the Kikuyu people in the 1920s and 1930s, announcing in 1929 that all those sending their children to their schools had to pledge not to allow their daughters to be circumcised (Kenyatta 1962: 125). Some delegates to a conference on African children in Geneva in 1931 referred to it as a "barbarous" and "heathen" custom (Kenyatta 1962: 126–127). Kikuyu nationalists appropriated the custom as a mark of loyalty to the new nation, merging this issue with other grievances about missionary influence and land seizures (Walley 1997: 425). Jomo Kenyatta (1962: 128), anthropologist and leader of the young national-ists and later President of Kenya, argued that circumcision and initiation of both males and females is fundamental to tribal law, religion, and morality. In his words, "The abolition of *irua* [circumcision] will destroy the tribal symbol which identifies the age-groups, and prevent the Gikuyu from perpetuating that spirit of collectivism and national solidarity which they have been able to maintain from time immemo-rial" (Kenyatta 1962: 130).

The celebration of such gendered social practices as fundamental to a new, post-colonial nationalism was a widespread reaction to criticisms about "backward" customs by colonial powers. Veiling, *sati* and child marriage in India, and concubi-nage in Hong Kong were also the objects of nineteenth-century reform movements that sought to protect women at the same time as they condemned the social and cultural practices of colonized people (see Mani 1990; 1998). Consequently, nationalists seeking to throw off colonial control often reasserted the value of these practices and defined them as fundamental to their national identity, much as Kenyatta did with female circumcision in Kenya (see Chatterjee 1989; Ahmed 1992; Walley 1997).

Since the 1970s, FGC has become a major international issue, defined as a health hazard, a form of gender oppression, a form of violence against women, and a human rights violation (see Boyle and Preves 2000; Boyle 2002). These reform efforts encountered resistance similar to that in the colonial era, couched in terms of the defense of culture and national identity. Since women are commonly imagined as the bearers of culture and its embodiment as they wear traditional clothing and maintain social and religious practices in the home, they often become symbols of national identity. Thus, since FGC defines virtuous womanhood, it also defines nationhood. As countries in which FGC is widespread confront intense and some-times arrogant Western critiques, it comes to symbolize the postcolonial nation. UNICEF data indicates that in countries where FGC is done by a minority, its inci-dence is diminishing, but where it is virtually universal, it is on the increase. It is in these countries that FGC comes to represent national identity. In these circum-stances, FGC rates remain high among rural poor as well as urban educated women.

In recent years, feminist critiques of FGC as a form of gender oppression have increasingly been rejected, leading activists to focus more on the health hazards of the practice (Boyle 2002). However, in response to these health critiques, urban edu-cated women in countries where the practice is widespread are having the surgery performed in hospital with anesthesia. For example, a diasporic African woman describes returning to her family's village where the surgery was performed for her by a nurse (Ahmadu 2000). However, medicalizing the surgery does not eliminate anti-FGC activists' concern about the practice.

During the 1970s and 1980s, some feminists in the West targeted this issue as a particularly egregious form of violence against women. The strident quality of their writing generated a backlash even among African feminists concerned with the problem. While it remains an important issue for women's human rights, in recent years the rhetoric has become more muted. Some of the early writings criticized these practices as backward and opposed to progress as well as a form of gender oppression, a denial of women's sexuality, and a human rights violation (e.g. Daly 1978; Hosken 1981; Morgan and Steinem 1983). Fran Hosken, for example, an American and one of the early leaders in this movement, argued in her influential book that female genital mutilation, as she called it, was a human rights violation:

> There is no doubt that the practices discussed here are a gross violation of human rights; they not only violate the human right to health of the victims, but they also represent a violation of the very essence and spirit of femaleness by drastically altering and curtailing the natural female potential, thus ensuring submission to male exploitation and demands. (Hosken 1982: 1)

> The fact that today, many thousands of helpless young girls continue to be subjected to these cruel operations of sexual castration every year is due to another kind of mutilation, or crippling of the human spirit, which is embedded in every culture. Though these operations affect the health of millions of females, they are carefully concealed by those directly involved – their own families – as well as those responsible for health in each country, and by international governmental and non-governmental organizations of all kinds, including the United Nations agencies, especially those concerned with health and development. (Hosken 1982: 2)

Hosken argued that this practice hindered economic development and modernization. She asserts that women cannot attain "liberation" and "freedom," and countries cannot become "modernized" or "developed," until the women of the country embrace a Western feminist conception of what it means to be a "free" and "liberated" woman.

> Modernization is the goal of all African and Middle Eastern governments today, of all assistance and cooperation programs of international development agencies, as well as of countless private, charitable organizations working all over Africa … Why then, are women singled out as keepers of tradition? Tradition is stressed when it comes to keeping women "in their place" – that means, without education, training, or modern tools; ignorant, illiterate, and isolated; and most of all, without the most important and basic facts on health, reproduction and sexuality, which every woman who is raising a family most urgently needs to know. How often have you heard a man: a politician, a professor or a president, address a group of women on the issues at hand, and then praise them as keepers of "our culture and tradition," and encourage them "to uphold the cherished values of the past, the family and home"? It happens all over the world and all the time. What the man on the podium really means is: stay out of politics – we

don't want women here; get back to the past where women had no voice and no vote. Go home: you should be grateful to serve your husband, the head of the family. (Hosken 1982: 8)

Hosken argues that female genital mutilation is the product of oppressive "culture" and "tradition":

Tradition is always the reason given anywhere in Africa and also in the Middle East for practicing excision and infibulation on children, who most often are subjected to these operations by force. If the goal of national development is modernization, then abolishment of damaging traditional practices which are responsible for countless deaths, the painful maiming of women's bodies, and an impediment to normal childbirth, surely must be a priority.[1] (1982: 10)

Yet Hosken also realizes that failure to perform the cutting will diminish if not eliminate a girl's chance at marriage. She tells the story of a woman in Somalia facing the dilemma of circumcising her daughters: "Whether a girl is operated on or not, she is a victim. 'I cannot sacrifice my child. Either way, she suffers. What am I do to?' she asked.

As a midwife, I know the terrible health results. As a mother, I know how the child suffers from being teased, insulted and excluded by her friends. She will face even worse problems later when the family of the man whom she will be given in marriage may turn her down as "unfit." How can we stop these operations as long as we know that if our girls are not operated, they will not find husbands and their lives will be ruined? (Hosken 1982: 129)

The movement against female genital cutting has been fueled by stories told by victims of their pain and suffering or of their desire to escape the knife. Stories presented by advocacy groups seek to elicit outrage and build support for their cause. For example, a 1993 report of the proceedings of a workshop funded by the Family Violence Prevention Fund and the Coalition for Immigrant and Refugee Rights and Services tells the story of a 23-year-old woman from Mali who resisted excision, the surgery that removes parts of the labia and the clitoris. A Muslim and the fourth of 11 children, Aminata lived from the age of 12 with her paternal aunt in the capital city, Bamoko. She was determined not to be excised, particularly after a friend died after three days of bleeding. When she was taken by her father and fiancé to be

---

[1]   Hosken continues: "Tradition, according to Webster, means to deliver, to hand down a doctrine, a belief, a custom from the past. Tradition is a contradiction of the goals of development loudly proclaimed by every African/Middle Eastern government. Tradition means the continuation of the past, the refusal to change or accept anything new. Tradition in rural Africa means the subordination of the individual to the family group, which is ruled by a man who makes all the decisions. It demands the subordination of the families to the collective village life, where all decisions are made by the elders and chiefs, who with a few exceptions, are always men. This hierarchical structure dominates village life and does not tolerate individual accomplishments or change" (1982: 10).

excised, she refused, and her father beat her severely. She fled the night before her wedding. Her aunt rejected her for bringing shame to the family, so she took refuge in the home of a friend from school, whose older sister worked for an airline company. The older sister helped her to flee the country, and in 1990 she arrived in France. This is her story, as told in the NGO report:

> My parents wanted me excised by force. I opposed them. By listening to my friends and my sisters who had been excised, I learned that this practice brought a lot of suffering and pain. A friend of mine had died several days after being excised.
>
> I was beaten and tortured. I was ostracized by the whole village. I was rejected by everyone. Even the aunt who adopted me when I was 12 years of age chastised me. No woman had ever refused to be excised. All my grandmothers had been excised. Why then was I refusing to be excised?
>
> I could not return to the village because I did not obey my parents. No person would dare look at me. I went to the house of my friend. Her sister, touched by my plight, helped me to go to France. There I sought political refugee status. I went to see Mme Boutet to show that I was not excised.
>
> (Overcome by emotion, Aminata stopped for a moment.)
>
> And then the doctor examined me and I explained the problem to her. I felt very alone. I was rejected by everyone. I no longer had a father and a mother. I saw myself very alone. With the help of Dr. Renee Boutet de Monvel, gynecologist of the COMEDE (Medical Committee for Exiles), I came to know Maitre Linda Weil-Curiel, who has been my advocate and who is also helping other women like me. There are many people who have given me help.
>
> What is the excision that is done to us? There are many women who have no support, there are many who have died, there is so much pain – all of which I can bear witness to. I wish all the women of the world would help us to fight and put a stop to the excision that goes on in my home country. (Diop 1993: 23)

When she filed for refugee status in France, the lower court denied her request but it was appealed to the highest court. In Mali, her mother has been repudiated by her father and in France, some of her compatriots have accused her of bringing shame to her people by disclosing her traditions to Europeans (Weil-Curiel 1993: 25). This story clearly shows the capacity of an independent-minded young woman to resist as well as the costs of resistance. And it shows the difficulty of winning refugee status even in countries that oppose the practice.

Another account of female genital cutting presents quite a different picture of women's response. This is one of several stories collected by a Somali and Swedish team in the early 1980s from urban Somali women who have experienced infibulation, the form of female circumcision in which the clitoris, labia minora, and inner parts of the labia majora are cut and the sides of the vulva stitched together, leaving only a small orifice as outlet for menstrual blood and urine. This is the form of FGC found most widely in Somalia, the Sudan, and Mali, but only about 20 percent of circumcised women around the world experience this extreme version (Warsame et al. 1985: 2). This operation is a crucial step in shaping Somali women as women, along with changes in hairstyle. Their genitals become more different from those of men and the women are constructed as virgins. One woman told a typical story of her operation at the age of 7. She told it to the researchers in the early 1980s when she was 28 and working as a typist in a government ministry, so it probably occurred in the early 1960s:

> When my older sister was circumcised, I was too young to remember anything, but later I heard a lot about girls being circumcised. When girls of my age were looking after the lambs, they would talk among themselves about their circumcision experiences and look at each other's genitals to see who had the smallest opening. If there was a girl in the group who was still uninfibulated, she would always feel ashamed since she had nothing to show the others. Every time the other girls proudly showed their infibulated genitals, I would feel ashamed because I was not yet circumcised. Whenever I touched the hair of infibulated girls, they would tell me not to touch them since I was "unclean" (because I had not yet been circumcised and shaved). After the infibulation, the girl's head is shaven as a rite of purification, but my hair was "dirty." One day I could not stand this any more. I took a razorblade and went to an isolated place. I tied my clitoris with a thread, and while pulling at the thread with one hand I tried to cut part of the clitoris. When I saw blood coming from the cut I stopped and went directly to my paternal aunt, my own mother was dead, and told her what I had done. I had heard my grandmother tell how she had tried to infibulate herself, in order to hasten the process, and how I had tried to repeat what my grandmother had done.
>
> ...
>
> After some weeks, I was infibulated together with seven other girls. I was seven years old, but some of the other girls were older. One of them was as old as seventeen. All seven girls wanted to be the first to be operated upon, because it is said that most of the pain goes to the last girl. Since I was the youngest, I was taken first. I did not struggle much during the operation, because I was held tightly by big, strong women, but I cried at the top of my voice and begged them to let me go. When the operation was finished, the operating woman asked my aunt whether to leave the opening as it was, upon which the aunt handed her a grain of millet and told her to compare it with the hole and see if the opening was bigger than the grain. The circumciser found that it was not small enough, so to be sure she put in another thorn and closed the opening even more tightly. Then my aunt was satisfied.
>
> After the operation, my aunt gathered me in her arms, put me in the shade of a big tree near the hut and left me there. Then she went back to help holding the other girls. When all seven girls were done, two of the other girls were laid beside me in the shade. The other four girls were taken to their own hamlets. My aunt and the mothers of the two other girls gave us some porridge and milk to eat, and afterwards went off to do some errands. They stayed away for some time, and the shade moved to the other side of the tree. We felt very hot, and our wounds were bleeding a lot. When the women returned and saw the blood, they blamed themselves for the mistake and took us to their huts.
>
> After four days the wound had healed and the thorns were removed.
>
> The night of the operation I could not urinate and I cried and cried. My aunt inspected me and saw that there was no room for the urine to pass. Early the next morning, my aunt went to fetch the woman who had carried out the operation. She opened the last stitch (thorn), and immediately the urine rushed out, but as the other thorns held the infibulated part, the urine did not do any damage to the infibulation.

> When I was able to resume my normal work, I felt proud, and whenever some girls asked me if I was infibulated, I did not have to hide my genitals. (Warsame et al. 1985: 5, 7–8)

This surgery occurs in a context of enormous emphasis on a girl's virginity, indicated by the small size of the opening. If a daughter or a sister has a broken infibulation, she will bring shame to her family and severely limit their ability to find her an acceptable husband. It will also reduce the gifts that her parents will receive for her, called bridewealth (Warsame et al. 1985: 9). A generous bridewealth brings honor to a bride's family, while a virgin bride is important to show a man's virility. His penetration of an infibulated woman in marriage is an important proof of his masculinity. Many of the Somali women interviewed described this as a painful experience almost as bad as the infibulation itself. One woman for whom this process lasted three months said it destroyed her marriage, so that she is now a strong opponent to excision and infibulation. For men also, the process may cause physical suffering, but men still prefer to marry "closed" women, who are thought of as virgins, since this is the only guarantee they have of their wives' chastity. Infibulation has an important cultural content as an act of purification and a protection against indecency and immorality. Even parents who are opposed to the practice face enormous pressures to do it in order to ensure that their daughters are able to marry and bear children. Although this practice is practically universal in Somalia even in the early 1980s, many women rejected the practice on the basis either of their education or of their own painful experiences. Men are typically not involved in the surgeries, but overall they support the practice in order to ensure marriages for their daughters and a good bride price. Nevertheless, even in the early 1980s, many women were ready to question the wisdom of the practice (Warsame et al. 1985: 11–17).

There are many other ways to understand and interpret this cultural practice. An anthropologist, Christine Walley, who was working as a teacher in western Kenya, attended a circumcision ceremony in 1988. One of her students took her down winding paths to the family compound, which they entered just before dusk.

> The compound was crowded with people of all ages, and many of the older guests were sitting on the ground drinking homemade grain beer, or buzaa, brewed especially for the occasion … The teenage girls wore skirts and the boys wore shorts of bright red fabric decorated with colored strips of cloth and white T-shirts emblazoned with "Datsun" or "Free Mandela" logos … As darkness fell, the increasingly drunken crowd surrounded the candidates and encouraged them by joining in the dancing and singing. The bright glow of pressure lamps cast a flickering light on the raucous, gyrating crowd as well as on the wooden faces of the initiates, which were masked with the expressionlessness expected of those awaiting circumcision. The dancing continued throughout the night; we were told that it would tire the novices and numb them for the pain to come. At dawn, the initiates were led by circuitous routes to a stream, and before being bathed in its water (a restricted part of the ceremony witnessed only by the initiated), they were harangued by their mothers and warned not to disgrace their relatives, living or dead, by showing cowardice. After being led back to the family

compound, they were immediately circumcised. The cutting was public and demonstrated to the community the bravery of the initiated. The boys were cut by a male circumciser while standing; the girls were excised by a woman as they sat with legs spread on the ground, their backs supported by their sponsors. The crucial test was for the initiate to show no pain, to neither change expression nor even blink, during the cutting. Remarkably enough to my friend and I, the initiates remained utterly stoic and expressionless throughout. We were told it is this ability to withstand the ordeal that confers adulthood, that allows one to marry and have children, that that bids one to one's age mates. (Walley 1997: 410)

After this ceremony, the initiates recuperated for a month, boys and girls separately. The girls were generally between 14 and 16 years old.

Walley points out the complexity of the way local schoolgirls thought about the experience of circumcision. On one hand, it was clearly a source of pride and self-confidence in their ability to withstand pain as well as "our custom" to keep unmarried girls from having sexual relations before marriage (Walley 1997: 411). Yet, in a class essay contest, some of these same girls condemned the practice as forbidden by the government and Christianity. Many recognized that it would diminish their sexual pleasure, and disagreed about whether they would continue the custom with their daughters. Walley (1997: 412) concludes that the meaning of the ceremony is complex and layered: it is both a painful public ordeal that reveals strength and fortitude, thus developing self-confidence and public respect as adults, but it comes at the price of women's decreased pleasure and containment of their sexuality.

Another anthropologist working in the Sudan in the late 1970s, Janice Boddy, argues that infibulation is a source of purification and cleanliness, a way of emphasizing the importance of women not as sexual partners but as the mothers of men and the founders of lineages (Boddy 1982, quoted in Walley 1997: 413). In this area, as in the country of Mali and other parts of west Africa, the cutting emphasizes the differences between men and women, even benefiting women by giving them greater control over their sexuality (Walley 1997: 415). In many of these societies women's sexuality is not repressed and women talk about sex and lust (Walley 1997: 415.) Thus there are many different ways of understanding this practice, and women who experience it are often encouraged to see it as a form of self-improvement and virtue. This does not diminish the pain and medical complications of the surgery, however.

Female genital cutting, like honor killing, is embedded in a kinship system that values female virginity and chastity outside marriage. It is found in patrilineal, patrilocal kinship systems in which descent runs through males but reproduction of the kin group depends on in-marrying women. The surgeries are necessary for a woman to marry, and serve to constrain her sexual behavior before and after marriage. It is an effort to guarantee that the children belong to the father and that the wife's sexual behavior will not challenge his claims to control her. Not all societies place such value on controlling women's sexuality, but in this chapter we have seen several quite different social practices that serve to regulate and control women's sexual lives. Ironically, it is the reproductive power of women that subjects them to these forms of violence.

## The Debate over FGC

The global human rights community has been clear in its denunciation of the practice. The World Health Organization declared:

> Female genital mutilation of any type has been recognized as a harmful practice and a violation of the human rights of girls and women. Human rights – civil, cultural, economic, political and social – are codified in several international and regional treaties. The legal regime is complemented by a series of political consensus documents, such as those resulting from the United Nations world conferences and summits, which reaffirm human rights and call upon governments to strive for their full respect, protection and fulfillment. Many of the United Nations human rights treaty monitoring bodies have addressed female genital mutilation in their concluding observations on how States are meeting their treaty obligations.
>
> The Committee on the Elimination of All Forms of Discrimination against Women, the Committee on the Rights of the Child and the Human Rights Committee have been active in condemning the practice and recommending measures to combat it, including the criminalization of the practice. The Committee on the Elimination of All Forms of Discrimination against Women issued its General Recommendation on Female Circumcision (General Recommendation No 14) that calls upon states to take appropriate and effective measures with a view to eradicating the practice and requests them to provide information about measures being taken to eliminate female genital mutilation in their reports to the Committee (Committee on the Elimination of All Forms of Discrimination against Women, 1990) ...
>
> This Interagency Statement expresses the common commitment of these organizations to continue working towards the elimination of female genital mutilation. Female genital mutilation is a dangerous practice, and a critical human rights issue.
>
> *The United Nations agencies confirm their commitment to support governments, communities and the women and girls concerned to achieve the abandonment of female genital mutilation within a generation.* (World Health Organization 2008: 8, 21; emphasis original)

Although the criticism of the international community has been intense in the last few decades, many local activists are also seeking to end the practice, some of whom have teamed up with international organizations. They tend to take a more nuanced and sensitive approach, usually referring to "female circumcision" or "female genital cutting" (see Toubia 1994a; 1994b; 1999). The practice has been widely prohibited: Burkina Faso, Ghana, Ivory Coast, Senegal, Tanzania, and Togo, as well as in the USA, UK, Australia, Canada, New Zealand, France, Norway, and Sweden, have passed laws criminalizing female circumcision (Toubia 1999: 94). However, prosecution has been lax in most countries. Even the countries of the African diaspora are ambivalent: Dembour (2001) describes the reluctance of French juries to punish mothers who circumcise their daughters, while in the USA, it was not until 2006 that the first conviction under a 1996 law banning FGC took place (Tuhus-Dubrow 2007). Some families in the US diaspora are glad these laws exist so that they can avoid circumcising their daughters, while others insist on continuing the practice, sometimes sending their daughters back to their natal villages for the surgery (Tuhus-Dubrow 2007; see Ahmadu 2000). Members of diasporic African communities have worked on eliminating FGC but at the same time objected to the strident tone of many critiques. In an interview in 1986, an African activist talked about the differences between her perspective and that of Western white feminists. Efua Graham, a Ghanaian living in Britain, says:

> Our group has been working since 1979. That came about through the work of a group of African women, activists, campaigning on female circumcision internationally. The network consisted of African women in Europe and Africa. The Minority Rights Group, an international human rights organization, was a catalyst for the group and supported it. In 1979, Minority Rights Group put together a report on the subject with contributions from women from Senegal, Sudan, Egypt, Kenya, Ghana, Somalia, Nigeria, and Benin. At that time there was very little publicity on the subject. Our goal was to put the subject on the agenda of government and private groups ... No one talked about female circumcision, there was a lot of taboo and controversy around it. You could not even think of doing grassroots work right then. Government agencies considered the subject too sensitive to assist education programs with funding. Our objective was to at least get the subject on policy makers' agendas internationally as an issue for women. We ... had problems with white feminists campaigning on the issue. They saw nothing but the issue of the mutilation of the women as the single most important problem facing African women. They could not propose any tangible way of dealing with the traditions. They could only say how terrible it was, how it signified male oppression. They could not see how it was interlinked with the depressed socio-economic position of women in Africa. They did not want to see how it was interlinked to the international economic order.
>
> Talking about women's liberation, women's sexuality, women's right to control their bodies will not get you the audience initially. If you want to enlist the support of the community, including religious leaders, you won't get anywhere starting with a women's liberation angle. The issue most people can identify with is health. A man can identify with his wife's health. If she is having severe tears during childbirth, a man will be concerned. Individual men are not wicked. They are only behaving in ways they have been brought up to behave through tradition and socialisation. Most men have no idea what women's reproductive functions are, what happens during childbirth or what circumcision involves. The operations are done secretly.
>
> Sometimes you need to start with the pressing need of the women, with the economics of survival. You then can fit in educational components on various aspects of health, including reproductive health, that include problems arising from female circumcision ... Perhaps in the long term we want laws, but laws are not worth much unless many people know what the issue is and the law can be enforced. In any country, the government cannot enforce a law against a family custom that 99% of the population is against. And in many villages, where education on the issue of female circumcision hasn't started, if you started with a law, it is a waste of time. (Anon. 1986)

She points out that an uncircumcised woman faces the prospect that she will be unacceptable as a wife and therefore faces economic suicide. If women had more education, more access to land and work, their choices would be broader (Graham, in Anon. 1986).

She advocates focusing on the women who are traditionally birth attendants and those who do the cutting:

> In West Africa, they usually command respect because of their knowledge of health. We must remember that the power women had in Africa had been eroded by colonialism, particularly with white men coming in and trying to force women to act like the women in their own societies. It is important to preserve the power of women, and not focus only on the negative aspects of what they do. We have to preserve our power base. We want to take out the negative elements and encourage the positive parts of traditional practices. For instance, the extended family system provides great support to women. Initiation rites are an advanced form of socialisation and education, and their positive elements should be preserved. (Anon. 1986)

Similarly, Nadia Toubia writing in the late 1980s criticized the approach of some Western activists:

> Over the last decade, the issue of female circumcision has received wide exposure by Western media and international organizations as well as national bodies. The West has acted as though they have suddenly discovered a dangerous epidemic which they then sensationalized in international women's forums, creating a backlash of over-sensitivity in the concerned communities. They have portrayed it as irrefutable evidence of the barbarism and vulgarity of underdeveloped countries, a point of view they have always promoted. It became a conclusive validation to the view of the primitiveness of Arabs, Muslims and Africans all in one blow. (Toubia 1988: 101)

She poses a basic question for the activist:

> Let us also question how a Sudanese mother (herself circumcised at the age of 4–8 years) can choose not to circumcise her daughter? She will alienate her from her peer group and from the other women in the family, for they are all circumcised. Even if the parents are convinced that they do not want to mutilate their daughter, how can they possibly antagonize the grandmothers, the aunts, and the whole family? It is necessary to think of ways to change the belief of the extended family and the group, and not restrict our arguments to individualistic conviction, for that is too weak against group pressures … Our efforts must be geared toward finding a language that will communicate to society as a whole. We have to convince the group that the benefits of this action (in this case stopping circumcision) will be for the society as a whole and not only for the individual. (1988: 102)

Clearly, FGC has been seen as cruelty to innocent and powerless children, an expression of patriarchy, a denial of women's sexuality, and a hazard to health. It is also seen as a ritual which tests girls on the path to becoming respected adult women, an expression of sexual modesty and family honor, and a necessary step to marriage. To refuse the surgery opens a girl to insults and humiliation as well as the possibility that no man will marry her. Mothers who desire the best for their daughters may circumcise them because they know that the uncircumcised woman faces marginality and isolation.

## Grass-Roots Initiatives

Some nongovernmental organizations have promoted innovative approaches to change such as persuading an entire village to give up the practice for all its daughters. One of the leading NGOs taking this approach, Tostan, has had great success in Senegal working with villages as a whole. According to the executive director, Molly Melching, they strive to get villages to agree collectively to cease circumcision and to issue a public declaration, while the villages into whom these women marry also agree collectively to marry uncircumcised women. Tostan has worked on education, literacy, and human rights programs in this region for many years as the basis for its work on FGC, and Melching herself has spent 30 years in Senegal. As of 2007, almost 1,700 villages in Senegal have agreed to end female genital cutting and child marriage (Leah Jarvis, "Tostan", www.cpnn-world.org, June 21, 2007; see www.tostan. org). This effort joins local village education programs, government leaders, and international and national donors, including major aid programs of the USA, Germany, and Sweden.

A UNIFEM-funded project followed a similar, grass-roots approach in Kenya, again with some success despite considerable resistance. In the late 1990s two local NGOs teamed up to develop an alternative rites project for girls to experience the rituals of the coming-of-age ceremony without cutting. Instead of the period of ritual seclusion after the cutting, for example, the program introduced an intensive training program for the girls on reproductive health, motherhood, women's empowerment, and women's rights. The project began in three villages where leaders had already been working and some mothers were supportive, but it has since expanded to a nationwide effort. The girls participating in the project faced considerable social pressure and exclusion, but because they were following this new strategy together, they received support from one another and from their families. The program provided training for men and boys as well, and some boys supported the girls during the ritual walk through the village. Although this is a small start, it shows the possibilities of locally organized and run programs that work within existing social practices and envision change as a collective rather than an individual process (Spindel et al. 2000: 23–33). Some programs have targeted cutters, seeking to persuade them to stop the practice.

## Conclusions

These descriptions of female circumcision show that there is significant variation in the practice itself and wide differences in how people talk about it. The critique of Western feminists in the late 1970s and early 1980s was grounded in colonial conceptions of backward, barbaric societies. More recent reform efforts have muted this extreme rhetoric and there are significant collaborations between international donors and activists and African feminists. Some African feminists urge Western feminists to support their efforts rather than assuming that they know best how to promote change. The examples discussed here show the possibilities of a more collaborative, respectful approach. Yet this issue continues to have an enormous capacity to generate outrage, particularly when it is presented in sensationalistic ways that build on pre-existing (although often unstated) assumptions about the "dark" continent and "primitive" customs. It seems likely that the issue titillates Westerners, who have long had a preoccupation with African women's sexuality. Yet for many African women, this practice is only one of the many issues they face, with pressing problems such as their need for clean water, adequate food, access to education, and prevention of common childhood diseases such as diarrhea taking on equal if not greater importance. Only if the beneficiaries of reform take a leading role in defining its terms and its projects will reforms respond to their most pressing needs. While there is no denying that female circumcision, particularly the most severe form, infibulation, seriously affects women's health and sexual and reproductive lives, it has occupied a disproportionately large place in the efforts to diminish gender violence worldwide.

### The Issue of Consent to Female Genital Cutting

One of the most difficult dilemmas for critics of FGC is the issue of choice. The surgeries are usually carried out by mothers and aunts and, as the readings suggest, sometimes with the consent of the young women themselves. Some young women are willing and even eager to conform to social expectations of virtuous adult womanhood. The following essay, written by a Wellesley College graduate from 2004, grapples with the comparison between FGC and eating disorders in the USA. Although the former is presented as forced on young women while the latter is chosen, on closer examination both contain elements of consent within the context of a society that values certain body images, whether a beautifully smooth vagina like a watermelon or a pencil-thin body. This does not mean that these practices are the same, but it does suggest that there is no bright line defining one practice as coerced and the other as chosen; instead both represent choices made within contexts that define the allocation of virtue and merit according to the way a woman shapes her body.

My name is Rebecca Goldberg. I am 22 years old, I am a committed activist against gender violence, and I am a survivor of anorexia. This is my story. It is the story of my journey to understand female genital cutting and to acknowledge and face the disfiguring and mutilating beauty practices of my own society and culture. At its heart, it is the story of my intimate relationship with and struggle against the misogynistic forces that have influenced my life. Like most stories, this story cannot speak for or to all women because it is uniquely shaped and colored by my own background and experiences. I hope, however, that sharing my experiences will help other women and men to begin to examine the social and cultural forces that influence all of our lives.

The first time I read about female genital cutting, I was 17 years old. Like any good young Western feminist, I was instantly filled with horror and righteous anger. The practice seemed both unimaginably painful and incomprehensibly misogynistic; I didn't think I could understand how any culture or society could insist that its women submit to such a gruesome and disfiguring operation. The explanations that both men and women gave in support of the practice seemed absurd and nonsensical. How could anyone really believe that such a bloody and painful ordeal was a mark of pride in their culture and traditions, a necessary step to make women pure and marriageable, or, perhaps most ridiculously, a way of making women more beautiful?

It seemed to me that the places where people conducted these surgeries must be radically different from the United States. The women who submitted to or even encouraged the mutilations, I imagined, could not be anything like the "liberated" women of my own society. I thought of these women with revulsion and a morbid fascination, imagining that they were bound by tradition, weakened by the mutilation they had endured, and unable to escape the gendered violence of their own cultures. I was appalled to think that any woman anywhere might accept and even support something so painful and disfiguring, something that seemed to be such a complete rejection of her own body and desires. I failed to notice that I was bound and, yes, even mutilated by very similar forces.

When I was 17, my main focus in life was starving myself into oblivion. I suffered from a strange form of tunnel vision in which I could see little beyond the reflection in the mirror and the glamorously emaciated bodies displayed on every magazine cover at the grocery store checkout stand. Everything from television shows to interactions with family, friends, and strangers seemed to be sending me the message that fat people, particularly fat women, are stupid, ugly, and lazy because they have gluttonously allowed their desires to overtake their lives. Feeding off these messages, I became convinced that the only way to be accepted by my society as beautiful, successful, and intelligent was to reduce the amount of space I occupied in the world.

All of my activities, dreams, and goals took a backseat to the all-consuming task of counting and re-counting the amount of calories I put into my body. Although I was a straight-A student with aspirations of attending college and making a positive difference in the world, I believed that the only way I could become truly successful was by starving and controlling myself into a non-threatening, non-existent physical form. Over the course of a year I became a sickly and withdrawn shadow of my former self. My hair began to fall out, my menstrual cycle ceased, and each day I was less and less able to concentrate on my classes, connect with my friends and family, or give energy to the activist causes for which I had once had a passion. Despite my skeletal and somewhat frightening appearance, however, I gained a strange sort of social and cultural prestige. Once teased for my chubby, unfashionable body, I was now the "perfect" female; I had conquered my desires, risen above the vulgar hunger and sloppiness of "ordinary" women, and reduced myself to a non-threatening waif.

After a year of focusing all of my energy on denying myself food, I finally realized that I had to choose between "perfection" and the rest of my life; I simply could not starve myself at the same time as getting an education, having relationships, and making a positive difference in the world. Due to a combination of will power, luck, and positive role models, I chose to leave my tiny and "perfect" anorexic box to face the complicated and messy world. I have now spent five long and bumpy years fighting to believe that I have a right to eat, to gain knowledge, and to be successful on my own terms. This struggle has helped to make me a lifelong activist against gender violence and inequality, and it has also helped me to fully understand the physical and psychological repercussions of anorexia. My hormone levels have never returned to normal, which means that I cannot produce a menstrual cycle on my own; my bone density is extremely low for a woman of my age, putting me at risk for early onset osteoporosis; and my circulatory and digestive systems both function poorly. Even more disturbing than my physical health problems, perhaps, is that a part of me still harbors the belief that I will never truly be successful unless I once again reduce myself to an anorexic shadow.

Am I "crazy" to believe that starving myself will make me beautiful and successful, the "perfect" woman? I used to think so. Anorexia, after all, is defined as an eating *dis*order, something that is out of order, separate and distinct from the eating patterns of "normal" US women. Over the last five years, however, I have come to realize that if I am "crazy," "sick," and "disordered," then most of my female family members, friends, and acquaintances must be crazy, sick, and disordered as well. The majority of women I have met in my life, from my female relatives to my college classmates, to the women I encounter at the grocery store, dedicate a huge portion of their energy and passion to controlling, reducing, and/or changing their physical forms.

The truth is that I am not alone in my struggle to believe I have a right to eat, to be healthy, and to be successful on my own terms. As many women reading this story already know, the majority of women and girls in the United States are engaged in an anguished and often dangerous battle against our bodies. Fueled by the belief that we will never be successful until we achieve our society's ideal of physical "perfection," we engage in a variety of unsafe beauty practices, including yo-yo dieting, self-induced vomiting and starvation, painful cosmetic surgery, and risky weight-loss surgery. The National Eating Disorders Association estimates that between 40 and 50 percent of women and girls are trying to lose weight by dieting at any one point during the year; 95 percent of these diets will eventually fail – the dieters will regain the weight they had lost, and many will begin a heart-damaging cycle of weight gain and loss, or yo-yo dieting.[2]

[2]   National Eating Disorders Association. "kNOw Dieting: Risks and Reasons to Stop." <www.nationaleatingdisorders.org/p.asp?WebPage_ID=321&Profile_ID=41142>, accessed November 8, 2004.

In desperation to keep off the unwanted weight, some of these women will develop serious eating disorders such as anorexia nervosa and bulimia nervosa, while others will react to the periods of semi-starvation that we call "dieting" by developing binge-eating behaviors.[3] For women whom the medical industry defines as "morbidly obese," failure to lose weight may lead them to try the expensive and risky procedure known as bariatric surgery, or weight loss surgery. Still other women, unsatisfied with the results they can achieve through dieting, exercise, and cosmetics, will put themselves under the plastic surgeon's knife in an effort to change the natural physical form of their faces and/or bodies. The combined impact of all of these practices is that one-half of our society puts their physical, mental, and emotional health at risk on a daily basis in pursuit of an elusive ideal of beauty. Perhaps the strangest aspect of this battle against our bodies is that most of us do not recognize it as a struggle at all, but regard it as a normal and even necessary aspect of our lives as women. For many of us, it is "obvious" that we can never become truly attractive, truly successful, or truly happy unless we lose those "extra" and "ugly" 5, or 10, or 100 pounds or change our perceived physical imperfections through cosmetic surgery.

Some skeptics reading this story may protest that excessive dieting and even surgery are rational and healthy responses to the fact that 30 percent of people in the USA are defined as obese and 4.9 percent are classified as morbidly obese.[4] They may point to the statistics published by the health insurance companies and numerous actors within the medical industry, all of which insist that people who are even modestly overweight are at risk for increased rates of mortality. In tune with the deafening chorus of disapproving doctors' voices and hysterical declarations from popular magazines, the skeptical reader may proclaim that obesity is a national epidemic, and that it must be addressed through any means available.

The problem with the skeptic's argument is that the majority of the "cures" that doctors and magazines prescribe for overweight, obesity, and other perceived physical imperfections have many negative side effects. Numerous medical studies document the risks and long-term health effects associated with dieting, diet products, weight loss surgery and cosmetic surgery, revealing the dangerous nature of our society's pursuit of thinness and physical perfection. There are so many examples of the harmful effects of dieting and other weight loss treatments, in fact, that it would be impossible to list them all within the short space of this story. If you find yourself alternately shocked, skeptical, and curious about the information I mention here, I encourage you to seek out more on the subject; you will likely be surprised by the amount of information you find to contradict the official party line of our fat-phobic and appearance-obsessed culture.

---

[3]  G. Terence Wilson, PhD. 1993. "Relation of Dieting and Voluntary Weight Loss to Psychological Functioning and Binge Eating." *Annals of Internal Medicine* 119: 727–730.

[4]  Robert G. Dluhy, MD, and Caren G. Solomon, MD, MPH. 2004. "Bariatric Surgery – Quick Fix or Long-Term Solution?" *New England Journal of Medicine* 351: 2751–2753.

It is unlikely that you have heard, for example, of the numerous medical studies that found that losing weight, especially in a cycle of weight loss and weight gain, or yo-yo dieting,[5] was strongly linked to increased rates of mortality from cardiovascular disease.[6] These findings held true even when they excluded subjects who smoked (a factor that is linked to both leanness and high mortality) and who had diseases that might have caused the weight loss, such as cancer. The tentative conclusion of these studies was that weight loss, particularly when it is part of a yo-yo cycle of weight loss and weight gain, puts fatal strain upon the heart and cardiovascular system.

Dieting has also been linked to a wide variety of other serious short- and long-term health problems. It can lead to gallstones; loss of muscle mass; excessive loss of the electrolytes sodium and potassium, which can cause poor coordination skills; slower mental reaction time owing to the lack of vital nutrients; and liver dysfunction.[7] In addition to these physical health complications, dieting among normal weight persons has been proven to cause feelings of failure, lowered self-esteem, and depressive symptoms.[8] Possibly due, in part, to these psychological consequences, dieting can also develop into a more serious eating disorder; nearly all individuals who suffer from bulimia nervosa, anorexia nervosa, or binge-eating disorder began to develop their eating disorder while they were on a diet.[9]

All of these findings directly contradict our society's prevailing belief that overweight and obesity inevitably lead to disease and death, and that we must therefore achieve a lean body at any cost. There is a grain of truth in this belief, for most studies seem to agree that health conditions such as high cholesterol and triglyceride levels, sleep apnea, type-2 diabetes, and heart disease[10] are linked to being overweight, and that losing a modest amount of weight does alleviate their symptoms.[11] For people who are of normal weight, however,

[5]   Steven Blair, PED, et al. 1993. "Body-Weight Change, All-Cause Mortality, and Cause-Specific Mortality in the Multiple Risk Factor Intervention Trial." *Annals of Internal Medicine* 119: 749–756.
[6]   Reubin Andres, MD, Denis Muller, MD, and John D. Sorkin. 1993. "Long-Term Effects of Change in Body Weight on All-Cause Mortality." *Annals of Internal Medicine* 119: 737–743. Elsie R. Pamuk, PhD, et al. 1993. "Weight Loss and Subsequent Death in a Cohort of U.S. Adults." *Annals of Internal Medicine* 119: 744–747.
[7]   F. Xavier Pi-Sunyer, MD. 1993. "Short Term Medical Benefits and Adverse Effects of Weight Loss." *Annals of Internal Medicine* 119: 722–725. National Eating Disorders Association. "kNOw Dieting: Risks and Reasons to Stop." <www.nationaleatingdisorders.org/p.asp?WebPage_ID=29>, accessed November 8, 2004.
[8]   G. Terence Wilson, PhD. 1993. "Relation of Dieting and Voluntary Weight Loss to Psychological Functioning and Binge Eating." *Annals of Internal Medicine* 119: 727–730.
[9]   National Eating Disorders Association. "kNOw Dieting: Risks and Reasons to Stop." www.nationaleatingdisorders.org/p.asp?WebPage_ID=321&Profile_ID=41142, accessed November 8, 2004.
[10]  F. Xavier Pi-Sunyer, MD. 1993. "Short Term Medical Benefits and Adverse Effects of Weight Loss." *Annals of Internal Medicine* 119: 722–725. A. H. Mokdad et al. 2003. "Prevalence of Obesity, Diabetes, and Obesity-Related Health Risk Factors." *Journal of the American Medical Association* 289: 76–79.
[11]  Lars Sjostrom, MD, et al. 2004. "Lifestyle, Diabetes, and Cardiovascular Risk Factors 10 Years after Bariatric Surgery." *New England Journal of Medicine* 351: 2683–2692.

and even for people who are mildly overweight but do not suffer from these conditions, it seems that losing weight is more of a health risk than a "magic pill" for robust well-being.

Diet drugs and weight loss, or bariatric, surgery have proven to be even more dangerous than dieting in and of itself. One of the deadliest examples is the drug fen/phen (fenfluramine/phentamine), which was released onto the market for public consumption in 1994 and was later found to be the cause of heart valve defects, fatal lung disease, schizophrenic behavior and brain damage.[12] A number of people died from these complications before the drug was removed from the market. Weight loss surgery, which has recently been heralded as the new "cure" for obesity by celebrities such as Carnie Wilson, Al Roker of NBC's *Today* show, and Randy Jackson of Fox's *American Idol*,[13] is also potentially deadly and almost guarantees various complications. The more severe procedure, called gastric bypass, typically leads to daily bouts of vomiting, dangerous nutritional deficiencies, and dumping syndrome; the slightly less extreme operation of gastric banding also tends to result in frequent vomiting.[14] Although both operations usually produce immediate weight loss and often alleviate conditions associated with obesity such as diabetes, high cholesterol, hypertension, etc., both also pose numerous fatal risks, including pulmonary embolism, respiratory failure, gastrointestinal leaks from the breakdown of the staple or suture line, stomal obstruction, and internal bleeding.[15] To date, the number of deaths and severe complications caused by the operations has not been officially documented,[16] but it seems clear that the risks may outweigh the benefits.

Like weight loss surgery, cosmetic surgeries bear a number of very real risks and dangers; unlike bariatric surgery, however, these operations impart almost no health benefits. Most cosmetic procedures are performed upon healthy individuals who wish to change a part of their body for purely aesthetic reasons, but nonetheless they can cause serious complications and even death. Women are disproportionately affected by these complications because they comprise over 80 percent of the patient base for most types of plastic surgery procedures.[17] Tumescent liposuction, for example, which has been promoted over the past few years as the newly improved and "safe" type of liposuction, has resulted in

[12]   Marilyn Wann. 1998. *FAT!SO?Because You Don't Have to Apologize for Your Size!* Berkeley, CA: Ten Speed Press.

[13]   Robert Steinbrook, MD. 2004. "Surgery for Severe Obesity." *New England Journal of Medicine* 350: 1075–1079.

[14]   Robert Steinbrook, MD. 2004. "Surgery for Severe Obesity." *New England Journal of Medicine* 350: 1075–1079.

[15]   Lars Sjostrom, MD, et al. 2004. "Lifestyle, Diabetes, and Cardiovascular Risk Factors 10 Years after Bariatric Surgery." *New England Journal of Medicine* 351: 2683–2692. Robert Steinbrook, MD. 2004. "Surgery for Severe Obesity." *New England Journal of Medicine* 350: 1075–1079.

[16]   Robert Steinbrook, MD. 2004. "Surgery for Severe Obesity." *New England Journal of Medicine* 350: 1075–1079.

[17]   American Society of Plastic Surgeons. "Plastic Surgery Statistics for 2003." <www.plasticsurgery.org/>, accessed February 11, 2005.

numerous deaths due to a toxic reaction to the lidocaine that is pumped into fatty areas of the body prior to surgery.[18] Serious complications have also been common in breast implant procedures. A study conducted in Olmsted County, Minnesota found that 178 of the 749 participants experienced severe problems such as capsular contracture, implant rupture, hematoma, and wound infection; all of these women had to undergo further surgical procedures to salvage their health.[19] Other health complications from cosmetic surgery procedures include fatal reactions to anesthesia; wound infection; persistent pain in the area of surgery; anemia; fat embolisms (when fat cells travel through the body and lodge somewhere, such as the lung) from liposuction; and injury to deeper structures such as blood vessels, nerves, and muscles.[20] Despite these very serious risks, the number of healthy people, mainly women, who scramble to have their nose, eyes, ears, and thighs cut open by a plastic surgeon rises every year.

What is going on here? If all of these statistics and studies on cosmetic operations, bariatric surgery, diet pills, and dieting clearly show that they are detrimental to our mental, emotional, and physical health, then why are so many of us rushing to embrace them on a daily basis? Why do we continue to pursue an elusive ideal of physical "perfection" even when this pursuit is obviously damaging to our health and well-being? Why, after five years of fighting off anorexia and working against gender violence and inequality, is it still difficult for me to believe that I can be happy and successful even when I am not starving myself? The answer, I have finally begun to understand, is that we all are caught within a web of deeply ingrained cultural norms which insist that we conform to a waifish and unhealthy standard of beauty. These cultural norms form the framework of our daily lives, and are therefore extremely difficult to ignore or reject. Although we might like to think of ourselves as "independent" and "liberated" women, and although we may even acknowledge that dieting and surgery are harmful to our bodies and psyches, it is difficult to give up these beauty practices while we live in a society that tells us we will never truly be happy, successful, and accepted until we achieve a narrowly defined ideal of beauty. The truth is that we women in the United States are, in many ways, "bound" and "mutilated" by the demands and expectations of our culture.

Now, as I look back upon my horrified reaction to FGC, I can see that my feelings of superiority and righteousness were both ungrounded and unjust. When I thought of FGC as "unimaginably painful" and "incomprehensibly misogynistic," I clearly failed to take into account the pain and misogyny that the women of my own culture inflict upon themselves on a daily basis through a variety of dangerous beauty practices. When I asserted that it was "absurd"

---

[18]   Rama B. Rao, MD, Susan F. Ely, MD, MPHTM, and Robert S. Hoffman, MD. 1999. "Deaths Related to Liposuction." *New England Journal of Medicine* 340: 1471–1474.
[19]   Sherine E. Gabriel, MD, MSc, et al. 1997. "Complications Leading to Surgery after Breast Implantation." *New England Journal of Medicine* 336: 677–682.
[20]   Magdalena Alagna. 2002. *Everything You Need to Know about the Dangers of Cosmetic Surgery.* New York: Rosen.

and "nonsensical" for anyone to believe that a bloody and painful practice such as FGC could be a mark of pride in their culture or a way of making women more beautiful, I should have realized that my own culture is dominated by similar beliefs. And, when I judged the women who underwent or supported FGC as either "crazy" or "weak," creatures who were radically different from the "liberated" women of my own culture, I bluntly disregarded the complicated and problematic experiences of women in my own culture.

Do I now understand why certain societies and cultures in Africa and other places around the world choose to circumcise women, and why some women support and promote the practice? The answer, of course, is no: there is no way that I, as an outsider, can fully understand the intricate mix of historical events, cultural patterns, and spiritual beliefs that shape and perpetuate FGC. What I can understand, however, is how a culture or society could come to embrace such a practice, for I live within a society that is convinced that a variety of painful and dangerous beauty practices are a normal and even necessary aspect of women's lives.

In order to become effective activists against gender violence both within our own society as well as in the context of other cultures, we must strive to become fully aware of the cultural forces that encourage us to hate and mutilate our bodies. We cannot successfully combat painful beauty practices in the United States until we admit that these practices are detrimental to our health. We also cannot become effective activists within other cultural contexts until we acknowledge that it is extremely difficult to gain perspective on these culturally condoned beauty rituals. Once we recognize how hard it can be to escape from our own society's maze of cultural expectations, we will also have to acknowledge that women of other cultures are not necessarily "crazy" or "weak" because they support or allow practices such as FGC. We can begin to understand that, much like ourselves, these women are responding to a complex set of cultural demands, deeply ingrained traditions, and historical realities, and may simply be doing what they feel is necessary to become successful and accepted within their society.

In essence, acknowledging the complicated and problematic nature of our own situation will make it impossible for us to continue to presume that we are "liberated" women who can act as "saviors" of women in other cultures and societies. Once we admit that we are not free of the misogynistic forces within our own society, we will also have to stop judging other women as if we were standing on the feminist high ground. Standing on equal grounding with women of other cultures will help us to enter into alliances that eschew the power imbalances that so often drive wedges between "first-world" and "third-world" women. Through these alliances, we may finally find the strength and the power to subvert and change the misogynistic forces that rule the lives of so many women around the globe. It is crucial, then, that we begin to recognize the reality of our own struggles, that we acknowledge the complexities inherent both within our own condition as well as within the situations of women in other cultures, and that we work to form equal and balanced partnerships with these women. Hopefully, my story can serve as a spark to this journey of self-examination and discovery.

## Questions for Further Discussion

1  Name some examples of "harmful traditional practices." Have they always been practiced the same way? What is the relationship between "traditional" practices, nationalism, and gender?
2  Why did some activists critique the Anglo-European response to FGC in the 1970s and 1980s? What are some of the recommendations posed by African activists working with FGC? How do locally organized efforts imagine change?
3  Compare the story of FGC told by the Somali woman who later worked as a government typist with that told by Rebecca Goldberg who practiced self-starvation. Instead of comparing one practice with the other, consider the contexts in which these practices took place. What conditions their choice to participate in these practices? What do their stories tell us about the way gender and violence is constructed across contexts? Are these stories comparable? Why or why not?

## Video Suggestions

*The Day I Will Never Forget*, by Kim Longinotto (England, 2002), 92 minutes

The practice of female genital cutting is as widely performed as it is contested in rural and urban Kenya. This film captures the complexity of FGC, its social significance, and the possibilities for social change through the candid perspectives of Africans themselves: pioneering activists who work to educate women about the practice to end it or make it safer, young women who favor and fear it, and elderly matriarchs who promote its continuance. We witness first-hand an FGC ceremony, and learn about the domestic legal battles that have emerged on behalf of young women who seek court injunctions to stop their parents from forcing the practice on them.

*Fire Eyes: Female Circumcision*, by Soraya Mire (USA, 1994), 60 minutes

Somali filmmaker Soraya Mire is familiar with female circumcision. At age 13, she underwent the practice and spent the following 20 years recovering from the physical and emotional scars it left. Her film examines the socio-economic, psychological, and medical consequences of FGC from many points of view, including those from Africa and the Anglo-European West. Testimony from biomedical practitioners details the types of female circumcision commonly performed, from Africa to southeast Asia, as well as the complications that may result.

*Gift of a Girl: Female Infanticide*, by Mayyasa Al-Malazi (USA, 1998), 24 minutes

This film documents the complexity of female infanticide in southern India. Every year thousands of baby girls are killed, partly because of the financial burden the dowry system places on families to marry off their daughters. Because many women lead a life of hardship, the killing of female babies is considered humane by some. In an effort to end the practice, URISE, a nongovernmental organization, is working in village associations called *sanghams* to support pregnant women and mothers in their decision to keep their daughters. When a baby girl is born, the *sanghams* celebrate her arrival with gifts to show that a girl is something to be valued.

# 7

# Women and Armed Conflict

Women are often at the heart of war, but usually not as soldiers. More often, they are its silent victims, killed in the crossfire, raped by conquering soldiers, or made into sexual slaves. They are often driven from their homes to become refugees, suffering the loss of sons, husbands, and brothers. They may be left to fend for themselves in destroyed neighborhoods or forced to flee to flimsy and insecure shelters in refugee camps, responsible for children without the support of their male kin. For these reasons, women are often the peacemakers, those who seek to build bridges over conflict. However, sometimes women incite men to violence and war and take on critical roles in promoting militarism and violence as mothers of martyrs. Moreover, men clearly bear the brunt of the violence of war as fighters, as targets of violence, as subjects of systems of interrogation and torture.

Despite the pervasiveness of violence against women in times of war and armed conflict, only recently has women's special vulnerability in wartime received global recognition. Even though rape is one of the oldest features of war, it was not until the late 1990s that international criminal tribunals began to focus on prosecuting rape as a crime of war. The international court set up in 1993 to adjudicate the war in Yugoslavia made its first conviction for rape as torture in 1998 (www.un.org/icty/cases-e/index-e.htm). The International Criminal Court (ICC), established in 2002 by the international community to handle major human rights violations and in operation by 2006, includes rape in wartime as part of its mandate (see Clarke 2007).

Rape, assault, and the killing of women is a common feature of war and ethnic conflict, whether in the Hindu–Muslim conflict in India, the Arab–African fighting in Darfur, a region in the Sudan in Africa, or the genocide in Rwanda. Military forces use sexualized forms of violence to establish control over subordinated populations, including those who are captured. Colonialism, created through military conquest, is maintained through violence, including rape and battery of subordinate group women by dominant-group men. Men of the conquering group can typically abuse or kill subordinate women with impunity. Indigenous peoples in the USA and

Canada suffer ongoing violence of this kind, as well as more systemic forms of violence such as forced sterilizations and the dumping of environmental toxins in their communities (see Smith 2005).

On the other hand, the toxic combination of racism and colonialism led to an elevated pattern of violence against men in subordinated groups. Conquered men suspected of sex with conquering-group women are sometimes lynched. This was a widespread practice in the late nineteenth and much of the twentieth century in the USA, where lynching of African American and Hispanic men for alleged violations of white women was widespread. African men in British colonial Africa were similarly suspected and punished. This chapter provides examples of gender violence that are part of larger social processes of conquest and control. The examples make clear that gender violence is fundamental to the way hierarchies of power are formed and maintained.

## War and Armed Conflict

Militarism is widely, if not universally, linked to men and masculinity. Soldiers are disproportionately men (Goldstein 2003), while societies that experience a high level of militarization tend to be more violent toward women in interpersonal relationships. Although some argue that males are inherently more violent than females, even labeling them "demonic" (Peterson and Wrangham 1997), Joshua Goldstein arrives at a more ambiguous conclusion. He explores a wide range of explanations for the disproportionate engagement of men with war, such as biological differences in strength, testosterone levels, endurance, and aggressiveness. He concludes that there are a few systematic gender differences, such as greater physical aggressiveness by males, but otherwise these variables overlap between men and women far more than they differ. Biologically rooted social patterns such as male bonding or greater male capacity to work in hierarchies show no clear and consistent pattern that accounts for differences in militarism. But he does find significant differences in the way societies promote images of a militarized masculinity. Militarized societies reward men who suppress their emotions and suspend social inhibitions against killing in order to excel in battle. They accord them the desirable status of manhood (Goldstein 2003: 331). Women are often willing to witness and celebrate male bravery in war. Goldstein concludes that the significant gender differences in war-making that he found lie in the prevalence of these gender ideologies and the socialization of children. In all societies, children are taught early in their lives the appropriate roles and behavior for masculine or feminine identities.

The famous study of the Yanomamo people in the Amazon, a horticultural people living deep in the forest, suggests a linkage between an environment of pervasive warfare and women's victimization by violence. In his research in the 1960s, Chagnon (1997) found that women are frequently raped and assaulted by the military forces opposing them. Raping women of the opponents' community serves to assert dominance over that community and humiliate its members. He suggested that in an environment of threat and pervasive warfare, traits of violence and assertiveness become celebrated dimensions of masculinity.

Sherene Razack's study of Canadian peacekeepers in Somalia in 1993 shows how even soldiers from a country that prides itself for its peacekeeping role in the world can slide into the same kinds of violence and abuse characteristic of this kind of militarized masculinity elsewhere. Peacekeeping soldiers from Canada entered Somalia expecting to be greeted with gratitude and warmth, but instead received suspicion and hostility. They were "surprised and outraged when they found ungrateful natives and a complicated conflict. In such an environment, violence directed at Somalis enabled some peacekeepers to manage their own fears and ignorance and to see themselves as men in control" (Razack 2004: 48). Canadian soldiers grew increasingly hostile to the Somalis as they discovered that they were not grateful for their help. Setting up a camp well stocked with water, food, and other desirable items in an area where these were all in short supply invited envy and thievery. Responding to the sense of threat, Canadian soldiers became more and more hostile and abusive, trying to "teach the Somalis a lesson." When higher-ranking military people gave tacit approval to abusing prisoners and shooting intruders, lower-ranked soldiers complied, leading to the death of a 16-year-old in custody and the shooting of another Somali at night. At one point, Canadian troops fired into an unarmed crowd. Yet the Canadians were in a relatively stable area and faced no aggressive events beyond thievery and rock-throwing by boys. The Somali militia had long since left the area, which was populated largely by starving refugees. No Canadian personnel were killed or wounded by Somalis (Razack 2004: 73). In fact, as the threat diminished, the more extreme incidents of peacekeeper violence occurred. Why did the Canadian soldiers become so aggressive and abusive toward the Somalis?

Razack (2004: 69) argues that part of the answer lies in the "imperial fantasies" the soldiers brought with them: the idea that they were in Africa to save Somalis from themselves, and that the only way to justify their presence was the existence of black savagery. They were also acting out, or "performing" (in the terms discussed in Chapter 1), a particular vision of masculinity in which physical violence against women and racial minorities is celebrated (Razack 2004: 56). This is a cultural understanding of masculinity developed in military contexts that sees violence as heroic and as essential for the support of the nation. In the Canadian case, this understanding of military masculinity drew on implicit understandings that Canada was a white country, forged out of violence against Indians (Razack 2004: 62). Similarly, in Britain during the age of imperialism in the nineteenth and twentieth centuries, manhood was defined by the violence white men had to use to protect, guard, and subdue brown subjects (Razack 2004: 63). In Somalia, enacting this racialized masculinity meant that abusing Somalis was a patriotic duty and a proof of manhood.

Two of the soldiers accused of the violence were part Aboriginal. Rather than arguing that racially subordinated males are more violent than white males to compensate for their subordinate status, Razack (2004: 90–91) thinks that both white and minority men are pulled into what she calls the "hegemonic masculinity" of imperialism, the taken-for-granted ideas about what constitutes masculinity in a colonial and postcolonial society. In white settler states like Canada (and the United States), this understanding of masculinity is implicitly white and directed against those who might threaten the nation, the not-white. Men of color as well as white men are seduced into performing white hegemonic masculinity. Men of color are, as one journalist put it, trying to "outwhite the white guys" (Razack 2004: 103).

In Somalia, violence was also common among the peacekeepers from the USA, Italy, and Belgium. The violence, ranging from racial slurs to torture and murder, was typically enacted in front of witnesses, often documented by videotapes and trophy photos and described in diaries. Anal rape and sodomy were common. As Razack (2004: 53) points out, this makes it difficult to argue that the violence was the result of soldiers pushed to extreme reactions by an aggressive and unwelcoming local population. Instead, it partakes of widespread sexualized patterns of dominance. These patterns are chillingly similar to those revealed in the American treatment of Iraqi prisoners in Abu Ghraib in 2004. Sexualized forms of abuse and torture such as stripping prisoners, forcing them to lie in a pile, or attaching a dog's leash to a man's neck as he lies prone while an American woman soldier holds the leash were captured in trophy photos and circulated to family and friends. These sexualized acts of violence and power clearly represent gendered performances of violence and humiliation.

## Militarized Societies, Nationalism, and Motherhood

Military culture, the set of norms and values found within military communities and focused on ideas of masculinity, sexuality, violence, and women, is conducive to rape, sexual harassment, and domestic violence, according to some activists and researchers (see overview in Adelman 2003). Research in the USA shows that domestic violence is a particularly severe social problem for the military, while scandals at the military academies in the early 2000s revealed widespread sexual harassment. There is also concern about the relationship between US military bases both inside and outside the country and cases of sexual harassment, rape, and domestic homicide around the bases, as well as prostitution and forms of sexual abuse (Enloe 1990). However, there is still debate about the nature of the relationship between militarism and various forms of gender violence, and it is not clear that military service in itself produces higher levels of gender violence in the home.

At the societal level, militarization celebrates violence, including its gendered forms. In the USA, the military is fairly isolated from the rest of the society, but in some countries the boundary between military and civilian sectors is blurred, so that militarization and militarized ideas of masculinity creep into mainstream society. Cynthia Enloe (2000: 3) defines militarization as a gradual process by which the individual and society come to be controlled by the military and to see militaristic ideas as fundamental to well-being. As militarization transforms individuals and societies, military needs and assumptions come to appear both valuable and normal. Some consider militarism a taken-for-granted worldview that legitimates and venerates organized violence as the way to achieve political goals (Adelman 2003: 5; see also Lutz 2002). It refers to the diffusion of military ideologies and values throughout society. "In a militarized society, one is always oriented toward war" (Adelman 2003: 6). Feminists have argued that militarism and its gender hierarchies are linked to men's violence against women. Its culture of violence seems to reach from armed conflict to relations in the home. Militarized masculinity can produce woman battering.

Israel is an example of a militarized society in which the boundaries between the military and society are highly permeable (Adelman 2003: 3). Israel exists in a state of perpetual preparedness for war, and has still not canceled the state of emergency declared at its founding in 1948. The army is the core of Israeli collectivity, and security is everyone's project. Men who are eligible for the military earn membership in the collectivity through their military service. Women, on the other hand, earn their membership through marriage and motherhood, by nurturing soldiers and raising soldier children, although they are also conscripted into the armed services (Adelman 2003: 9). Yet those who are Palestinian citizens of Israel or Palestinians in the occupied territories experience this militarism differently, as a form of symbolic and physical violence (Adelman 2003: 11).

In the 1990s, some Israelis began to draw links between men's military service in the occupied territories and domestic life in Israel, arguing that this experience had normalized violence and legitimated its role in solving problems and dealing with differences. Although the extent to which the violence of soldiering is brought home is debated in Israel, the pervasive availability of weapons issued by the Israeli Defense Force was acknowledged by a special report to the minister of public security in 1998 (Adelman 2003: 18). Both Israeli and Palestinian activists in the field of domestic violence agree that militarism and the occupation increased the number of women seeking help for violence and most likely added to the incidence of violence itself. At the same time, the public celebration of victims of political violence served to privatize and diminish the importance of other victims of violence, whose suffering does not equally symbolize the threats to the nation as a whole. Police officers still view domestic violence as a "family conflict" situation that they would rather avoid. Arab women have particular difficulty getting police help since they are often viewed as complicit with terrorists or as accustomed to violent treatment (Adelman et al. 2003).

The military itself makes pervasive use of gendered metaphors to assess morality and good behavior. For example, in Carol Cohn's study of the way defense intellectuals in the USA talk to each other, she finds that gendered images are fundamental to the way they evaluate military strategies. She uses the term "gender discourse" to describe how people in this security/defense community refer to actions as masculine or feminine in order to judge them as good or bad. For example, the approved speaking style is dispassionate and cool, while the person who becomes emotionally intense is dismissed as a "hysterical housewife," clearly a gendered image of a person without legitimate opinions. Men who worry about death rates in war consider themselves to be acting like women (Cohn 1993: 331).

Cohn gives an example of the dominance of these gendered modes of thinking in an account of her participation in a simulated war exercise. The participants are divided into teams and cannot negotiate with each other directly but must simply use military tactics. Her team focused on protecting the civilian population and did not retaliate to an attack of tactical nuclear weapons. In the discussion after the exercise, the other team called her team "wimps," suggesting that they lacked the kind of masculinity that would have led them to attack back vigorously. The author describes how this label served to silence her group, found wanting in this crucial dimension of masculinity. Another commonly used term is "pussy," referring both to domesticated, and therefore demasculinized, pets and women's genitalia. The term is used when someone begins to worry about the loss of life on the other side, so that a defense intellectual might say, "What kind of pussy are you, anyway?" A few comments of this genre, and those who might be concerned about excessive loss of enemy life learn to remain silent (Cohn 1993: 337).

Here, gendered language serves powerfully to police behavior that does not conform to social conceptions of masculinity within the sphere of war, humiliating and silencing those who appear to act in ways interpreted as less masculine or even feminine. It can also serve to denigrate the opinions of others, as occurred when a US defense intellectual referred to German politicians concerned about the popular opposition to deploying Euromissiles by saying, "Those Krauts are a bunch of limp-dicked wimps" (Cohn 1993: 337). Some US defense intellectuals referred to NATO allies as "Euro-fags" when they disagreed with US policies such as bombing Libya. During the Gulf War of 1991, popular bumper stickers in the USA read "Saddam, Bend Over," while a widely distributed cartoon portrayed an enormous missile entering Saddam Hussein's anus while he was bent over in prayer. Clearly, the idea of anal penetration is used to feminize and weaken an enemy. Over and over, the US military was depicted as achieving a humiliating defeat of Iraq through anal penetration of Saddam Hussein's body as a result of the more powerful and manly qualities of the USA. Failure to attack is also described in gendered terms: for example, a well-known academic security affairs specialist was quoted as saying that "under Jimmy Carter, the United States is spreading its legs for the Soviet Union" (Cohn 1993: 338).

Such comments shift discussions about war and military policy from rationality to masculinity. In this context, debates are shaped by where one positions oneself, either as masculine, therefore rational and strong, or feminine and weak. Those who take the latter path find that their opinions are ignored. Simply bringing more women into national security discussions would not help, since any views interpreted as "feminine" are dismissed regardless of who asserts them. Cohn's point is that gendered labels provide interpretations of behavior that are so closely linked to valued and disvalued identities that they create spaces of silence and non-action. Individuals fear to say or act in ways that will earn them humiliation and dismissal for not being masculine enough. In this way, culture shapes what people can and cannot do. As societies become more militarized, such gendered cultural categories tend to spread more widely in the society.

Although women often serve as peacemakers, they also contribute to male violence. Notions that women have some essential qualities of peacemaking are overly simplistic, as are ideas that men are inherently violent and incapable of making peace. Women actively incite men to war. For example, in the conservative Hindu nationalist movement which rose to national political leadership in India in the late twentieth century, women encouraged men to act in violent ways in the service of the nation. In a famous speech, a young woman ascetic, Sadhvi Rithambhara, used sustained passion, anger, and references to masculinity to deliver a call to Hindu men to arise and kill Muslims (Sarkar 2001: 268–288). She demanded that Hindu men take vengeance against Muslims to protect a sacralized nation and evoked images of combative masculinity juxtaposed with emasculation and eunuchs. In the speech, Rithambhara insists on violence, but frames her demand within a principle of benevolence: it is the Muslims who have inflamed a fundamentally peaceful Ram and his Hindu community (Sarkar 2001: 276). Portraying the country as sacred and vulnerable, threatened by Muslim neighbors outside and treacherous Muslims within, she preserves the vision of the nation as a unified whole and obscures divisions by caste and class (Sarkar 2001: 279). Women are part of this vision also. They are to fill their hearts with anger and take a place in the struggle, but Rithambhara is clear that their role is to produce sons who will kill Muslims. She calls women mothers and finally wombs. Mothering becomes an act of anger; the woman conceives and nurtures her sons as instruments of revenge. Women are to give birth to masculine violence, but it is the men who are violent: "Make yourselves into a clenched fist, my brothers!" (Sarkar 2001: 284).

This taped speech, recorded in 1990, was widely replayed in Hindu temples and at meetings organized by the religious wing of this movement. It contributed to renewed violence by Hindu groups against Muslims. The fact that these sentiments were delivered by a woman of an apparently sacred and disinterested status greatly increased their impact. This ideology celebrating masculine violence in defense of the sacred nation, along with feminine celebration of this violence, has contributed to ongoing tensions and periodic eruptions of communal violence.

## Ethnic Conflict and Sexualized Violence: The Carnage in Gujarat

In 2002 the latest in a series of violent rampages of Hindus against Muslims took place in several cities in Gujarat, a western province of India and one of its most industrialized states. This district is predominantly Hindu, although about 8 percent are Muslims. There have been episodes of religious conflict, called communal conflict in India, throughout the twentieth century. The 2002 attacks were set off by an alleged attack by Muslims on a train carrying Hindu pilgrims, but what actually happened was not clear. A fire in the train killed 59 men and women. The Gujarat government, under the control of the right-wing Hindu nationalist party, the Bharatiya Janata Party (BJP), quickly announced that Muslims were responsible. Some blamed local Muslim residents, others Islamic terrorists from adjacent Pakistan. The accusation unleashed a violent assault on the Muslim community across the state of Gujarat. Within 72 hours, some 2,000 people were killed according to one report, although the official figure was 762. About 113,000 were driven to relief camps. There was widespread destruction of Muslim property in terms of hotels, trucks, businesses, and mosques that were burnt or destroyed. There are indications that the attack was pre-planned: rioters carried lists of Muslim families by address or houses were pre-marked. Arms had been distributed widely to the public in advance. These points are described in an international, feminist report on the violence that offers detailed evidence of the extent of rape and assault on women as part of the violence (International Initiative for Justice in Gujarat (IIJ) 2003). This report also notes that there was little if any effort by state institutions to contain the violence or to provide humanitarian or medical support.

The IIJ report, describing hearings held by a panel of jurists, activists, lawyers, writers, and academics from around the world, examines the prominent role sexual violence played in this conflict (IIJ 2003: 6). Women caught in the conflict described rapes, especially gang rapes:

> We went to AA5 area. Young men came and started beating us and asked us to leave. Then we went into AA6 area. Again the people from AA6 area started beating us up. We again started running. We saw smoke, they told us tyres are burning. Lots of women, children were running. We went running there, we saw on the road between AA6 area and the State Transport depot, many girls were stripped and were being raped. Girls were shouting. I saw 4–5 girls being raped ... Hindu men from AA6 area were doing all this ... While raping the girls, the men were shouting *har har mahadev*. They were saying, "Go to Pakistan, why are you in Hindustan?" (Woman survivor from Ahmedabad, IIJ 2003: 33).

> They cut off the breasts of her (neighbour's) daughter, it is difficult to forget, it still swims in my vision. I have lost my mental peace. (Village survivor, IIJ 2003: 33)

> My father-in-law, a retired schoolteacher, refused to leave the village with the other Muslim families who fled to PV3 on February 28th. He believed that no one would harm us. From the 28th about 13 members of my family sought refuge in various people's houses and the fields. On Sunday afternoon (March 3rd) the hut we were hiding in was attacked. We ran in different directions and hid in the field. But the mob found some of us and started attacking. I could hear various members of my family shouting for mercy as they were attacked. I recognized two people from my village – Gano Baria and Sunil – pulling away my daughter. She screamed, telling the men to get off her and leave her alone. The screams and cries of Ruqaiya, Suhana, Shabana, begging for the *izzat* (honor) could clearly be heard. My mind was seething

with fear and fury. I could do nothing to help my daughter from being assaulted sexually and tortured to death. My daughter was like a flower, still to experience life. Why did they have to do this to her? What kind of men are these? The monsters tore my beloved daughter to pieces. After a while, the mob was saying, "Cut them to pieces, leave no evidence." I saw fires being lit. After some time the mob started leaving. And it became quiet. (Testimony in a report in Ahmedabad, IIJ 2003: 33–34)

The report argues that these events were pre-planned, and that the police, who witnessed the violence, did nothing. Some reported that the police themselves were violent, aiding in the attacks. The event was framed as a defense of "real Hindu men." One activist reported an incident where Hindu men exposed their penises and said, "Your men are weak, we're strong, you're not strong enough to fuck your own women" (IIJ 2003: 36). Women joined in the violence and looting as well. One woman testified: "X's daughter was pulling women by hair and throwing them in fire ... We saw women from AA6 area pouring kerosene or some chemical powder so the bodies used to burn" (IIJ 2003: 37). In addition to these acts of physical and sexual violence, Muslim women were subjected to taunts, threats, and many other forms of harassment.

These acts of violence reflected the idea of Muslim men as the enemy "other" and of the use of sexual violence to humiliate them and at the same time recoup the strength of the emasculated Hindu society. Rapes were often carried out publicly or in front of family members in order to subjugate the entire community. Rape served not only to humiliate but to impregnate Muslim women with Hindu children, a response to fears about allegedly greater rates of reproduction among Muslim families. As the report points out, one consequence of this violence targeted at young women and girls has been to increase early marriages, restrictions on girls' mobility, and their withdrawal from school and work as they confront their real lack of safety (IIJ 2003: 41). In this situation, attacking and raping women was a desirable strategy for undermining the honor of the other community and asserting dominance over them through the enactment of a violent and sexually predatory masculinity. Here, however, the state was complicit. The government of Gujarat has not yet moved to redress or punish these offenses. This inaction fuels women's fear of speaking out and reporting the abuse they have suffered. Instead, the panel found that many remain silent, reluctant to talk about their experiences of abuse even a year later (IIJ 2003: 44–45).

From the perspective of perpetrators, sexual violence in times of armed conflict can come to seem normal, even banal. A statement by a Peruvian soldier sent from the coast to control the Maoist guerillas of the Shining Path in the Andean highlands reveals the everyday ordinariness of gender violence in war, as well as some discomfort by a perpetrator. In 1982 the Peruvian military was engaged in an effort to contain a violent peasant uprising in highland Peru. A navy veteran sent to contain it offers this story. It takes for granted attitudes of coastal Peruvians toward the Indian populations of the highlands, expressed through the term *chola*, Andean woman, as well as a chilling indifference to the woman's suffering:

I'm going to tell you an anecdote. One day we had been on patrol for fifteen days. The patrol leader was a complete asshole, an imbecile, an idiot who had been a desk jockey his whole life, but they made him a leader because he had seniority. One day, they gave us a *chola* to waste. Great, so where can we do it? We looked for and found a deserted house. But it had all the conveniences, furniture, a television. That's because we were in a drug zone. We installed ourselves there, and one by one we gave it to the poor *chola*. I remember that beforehand the guys had dressed her well with her little dress, and they made everything just right. I remember too that the patrol leader didn't want us to touch her, and I told him, "You are really fucked, the order's been given, we've got to waste this *chola* and nothing more." I remember her saying, "I'm a virgin, I'm a virgin." Get out of here, *chola*. Of course she wasn't a virgin. Here one learns to be a shit. Afterwards, the boys played her like a yo-yo. Then we wasted her. ("Pancho" 2005: 361)

## Genocide and Rape in Rwanda: A Case Study

The 1994 genocide in Rwanda presents another vivid illustration of the centrality of sexual violence to conflict.[1] Over a 100-day period from April to June 1994, more than 800,000 Rwandans, mostly adult males, were massacred in violent conflicts between the majority Hutu and the minority Tutsi ethnic groups. A group of Hutu political leaders eager to create a purely Hutu Rwandan nation were the masterminds behind the violence. Not only Tutsis but also Hutus who advocated power sharing and a multi-ethnic coexistence were targets. Since these acts were committed with the intent of obliterating another group, they constitute genocide, as defined in the UN Convention on Genocide.[2] Although significantly fewer women were killed than men, women and girls were subjected to rape and other forms of sexual abuse (see Mamdani 2002; Power 2002).

Several studies have estimated the extent of rape during the genocide, with astounding results. A 1996 report by the United Nation's Special Rapporteur on Rwanda estimated that at least 250,000 women were raped during the genocide.[3]

---

[1]   I am grateful to Nur Amali Ibrahim for research and writing for this section.

[2]   Genocide is defined in the United Nation's 1948 Convention for the Prevention of Genocide as "acts committed with intent to destroy, in whole or in part, a national, ethnical, racial or religious group, as such: (a) Killing members of the group; (b) Causing serious bodily or mental harm to members of the group; (c) Deliberately inflicting on the group conditions of life calculated to bring about its physical destruction in whole or in part; (d) Imposing measures intended to prevent births within the group; (e) Forcibly transferring children of the group to another group."

[3]   "Report on the Situation of Human Rights in Rwanda," submitted by Mr. René Degni-Segui, Special Rapporteur of the Commission on Human Rights, under paragraph 20 of the resolution S-3/1 of 25 May 1994, E/CN.4/1996/68, January 29, 1996, p. 7; cited in Human Rights Watch, Africa 1996. The estimates were based on extrapolations of the number of recorded pregnancies resulting from rapes during the genocide.

Another study suggests that a high proportion of Rwandan women were raped during the genocide. This 1999 study, conducted by the Association of Widows of the Genocide, reported that of a sample of 1,125 women living in the prefectures of Kigali, Butare, and Kibundo, approximately 74.5 percent had suffered some form of sexual violence during the genocide (Association of Widows of the Genocide (AVEGA) 1999). These rapes were not simply random by-products of the chaotic situation in Rwanda, but were deliberately and efficiently committed as part of the extremist Hutu genocidal strategy. As a weapon of genocide, rape was no less brutal than guns or machetes: many rape victims eventually became infected by HIV or had their reproductive organs so severely damaged that they could no longer bear the next generation of Tutsis.

Why was rape so widespread during the Rwandan genocide? How does it contribute to a genocidal policy? As this chapter shows, sexual violence has long been a deliberate and carefully planned military tactic, as in the forced sexual enslavement of Korean women (also widely known as "comfort women") by Japanese soldiers during World War II, or the rapes of Bosnian women by Serbian soldiers in the Balkan wars of the early 1990s. War rapes are not simply the product of overaggressive males terrorizing victimized women, nor are they part of "ancient hatreds" or "African tribal savagery." Such explanations fail to take into account the specific factors and circumstances behind rape during times of war and conflict. As this case study shows, the particular historical context, social structure, and ideology of racial purity allowed rape to occur on a massive scale.

## Rape as a form of genocide

The Rwandan genocide was essentially an ethnic conflict orchestrated by extremist Hutu political leaders who were determined to maintain a Hutu monopoly over political power in Rwanda. Most violence came from soldiers in the military and members of the militia group known as the Interahamwe.[4] As the genocide progressed, ordinary citizens became involved as well. While Tutsi men were the primary targets of the Hutu militia in the first month of the conflict, women were systematically targeted after May 1994 (Human Rights Watch, Africa 1996). Evidence presented at the International Criminal Tribunal of Rwanda (ICTR), an international court established in November 1994 to address the atrocities committed in Rwanda, revealed that top Hutu political leaders gave orders to the militia to commit the rapes. In 1998 the ICTR found Jean-Paul Akayesu, a former Rwandan mayor, guilty of nine counts of genocide, crimes against humanity, and war crimes (see International Criminal Tribunal of Rwanda website at http://69.94.11.53/main.htm). This verdict was a

---

[4]    The Interahamwe consisted of mainly young Hutu men, and many of its members were even as young as pre-pubescent teens. The group was formed by Hutu members of the Rwandan government in the years leading to the genocide (International Criminal Tribunal of Rwanda website, http://69.94.11.53/main.htm).

dramatic new development in international law: it was the first time rape was defined by an international court as an act of genocide (Human Rights Watch 1998).

During the genocide, Hutu political leaders used the extremist Hutu radio station, Radio Libre des Milles Collines, to command the militia to commit violence against the Tutsis.[5] The Radio Milles Collines also disseminated anti-Tutsi hate propaganda to rouse anger among the Hutu militia and incite them to violence (Power 2002). To encourage the militia to rape Tutsi women, journalists from the Radio Milles Collines painted an extremely pejorative and alarmist picture of Tutsi women. They accused Tutsis of using their women to infiltrate the Hutu ethnic group by making Hutu men fall in love with them. The radio broadcasts portrayed Tutsi women as beautiful but very arrogant; allegedly often rejecting Hutu men they thought were ugly (Human Rights Watch, Africa 1996: 16–18). Tutsi women were therefore cast as seductress-spies who were wickedly trying to bring about the downfall of the Hutus. Moreover, the radio station broadcast the names of Tutsis to be targeted, along with their hiding places. Since many Interahamwe carried portable radios while they hunted for Tutsis, they could respond quickly to this information. The Radio Milles Collines therefore played an instrumental role in the perpetration of rapes and murders during the genocide.

The sexual violence against Rwandan women was chillingly systematic. Members of the Interahamwe set up checkpoints at roads across Rwanda to check the identity cards of all persons passing through. Those with Hutu identity cards could pass through unharmed. However, Tutsi were greeted with unimaginable terror. Tutsi men were usually immediately killed – hacked to death by machetes or shot – while Tutsi women were generally raped and/or killed. In addition to many Tutsi women being raped at checkpoints, some were raped in their villages by Hutu neighbors who were militia members. In such cases, the victims often knew their perpetrators. Most of the women raped during the genocide were Tutsi, but some Hutu women were violated if they were married to Tutsis, protected Tutsis, or were simply caught in the general chaos and mayhem (Human Rights Watch, Africa 1996: 41). Towards the end of the genocide, when the Tutsi rebel group Rwandan Patriotic Front (RPF) began gaining control over Rwanda, some RPF soldiers committed sexual violence against Hutu women as a form of reprisal (Amnesty International 2004: 2). Thus women on both sides of the conflict suffered sexual violence.

Testimonies collected from Rwandan women give us a glimpse into some of the atrocities committed during the genocide. One victim who was raped in April 1994 gave the following testimony:

> The next day, they killed all the men and boys. I was left with my baby and the three girls. At the riverside, I was raped by a group of Interahamwe one after another. I know

---

[5]    The Hutu extremist station Radio Libre des Milles Collines, which was founded in 1993 by leading Hutu extremists in the Rwandan government in response to reforms that had allowed moderates to take positions in the administration (Metzl 1997: 630), spread hate propaganda against the Tutsis, and also broadcast the names of Tutsis who were to be hunted down and murdered (Power 2002). Radio broadcasts also denigrated the Tutsis and warned Hutus that the Tutsis were planning to take control of the country by enslaving the Hutus.

all of them ... After they finished raping me, they threw me in the river to die along with my children. My children all drowned, but the river threw me back. I floated back to the riverside. (Human Rights Watch, Africa 1996: 42).

In addition to being raped, some women also had their genitals mutilated, a symbolic and physical destruction of the women's capability to reproduce the next generation of Tutsis. A witness who saw rape and mutilation happen during the genocide gave the following account:

> About ten of them (the Interahamwe) would gang-rape a woman, and when they had finished, they would kill her by pushing a sharpened stick the size of a broomstick into her vagina until she was bleeding and almost dead. I saw them do this to several women. (Human Rights Watch, Africa 1996: 64)

Apart from mutilating women's genitals, the perpetrators sometimes severed body parts which were thought to be characteristically Tutsi, such as thin noses and long fingers.

Another form of sexual violence was collective sexual slavery. Women were held captive in a compound to sexually service their captors. Some women became individual sexual slaves, singled out to belong to a particular captor. Others were forced to marry and were called "wives" of their Hutu "husbands" even though many were coerced into such arrangements. One woman who was forced to marry an Interahamwe member said: "You know ... we call these men our husbands. But they were not a true love. I hated this man. Maybe you could even be killed by them ... This happened to a lot of young girls – even school girls around eighteen years old were kept like this" (Human Rights Watch, Africa 1996: 57).

## Understanding sexual violence in wartime

During the Rwandan genocide, many international journalists attributed the violence to essentialized cultural factors such as atavistic tribal savagery. Media reports frequently made references to Africa's "heart of darkness," "the Apocalypse," "the Hell," and "the Devils of Rwanda" when offering explanations for the genocide. However, such reports failed to consider that there were specific causes, circumstances, and culprits behind the genocide. A fundamental factor is the longstanding rivalry between the Hutus and the Tutsis and the way that enmity was exacerbated by German and Belgian colonial leaders. The Europeans favored different ethnic groups at different moments of colonial rule as a strategy for maintaining colonial power over Rwanda. After Rwanda's independence from colonial rule in 1962, Hutu and Tutsi political leaders continued to jostle for control over the country, often with bloody consequences. Therefore, the genocidal killings and rapes in 1994 had a specific genealogy in terms of the struggle for political power (see Mamdani 2002).

In addition, evidence presented at the ICTR showed that the extremist Hutu government had taken various calculated steps, such as forming the Interahamwe and setting up the Radio Milles Collines a few years before 1994 in order to prepare for the genocide. The killings and rapes that took place in Rwanda in 1994 were not quintessentially "African," but were historically conditioned, politically motivated, state generated, and carefully planned.

While vast numbers of Rwandan women were subjected to terrible atrocities during the genocide, it is important that we do not cast Rwandan women in the singular role of victim. Rwandan women are not an undifferentiated group, nor did they experience the genocide the same way. Wealthy women were able to leave the country when their safety was threatened, but most Rwandan women were too poor to escape. One person who managed to escape from Rwanda while the genocide was taking place was Monique Mujawamariya, the president of the Rwandan Association for the Defence of Human Rights and Public Liberties. To leave the country, she bribed some Hutu soldiers with large sums of money. She eventually made her way to Canada, where she lobbied the United Nations and the international community to intervene in the crisis in Rwanda.

Some women aligned with the extremist Hutu faction were aggressors during the genocide. For example, Pauline Nyiramasuhuko, the Minister for Women and the Family in the Rwandan government, visited locations where Tutsis were detained and personally supervised the selection of people to be executed. Other women assisted the militia by identifying the people that were to be targeted and cheering the militia men on while they carried out rampages of killing and raping. Some women were reported as committing murders and looting the possessions of victims who had been murdered (African Rights 1995). Their complicity in the genocidal campaign is complicated, however. Some were probably firm believers in and supporters of the Hutu nationalist project, while others may have been threatened to comply on pain of death. Rwandan women's ethnicity, class, and other characteristics affected their position within the volatile and complex power relations of the genocide. Powerless women were more often raped and/or killed while women of higher social class or with better connections aligned themselves with people in power and escaped violence.

Like the women, Rwandan men also experienced the genocidal violence in different ways. Even though males were the primary aggressors – rapists and murderers – in the genocide, most of the people killed by the militia were also men (Lentin 1997; El-Bushra 2000). Therefore, just as there is no undifferentiated role of female victim, there is no single role for the male aggressor in the genocide. Most women in the genocide were targeted not because they were *women*, but because they were *Tutsi women*. Rape committed during the genocide was seen by the perpetrators as an assault not against the individual woman but on her ethnic group (see Kesic 2000: 31).

The sexual violence of the genocide was facilitated by the social structure in Rwanda. Traditionally, women occupied a subordinate position in Rwandan society. A study conducted by the Human Rights Watch listed some of the challenges faced by Rwandan women in their everyday lives prior to the genocide. For instance, there were limited economic opportunities for women outside the home (women were generally thought to be child bearers and little more); women were under-represented in education and politics; and there were discriminatory policies which denied women access to credit and landowning (Human Rights Watch, Africa 1996). This overarching structure of discrimination against women, combined with a murderous nationalist crusade, might explain why gender violence was committed on such a massive scale during the genocide. The extremist Hutu nationalist project requires obliterating *Tutsis*, and when it connects to the patriarchal social structure that dominates and silences *women*, it condemns *Tutsi women* to the same treatment. Kesic (2000) argues that a social structure that subordinates women merges well with a nationalist project because they share many structural similarities. Both naturalize power inequalities, promote a sense of "this is how it is meant to be," and imply the domination of one social group while silencing and conquering the bodies and territories of the other (Kesic 2000: 25).

Although the genocide ended more than a decade ago, Rwandan women are still suffering its consequences. To witness the killings of one's husband, brothers, and children, to survive when one's entire family has been killed, and to be displaced from one's home are some of the tragedies that Rwandan women face. Rapes bring problems such as shame, unwanted pregnancies, and HIV infection. Great social stigma exists against rape in Rwanda, such that a woman who reveals that she has been raped faces the likelihood of being shunned by her family members and community. Many rape victims choose to suffer in silence instead. Since abortion is illegal in Rwanda, pregnant rape victims must decide between carrying the baby to full term or having an illegal abortion. Of the women who were raped during the genocide, about 70 per cent are estimated to have been infected with HIV (Amnesty International 2004: 3). It is possible that some of these women were already infected because the rate of HIV infection in Rwanda is high, yet large numbers of women were tested for HIV only after the genocide. As in many other societies worldwide, people infected with HIV face stigma and discrimination in Rwanda. Many rape victims with HIV infection have not been able to gain easy access to HIV medication, given that Rwanda's medical infrastructure has been greatly devastated by the genocide (Amnesty International 2004; Meintjes et al. 2001).

While the genocide brought much grief to many Rwandan women and its effects still persist, the genocide also provided them opportunities to work toward changes in society. Because the majority of those killed during the genocide were men, the female population in Rwanda today significantly outnumbers the male population. About 70 per cent of the population is female. Women are called on to fill traditionally male roles such as heads of families, community leaders, and political elites (see Acquaro and Sherman 2005). Thus, despite the suffering and devastation of the genocide, it has paradoxically had some benefits for women.

Rape is usually understood as an interpersonal form of violence, but the Rwandan genocide shows clearly its political uses. The violence was an attempt by a ruling group to maintain its control and power over the nation. These rapes were not simply incidents of masculine aggression but were infused with ideas of ethnic power and subordination. Violating the woman was the same as attacking the ethnic group to which she belonged. Pre-existing social structures which placed women in subordinate roles in relation to men rendered rape more effective as a strategy for attacking men of the other group and legitimating their subordination in the act of sexual violence. The rapes which took place during the Rwandan genocide were motivated largely by political ambition and made possible by the existence of certain structures and ideas which made it thinkable and even palatable to commit violence against women.

## Refugees and Violence

During the post-Cold War period, the number of refugees and internally displaced persons has risen dramatically as people flee ethnic warfare, genocide, political turmoil, and natural disasters.[6] War is still the primary reason for displacement. Estimates of the world refugee population vary from 30 to 45 million people, of whom perhaps 70–75 percent are women and children (Wali 1995: 336; US Committee for Refugees and Immigrants 2004). Of these, according to the 2004 World Refugee Survey of the United States Refugee Commission report, 12 million were refugees in a foreign country and 24 million displaced within their own country. This survey found that 7.35 million had been "warehoused" in camps and settlements for over ten years. The largest numbers of displaced people are in Africa and the Middle East, with Sudan having the largest group of internally displaced people, approximately 5 million. Poor postcolonial countries with internal strife clearly have limited resources to assist refugees. Only about 17.1 million of these people fall under the umbrella of the United Nations High Commission for Refugees (UNHCR). About half of all adult and child refugees are female, although the common practice of estimating the proportion of refugees who are women and children suggests that there are higher numbers of women. However, demographic information on refugees is very difficult to obtain and quite fragmentary. Because displacement usually begins from war, men often leave while women are left to struggle to preserve their families. After they flee, they are deprived of the support of extended family and neighbors even as they become responsible for families in camps and settlements.

Situations of violence and flight, whether across borders as refugees or internally as displaced persons, exacerbate women's vulnerability to violence. Refugee women are vulnerable because of the disruption of community and housing resources and because those who have fled within their country must depend on their own governments for support, yet these governments often ignore or even sanction violence

---

[6]   Dante Costa did research and writing for this section, for which I am very appreciative.

against them, as in Gujarat and Rwanda. Once in refugee camps in another country, women are often malnourished because male refugees receive more food and medical attention. Some international and Western relief agencies exacerbate the problem by granting food, relief, and protection to male refugees (Wali 1995: 337). This discriminatory treatment may be justified as "culturally appropriate." Sometimes camp administrators and border guards assigned to protect refugee women fleeing across borders rape them. Reproductive health is a particularly serious concern for refugee women because they face dangers of sexual violence and the transmission of HIV/AIDS. Many refugees are women of child-bearing age yet health services are often lacking. Some face forced pregnancy as dominant military forces use them to "reproduce the nation" (Macklin 2004: 94).

In refugee camps, women are still vulnerable to sexual violence, as they were in wartime, from men in the receiving community, men in the camp, or even local police forces. A common problem is women's need to leave the camp for distant latrines or to forage for firewood, opening them up to attack. Forms of male privilege that governed women's lives before displacement are exacerbated in the refugee context at the same time as their vulnerability to attack is increased. There is gradual recognition of the particular difficulties faced by women refugees, but the concept of a refugee developed in the years after World War II assumed that the refugee was a heterosexual male fleeing persecution. Gender was not included as a basis for persecution in the 1951 Convention Relating to the Status of Refugees and has not developed as a clear and unambiguous category for relief.

It is becoming increasingly clear that there are critical linkages between housing and women's vulnerability to violence. Housing in refugee camps is typically minimal and flimsy. Refugees are easily preyed on by soldiers, local residents, or even camp police. Local law enforcement is likely to be ineffective. When refugees or internally displaced persons seek to return to their homes, they often find them occupied by others or destroyed, so that they must live in substandard conditions where the lack of privacy and limited space increases their vulnerability to violence. Recognizing the link between women's access to housing and their vulnerability to violence in the family in situations of armed conflict, the United Nations Special Rapporteur on Adequate Housing met with several Asia/Pacific NGOs in 2003 to discuss the linkages between violence against women and women's right to adequate housing. They also discussed land inheritance and gender-based housing discrimination. The Special Rapporteur reported on this issue at the 2005 UN Human Rights Commission meeting (Aggarwal et al. 2004).

The crisis for refugee women is powerfully exemplified by the situation in Darfur, a region in western Sudan. Here, a conflict between Arab militias and African rebel factions which began in early 2003 has produced an enormous level of death, displacement, and violence against women. Most of the 1 million displaced Darfurian villagers are living in camps elsewhere in Darfur, but between 120,000 and 200,000 had crossed into the neighboring country of Chad by 2005, according to Amnesty International (Amnesty International 2005b). Some refugees move from camp to camp in search of safety. Among those that have found minimal safety in UNCHR refugee and IDP camps in the past, women significantly outnumber men and are typically heads of households (Hyndman 2000: 105).

Rape has been a pervasive tool of war and means of displacement, with estimates from Amnesty International and Human Rights Watch of thousands of women raped in Darfur. Yet women rarely report rapes or seek medical, psychological, or legal assistance because of the shame and stigma of public exposure and the lack of faith in legal penalties. A *New York Times* news report notes that the pervasive violence women experience includes not only rape, but also verbal abuse and threats, robbery, whipping with animal whips, and gunshots to the ankles, a sign that women's attackers tried to keep them from fleeing (Sengupta 2004: A1, A9). Women are most vulnerable when they trek to gather firewood, an ongoing problem since wood has not been supplied by humanitarian assistance programs and is in scarce supply. This is defined as women's work in the family unit. One woman in a refugee camp in eastern Chad, just over the border from Sudan, said, weeping, that she had been sexually assaulted by five men, all in military clothes, during an attack on her hometown. Under her veil she had a long gash on her cheek. Amnesty International reported that some women had been raped in front of their relatives. Yet local law enforcement is unreliable, and little is done. Refugees in Chad reported in 2004 that it was common for the Sudanese military and Arab militiamen to attack villages and rape women as they tried to flee. One woman described being chased down by two men on horseback as she ran from an attack on her village and being raped by one while the other held a gun to her head. She was pregnant at the time (Sengupta 2004: A1, A9).

But even when they reach refugee camps, they are not safe. A UN refugee agency reported that 13 women had been raped over a period of ten days just beyond a displaced people's camp in Darfur. A 13-year-old girl told the African Union's cease-fire commission that three men found her as she was gathering firewood, called her a rebel, and took turns raping her. Another woman on her way to a farm on the outskirts of a town was stopped by four men on horseback and camel who accused her of looking like a member of the rebel faction and beat her with the butts of their rifles, then took turns raping her. She no longer goes outside to collect firewood, she says, and her children, aged 4 to 15, subsist on aid rations. When people go out, she says, they get beaten and raped. The head of the African Union in the area said that rape was very common, almost on a daily basis. Yet, the Sudanese government denies that its soldiers would do such a thing, and the African Union military delegation has no authority beyond monitoring the ceasefire (Sengupta 2004: A9). As is so often the case in situations of warfare, women become the pawns between rival militaries, with rape and assault a favored way for each group to attack the other. Their suffering is largely silenced and ignored, a common but unrecognized tragedy of war.

However, despite the challenges women face as refugees from war, they should not be viewed as simply helpless, victimized, and unable to better their situation given the opportunity. As Harrell-Bond and Voutira (1992: 7) note, the relationship between refugees and relief agencies is very unequal and can promote dependency, but experiments in which women are asked to locate latrines and make other important decisions about camp life have proved successful in diminishing vulnerability. Unknown numbers of women have managed to recreate their lives after displacement, disappearing from the spectrum of refugees. However, such success stories occur despite, not because of, the conditions with which refugee women are forced to cope.

## International Law and Rape as a Crime of War

Although rape has long been a dimension of war, only recently has the international community taken the offense seriously as a war crime. Even when rape has been widespread and systemic, as it was when German women were raped by the conquering Russian army in World War II or 200,000 to 400,000 Korean and other east Asian women were enslaved as "comfort women" by the Japanese army in the same war, it has not been viewed as a serious offense (Copelon 1994: 197). Estimates for rapes in Rwanda run to 50,000 and in Bosnia 20,000, although precise figures are impossible given women's reluctance to report violations and face the inevitable censure and stigma.

In the past, rape was often considered a violation of a man's honor and property and the victim was the humiliated and emasculated male, not the woman herself. The Geneva Conventions of 1949 move away from this position to some extent, but still define rape as a crime against the honor and dignity of women (Copelon 1994: 201). This reflects the idea that honor depends on chastity and ignores the ways in which rape is an act of violence against women. The Geneva Conventions do not include rape within the category of "grave breaches," the only offenses that are subject to universal jurisdiction and that obligate every nation to bring the perpetrators to justice. Kelly Askin, a scholar who has worked extensively on rape as a war crime, observes that there is a tendency to ignore sex-based crimes which are inevitably personal, with less visible injuries, and victims who are often uncomfortable about revealing them (Askin 2003: 346). The feminist legal scholar Rhonda Copelon (1994: 201) argues that rape should be explicitly recognized as a form of torture, and thus a "grave breach."

A historic decision by the ICTR tribunal investigating the Rwanda genocide recognized rape as a war crime for the first time. This 1998 decision convicted Jean-Paul Akayesu of failing to stop rape and murder by his subordinates (Cahn 2004: 27). The widespread incidence of rape in the Bosnian war in the early 1990s, in conjunction with practices of "ethnic cleansing" drew world attention to the problem of mass rape, although only in conjunction with genocidal assaults on the entire population of Bosnian Muslims. Even as "genocidal rape" gained attention, ordinary rape was viewed as less important. In 2002, however, three Bosnia Serbs were convicted by the International Tribunal for Yugoslavia of sexual assault on Muslim women at rape camps, defining rape and sexual enslavement as crimes against humanity. The head of Amnesty International USA noted that sexual enslavement in armed conflict is now legally acknowledged as a crime against humanity, which will make it more difficult for perpetrators to act with impunity. Although there was debate in the court about whether the prosecutor had to prove that the rapes were widespread or whether they took place in the context of a widespread and systematic attack, the judge decided that the latter standard was adequate (Hagen and Levi 2005: 1520), thus moving toward understanding individual rape, not only genocidal rape, as a serious war crime.

The Rome Statute, which created the International Criminal Court, the first permanent court to try cases of genocide, war crimes, and crimes against humanity, defined rape and other serious forms of sexual slavery as "crimes against humanity" when committed as part of a broad attack against civilians, and as "war crimes" when committed as part of a plan or when there are massive numbers of rapes (Cahn 2004: 27). Sexual and gender-based violence are included as severe human rights abuses, along with state-sanctioned beatings of women who fail to dress in a certain way, rape, sexual slavery, forced pregnancy, sexual violence, enforced prostitution, and enforced sterilization when they occur in the context of armed conflict or as crimes against humanity. Trafficking of women and gender-based persecution are also defined as crimes against humanity when committed as part of a widespread or systematic attack against civilians.

The court came into full operation in 2006 with jurisdiction over its signatory countries, which at the time did not include the USA. The court takes a case only when national judicial systems are unwilling or unable to prosecute the alleged criminals. In 2007 the ICC announced that one of its first cases would focus on rape. It plans to investigate a government crackdown in 2002 and 2003 that followed a coup attempt in the Central African Republic. There were at least 600 rapes as well as killings, beatings, and other abuses. The prosecutor believes it was a mass campaign and is seeking to indict the organizers rather than the rapists themselves. This investigation is unusual since it focuses primarily on rape rather than killing (Polgreen and Simons 2007: A6).

Thus, through changes in statutes and through the experience of trying war crimes (see Hagen and Levi 2005), international law has come to define rape in the context of armed conflict as a serious violation. This success does not mean such cases will be handled successfully in large numbers, however. International tribunals are slow and expensive and can handle only a small number of cases. Women who have been raped by enemy soldiers are usually reluctant to reveal their violation, fearing hostility and shame from relatives and neighbors. Despite the importance of these rulings within international law, women are still vulnerable to rapes, to bearing the children of rapes, and to a wide array of forms of sexual enslavement and violation during wartime. By and large, rape is defined as a war crime only when it occurs in the context of systematic and widespread sexual violence and armed conflict. However, there are clearly indications that the international community has finally recognized that sexual violence is a serious violation in the context of armed conflict and is moving toward defining the violations of even individual women as serious offenses.

## Conclusions

The case studies in this chapter demonstrate that although both men and women suffer during incidents of war, armed conflict, and ethnic and racial violence, women are particularly harmed. They are more likely to be displaced and housed in refugee camps than adult males, they are often raped, and they often suffer other forms of violence. Militarized societies celebrate a violent form of masculinity which sometimes increases the violence women experience. The examples from the Hindu–Muslim conflict in Gujarat and the genocide in Rwanda both show the importance of gendered discourses and violence in inciting conflict and the centrality of gender violence in the fighting. However, it is also clear that men suffer as well as women, and that women are not necessarily bystanders to these connections, since some women take central roles in articulating the need for men to go to war to defend women and the homeland, as the example from the Hindu right showed.

What these examples all show, in sum, is the power of gendered language to incite violence and justify rape and murder. They show the intimate relationship between religious and ethnic conflict and gendered language. Clearly, using gendered discourse and gendered forms of violence exacerbates and magnifies other kinds of hostilities. And equally clearly, these forms of structural violence have a powerful gendered dimension. As in the case of the metaphors typically employed by American defense intellectuals, the power of images of an aggressive military masculinity to define desirable behavior and condemn other behavior as "weak" and "feminine" is enormous. Gendered images reinforce militarist behavior.

However, with the emergence of an international criminal court system, the international community is beginning to focus on the gendered dimension of these conflicts and endeavoring to punish the perpetrators. Despite the example of the Canadian peacekeepers in Somalia, there are significant efforts to use UN peacekeepers to diminish some of the damage of ethnic conflict. In 2003 a coalition of NGOs persuaded the UN Security Council to pass a resolution advocating the incorporation of women in peacekeeping missions. The UN has recently established an office to promote this initiative, and there are some early indications of successful missions that include women in leadership roles.

## Questions for Further Discussion

1   To what degree is power embedded in, incited, and reproduced in the way we speak? Explain why gendered metaphors are linked to and harden particular values about masculinity and femininity. What are the consequences of their use? Can you think of other examples of everyday language that normalize gender violence?

2   In Chapter 6, we learned that "traditional" gendered practices are connected to nationhood. How are armed conflict, military policy, and other acts of conquest

also linked to gender, violence, and the nation? Consider how sexualized patterns of dominance are celebrated in society and used to humiliate others.

3   Armed conflict exacerbates women's vulnerability to violence. Explain why rape and forced relocation, like bullets and bombs, are tools of war. Why have they been long ignored, and why are women still silenced? Drawing on previous chapters, explain why you think international law may or may not make a difference in the lives of survivors.

## Video Suggestions

*Afghanistan Unveiled*, by Brigitte Brault and Aina Women Filming Group
(Afghanistan, 2003), 52 minutes

After the fall of the Taliban, a team of young Afghani women, many in their teens, trained as photojournalists. Except for one, none were able to study or pursue a career while the Taliban was in power. Camera in hand, they travel for the first time outside the capital, Kabul, to document the experience of other women under the Taliban and during the US military campaign. In this rare footage, we meet Kuchi and Hazara women, the latter of whom because of their poverty have been reduced to live in caves, their husbands and sons exterminated by the Taliban. We also journey to Herat, Jalalabad, and Badakshan, places where it was difficult to find women who would speak and be seen on camera at all.

*Calling the Ghosts: A Story about Rape, War and Women*, by Mandy Jacobson
and Karmen Jelincic (Croatia/USA, 1996), 63 minutes

Jadranka Cigelj and Nusreta Sivac, childhood friends and lawyers, led ordinary lives in Bosnia-Herzegovina until one day in 1992 when their coworkers, neighbors, and acquaintances became their tormentors. In a moving account of their first-hand experience at the Serb concentration camp of Omarska, this film documents their story of systematic torture, humiliation, and rape. Once released, they were shuttled to Croatia, where they turned their struggle for survival into a fight for justice: together, they amassed stories of brutality and successfully lobbied the UN Tribunal at the Hague to include rape as part of international humanitarian law.

*A Duty to Protect: Justice for Child Soldiers in the D.R.C.*, by WITNESS
with Association des Jeunes pour le Developpement Integre-Kalundu
(AJEDI-Ka) (USA, 2005), 14 minutes

Mafille and January are two girls who were recruited into the military at 13 and 10 years of age, respectively. Children in the eastern Democratic Republic of Congo comprise an estimated 60 percent of combatants in a region that has experienced a brutal civil war since 1998. *A Duty to Protect* tells their story of gender violence, sexual exploitation, masculine bravado, and the complexity of conflict and recruitment in a country where poverty and a lack of social services are endemic. Available online at www.youtube.com/watch?v=FIWIQ4Wt4o8&feature=user.

*God Sleeps in Rwanda*, by Kimberlee Acquaro and Stacy Sherman
(Rwanda/USA, 2005), 30 minutes

The 1994 Rwandan genocide left in its aftermath a country that is 70 percent female. Academy Award Nominee for Best Documentary Short, *God Sleeps in Rwanda* is a poignant story of loss and redemption told through the lens of five women who face an extraordinary burden and an unprecedented opportunity to rebuild their country. An HIV-positive policewoman; widowed mother of four; an aspiring lawyer; a teenage head of household who has on her own raised her four siblings; an orphaned woman turned top development official – these are the women who are redefining gendered power relations since the bloodshed ended.

*The Women Outside: Korean Women and the U.S. Military*, by J. T. Takagi
and Hye Jung Park (USA, 1995), 52 minutes

When the US military came to the southern Korean peninsula after World War II, an industry of a gendered kind emerged. As many as 27,000 women work in the military brothels and clubs that "service" American GIs. But these women, many poor and illiterate, remain "outside," subordinated to the whims of US military personnel and stigmatized in their home country. This film documents their lives, from the outskirts of Seoul to cities in America, and questions US military policy, South Korea's economic dependence on these zones of sexualized labor, and, more generally, the role of women in global geopolitics.

# 8

# Conclusions

Gender violence is clearly an old problem and one that occurs around the world. Yet only recently has it attracted serious national and international attention. As this book shows, feminist social movements seeking to understand women's subordination in the 1960s and 1970s recognized the importance of violence as a fundamental source of inequality in gendered relationships. The particular issues that galvanized movements against gender violence in various countries differed, but important similarities in ideas and politics connected the disparate movements. By exchanging theories and ideas about the nature of gender, violence, and ways of diminishing it across national borders, feminists influenced each other's thinking and actions. Gradually, they formed an international movement.

The current international understanding of gender-based violence as a human rights violation is one of the important products of this vibrant global exchange. It has expanded the range of actions considered gender violence and created new global alliances and mechanisms for reducing violence in a wide variety of situations from female genital cutting to illegal immigrant women. For example, village collectives in Senegal have refused to do further genital surgeries, while the VAWA Act in the USA offers special protections to undocumented battered women. Perhaps most important, gender violence is now recognized around the world as a significant social problem. It is widely discussed as a public concern that warrants state and private intervention.

Gender violence refers to a highly diverse set of actions ranging from interpersonal violence within the home to rape of men or women in police custody or prison. It is violence whose meaning depends on the gendered identities of the parties. Gender violence is violence that is comprehensible because of the gender of the interaction. For example, when a man hits his wife because he suspects she has been flirting with someone, his actions are shaped by his sense of masculine entitlement to control her. When the American soldiers in the Abu Ghraib prison in Iraq stripped Iraqi soldiers naked and forced them to lie in a pile, they were using ideas of proper and improper masculine behavior to humiliate them. When a family kills a daughter for flirting with a man, they are endeavoring to recover from the dishonor she imposed on them by violating the proper modesty of women. When the police in New York City anally raped a black man with a broom handle, they were insulting and injuring him in a gendered way. When a man discovers that the female prostitute he is with has male genitalia, his assault on this person is a way to recover what he imagines is his lost masculinity.

As social movements against gender violence grow and coalesce into an international movement, the scope of actions considered to be gender violence continues to grow. Since the conception of violence against women as a major social problem grew out of social movements in the first place, it is understandable that as these movements develop and expand, new issues appear. Some of the more recent issues are sex trafficking, rape in wartime and during armed ethnic conflict, widowhood rituals, and violence against transgendered people. Whether the continual addition of new categories to the definition of violence against women will expand its audience or doom it to incoherence remains to be seen. At this point, the new categories to be included in the definition are extremely diverse and wide-ranging.

## Rethinking Gender

The emergence of gender violence as a social problem was deeply influenced by theoretical developments in the analysis of gender. Movements against gender violence were inspired by ideas developed in new women's studies programs in universities around the world, as happened in India, China, and the USA. Of course, scholars in these programs often worked closely with movement activists as well. The intellectual ferment of the 1960s to 1980s produced critical changes in the analysis of gender. After an initial period that focused on adding women to descriptions of social life, social scientists started to explore gender as a social phenomenon. Instead of viewing male/female differences as based on sex and therefore biological and fixed, new feminist scholarship developed the concept of gender as a way of describing identities that are socially constructed. Talking about male/female differences as based on gender rather than sex emphasized the culturally determined and variable nature of this identity. By locating gender in the social world rather than the biological realm, as the term "sex" did, theorists were able to appreciate variations in the way gender was defined in different contexts. Moreover, the shift from sex to gender moved the analysis of gender difference beyond the narrow focus on reproduction to the myriad ways that gender shaped male as well as female identity and experience. Women's studies programs became gender studies programs.

With the transition from thinking of gender as a role to a performance, theorists began to focus on how gender is enacted for various audiences rather than analyzing it as a set of stable identities with rights and duties. Instead of viewing humans as simply male or female, the performative perspective emphasizes the multiple ways masculinity or femininity is performed. Gender is no longer a binary set of categories but a repertoire of signs and images that are used to perform gender and that vary over time and with the features of a particular situation. Performances resist binary categorization. This theoretical approach suggests that gender falls along a continuum, with individuals enacting gendered identities in a wide variety of ways along this continuum. Sexuality emerges as an important dimension of the performance of gender, again with a fluid and multiple set of performative possibilities. Just as sex differences are no longer a simple binary, so sexuality takes on a wide variety of forms.

These new theoretical developments challenged movement ideas that gender violence is simply an expression of patriarchy. Studies of non-heterosexual battering revealed that interpersonal violence occurs between same-sex couples and that there are forms of gender violence that target non-heteronormative expressions of gender. Clearly, gender violence is not just a way of expressing male power over women.

Nor are men and women simple categories of identity and action. As essentialist ideas of gender gave way to more intersectional models, the importance of race and class variation took on greater importance. This theoretical development reflected and informed concerns that the violence against women movement in the USA was exclusively white and middle class. As they grappled with this limitation, feminists sought to expand their frameworks and programs to include people of differing language, ethnicity, race, and sexuality. Similar issues confronted the movement in India, where the movement was led by urban, educated women but gradually expanded to incorporate a broader range of perspectives and concerns.

While the disproportionate voice of women privileged by race, caste, and class position is still a difficult issue, the women's movement has made significant progress in recognizing and dealing with the problem. Work in critical race theory on gender violence has contributed significantly to these developments as well (see, e.g., Bhattacharjee 1997; Mama 1997; Razack 2000a; 2000b; Wing 2000). Many women's centers are deeply committed to an intersectional approach to gender. Services for battered women who come from a range of nationalities, races, and sexualities are more available than in the past. The Incite! organization that grew out of the Color of Violence conferences has contributed significantly to expanding the framework of gender violence to a more intersectional model (see Smith 2005; Incite! 2006). Although the international movement lags behind, there are pioneers attempting to apply intersectional analysis to the global field as well.

## Rethinking Violence

In addition to these changes in theories of gender, conceptions of violence have also changed since 1970. The meaning of violence has expanded from blows and physical injury to a wide array of assaults on self-esteem, personal possessions, and emotional and financial well-being. Threats, fear, insecurity, and more indirect harms are seen as important. Theories of violence recognize that this is a system of mean-ing, so that it is important to see how and why individuals come to see themselves as facing danger and the risk of harm. Narratives of danger play an important role in creating a world of fear and anxiety. One transgendered group, for example, has catalogued murders and assaults on transgendered people, both as a warning and to build a social movement. Although the early years of the US battered women's move-ment separated rape and domestic violence, the contemporary movement focuses more clearly on sexual violence, recognizing the intimate connections between sex and violence.

Interpersonal violence is intimately connected to structural violence, as this book demonstrates. Structural violence refers to injuries and assaults that are produced by collective actions and institutions. It includes the violence following conquest and dislocation suffered by indigenous peoples; the use of violence to reinforce differ-ences of caste and class; violent forms of racial, ethnic, and religious discrimination and exclusion; and the violent consequences of poverty and the inability to support oneself. Contemporary labor markets that require massive migration of single young women or child labor, often with job opportunities on one side of a border and poverty on the other and a harsh border patrol in the middle, provide situations rife with violence. There are frequently gendered dimensions to structural violence, as occurs when women are disproportionately refugees after armed conflict. Interpersonal violence in gendered relationships is often embedded in these larger systems of inequality and violence.

Interpersonal gender violence often maintains structural inequalities. The caste system in India, for example, is supported by routine practices of rape and violence against lower-caste women by upper-caste men, assaults that humiliate the man and his caste at the same time as they injure and violate the woman. Racial minorities were long subject to disproportionate violence in the USA, often targeting the women of the community. During warfare, rape and other forms of sexual violation and gender violence are commonplace as means of defeating enemies and enacting militarized versions of masculinity. As women and children flee, they become vul-nerable as refugees and internally displaced persons. Raping or otherwise violating women during armed conflict not only injures and perhaps kills women and pro-duces illegitimate children, but also angers and humiliates women's husbands, brothers, and other men of their nation or ethnic/religious community.

Controlling women's sexuality and reproduction through violence or threats of violence in the family supports family structures based on the power of the male head. Ideas about women's sexual modesty and virtue legitimate patriarchal control of women and violent retaliation for lapses. Women come to see these actions as fundamental to the way they perform gender. Comparing why women might acqui-esce to female genital cutting or to anorexic eating patterns demonstrates how blurred the distinction is between consent and coercion. In all societies, members consent to identities that they consider to be ideal. Those who resist experience coer-cion. This extends to American women pressured to be thin and American men who feel they must be aggressive and controlling toward women to show that they are "real men." As Chapter 7 showed, even war games celebrate a "masculine" show of force and make fun of a "feminine" tendency to negotiate.

The chapters in the book show that interpersonal violence cannot be understood separately from these forms of institutional or social violence. Moreover, they make clear that no general theory of violence against women is adequate to explain this diverse phenomenon. Violence against women is a complicated form of behavior that is situated in particular economic and cultural contexts and never separate from larger systems of power and inequality. It has multiple causes from the emotional to the cultural to the structural. Both individual features of emotionality and anger and the collective use of violence in social life shape the particular forms gender violence assumes in any location.

Gender violence is inherently difficult to measure. Because it is an injury that the victim sees as unacceptable, whether or not a person thinks she has experienced it is a matter of interpretation. A person could interpret a slap or kick as punishment, love, hazing, or fighting. If so, she will probably deny that she has experienced gender violence. Victimization surveys of gender violence that ask people if they have experienced gender violence only count what people think is gender violence. If they think an incident is simply fighting or normal behavior, they will probably not report it. Measurements that use calls for help depend on the victim not only interpreting the experience as illegal violence but also deciding that it makes sense to ask an institution for help. Of course, it must be an institution that collects data on these requests. An abused person who summons state assistance such as the police must have some hope that the police will intervene constructively. But is there a police force? Can they be trusted? Will they do anything? Is what they will do what the victim wants? Any of these factors could deter calling for help, but unless the person calls, the incident will not be counted. All of these interpretive, cultural, and institutional factors affect the accuracy of measurements of gender violence based on surveys or requests for help. Clearly, because gender violence includes both harm and an interpretation of the meaning of the harm, measuring gender violence is a subjective and culturally shaped process.

## An Anthropological Perspective on Gender Violence

This book offers a social science perspective on gender violence, one rooted in particular in anthropology. The range of particular forms of gender violence it considered exemplify this approach and show its strengths. Chapter 1 articulated the four dimensions of an anthropological perspective, which the rest of the book has illustrated. First, it argues that issues are created by social movements and political debates, subject to change over time. Clearly, the definition of gender violence as a social problem grew out of a series of national movements that coalesced into a global movement in the 1990s. It continues to grow and develop as activists think about the implications of defining gender violence as a human rights violation and as new issues emerge under that framework, such as sex trafficking. With the emergence of a human rights perspective, new coalitions have developed among activists in different countries. At the same time, the human rights perspective is reshaping the US movement, putting greater emphasis on social and economic rights to housing and economic support. While some activists work to develop the human rights perspective, others in the battered women's movement have turned to more therapeutic and interpersonal ways of defining the problem, emphasizing counseling and conflict resolution skills.

The wide range of issues and approaches now used to define and intervene in gender violence shows the creativity of social movements but also the risks of a movement-generated definition of the problem. It has produced a very broad definition of gender violence that has some conceptual incoherence and builds on a wide variety of theories about the phenomenon and modes of intervention. It has not resolved the problem of establishing a universal standard for unacceptable forms of gender violence that simultaneously validates cultural difference. Nor has it succeeded in specifying prohibited forms of violence while also understanding these practices within their social and cultural context. Instead, practices such as honor killing and female genital cutting are condemned without taking into account the systems of kinship and ideologies of sexuality within which they operate. A contextual analysis does not preclude critique, of course, but it does suggest a more nuanced perspective on the problem.

Such a contextual analysis is a second feature of the anthropological perspective, which understands gender as a performance for audiences in various contexts. These performances are done by individuals, but the repertoires of each performance and the expectations of audiences are collective, part of the culture of particular groups. Communities vary greatly as to which performances are acclaimed and which condemned. Gender violence is a performance directed at certain audiences, either the person subject to the violence or others surrounding it. In militarized societies that value violence as an expression of heroism, the performance of a violent masculinity against either men or women may produce acclaim. The marauding groups of young men that terrorize transgendered individuals or gay and lesbian men and women may see themselves as performing a kind of masculinity that will be praised by some audiences. The conversation in the men's violence prevention program in Hilo, Hawai'i provides another illustration of a gender performance, done for the other men in the room as well as the facilitator, which both celebrates and denies the violence they have carried out.

The third principle, that interpersonal behavior must be understood within wider contexts of power and meaning, emphasizes the importance of linking interpersonal gender violence and structural violence. As the case studies of rape in wartime, police rape of women in custody, rape of lower-caste women by higher-caste men in India, and the use of sexual violence during the assault on Muslims in Gujarat indicate, interpersonal gender violence serves as a mode of establishing and maintaining systems of inequality. At the same time, vulnerability to violence varies with a person's position of power. It is typically the marginalized, excluded, poor, and female who are targeted for violence. Perpetrators often escape consequences for their actions. In these situations, the violence reproduces existing inequalities. Threats of violence can constrain behavior even when the violence is not actually carried out, as occurs when women fear honor killings. Threats of violence or stories about violence reinforce these inequalities.

Finally, the anthropological perspective is comparative. This book shows the value of expanding the analysis of gender violence from the situation in the United States to a more international perspective and emphasizes gender violence as a global phenomenon. Even in one country, of course, there are significant variations depending on a person's race, economic situation, and legal status. The analysis of the effect of illegal immigrant status shows clearly the variations in the experience of gender violence among migrants depending on whether they are legal or not. Although much of this book has discussed forms of violence against women, there are important comparisons with forms of gendered violence against men. As the example of the Canadian peacemakers indicated, certain performances of masculinity target other men, such as those defined as "savage" or "less civilized" in the name of establishing a "civilized" form of order. The comparative approach exposes similarities and differences, making the familiar strange and the strange familiar. While a man who slaps his wife seems familiar to many Americans, as one instance of a global practice by which men assert control over women, it is a strange form of behavior. On the other hand, the practice of surgically altering a woman's genitalia to preserve her sexual modesty may seem strange, but enhancing breasts, reducing noses and buttocks, or starving oneself to produce a thin body are equally strange.

The anthropological approach, which sees gender violence as socially produced, performed, contextually defined, and existing in many different situations and contexts, provides a valuable way to understand what gender violence is, how its definition is changing, and how modes of approaching it are changing. This approach does not explain why one or another person uses gender violence against another; it takes a broader, more collective approach. However, it does explain why a performance of gender violence is celebrated in one context and condemned in another. And it shows clearly that efforts to change gender violence must understand the practice in terms of audiences that support it, the institutions that treat it lightly, and the structures of inequality that benefit from the kinds of control and power that it provides.

## Gender Violence and Inequality

This book argues for an analysis of gender violence situated within larger structures of inequality, but there are many scholars and activists working on gender violence that focus more specifically on its interpersonal dimensions. The early leaders of the battered women's movement came from Marxist, socialist, and feminist backgrounds and thought that changing women's position required changing society as a whole.

However, as shelters, women's centers, and intervention programs became more established and supported by government funding, the understanding of gender violence as a product of incompetence in interpersonal interaction, an inability to manage anger and violence, and a failure in family relationships grew more prominent. Instead of critiquing social inequalities, many scholars, activists, and service providers now focus on personality factors that produce violence, family dynamics that perpetuate violence across generations, and forms of conflict management that will deflect violent fights. Interventions are based on counseling, conflict management training, violence control programs, and removing children from violent households. Despite the value of these interventions, they neglect the larger social issue that inspired the movement in the first place: the concern with inequalities on the basis of race, class, and gender.

The international movement has retained this structural perspective more substantially than the US domestic movement. Moreover, the international movement is more skeptical about the role of the state than the social services segment of the US movement. Much of the current intervention relies on state activity without an extensive analysis of the state's interest in preventing gender violence or its complicit support for a very limited form of intervention. It is largely at the international level that such questions are now being addressed.

Even the socialist-feminist originators of the gender violence movement relied on the law, however. As we have seen, the initial modes of intervention were passing laws and creating safe spaces. The former soon encountered the inadequacy of legal reforms in the absence of effective implementation strategies. During the 1980s and 1990s, activists in the USA worked energetically to improve police, prosecutor, and judicial responses to gender violence. But, if law is part of patriarchal institutions, can it change the situation? Moreover, if gender violence is embedded within and reflects larger structures of inequality and violence, how can any society diminish interpersonal forms of violence without attending to these larger patterns? Can gender violence in families be tackled without simultaneous efforts to deal with global conflict, economic inequality, and a lack of social justice? Activists around the world have adopted a similar approach to criminalizing gender violence, despite skepticism about the state. Both American and international activists share misgivings about the capacity of the state to transform gender hierarchies in the absence of larger social changes.

This book shows that clearly it cannot. Its analysis challenges us to think broadly about gender violence, to see it as a manifestation of other forms of violence, and to confront these larger systems as well. In some ways, it returns to the roots of the battered women's movement, which questioned not only the notion that men have the right to hit their wives to discipline them, but also the inequalities produced by capitalism, by male political hierarchies, and by inequalities of race and class. Such perspectives have lasted longer in the international movement than in the American one, but must remain fundamental to all of them. A society that is free of violence against women can happen only when it is free of other forms of violence as well.

# References

Abdullah, Hussaina J. 2002. "Religious Revivalism, Human Rights Activism and the Struggle for Women's Rights in Nigeria." In Abdullahi An-Na'im (ed.), *Cultural Transformation and Human Rights in Africa*. London: Zed Books. Pp. 151–191.

Abu-Lughod, Lila. 1986. *Veiled Sentiments: Honor and Poetry in a Bedouin Society*. Berkeley: University of California Press.

Abu-Odeh, Lama. 2000. "Crimes of Honor and the Construction of Gender in Arab Society." In Pinar Ilkkaracan (ed.), *Women and Sexuality in Muslim Societies*. Istanbul: Women for Women's Human Rights (WWHR).

Acquaro, Kimberlee, and Stacy Sherman (dirs.). 2005. *God Sleeps in Rwanda*. Documentary film, 28 minutes.

Adelman, Madelaine. 2003. "The Military, Militarism, and the Militarization of Domestic Violence." *Violence against Women* 9(10): 1–35.

Adelman, Madelaine. 2004. "The Battering State: Towards a Political Economy of Domestic Violence." *Journal of Poverty* 8(3): 55–74.

Adelman, Madelaine, Edna Erez, and Nadera Shalhoub-Kevorkian. 2003. "Policing Violence against Minority Women in Multicultural Societies: 'Community' and the Politics of Exclusion." *Police and Society* 7: 103–131.

African Rights. 1995. *Rwanda – Not So Innocent: When Women Become Killers*. London: African Rights.

Aggarwal, Alison Gita, Asia Pacific Forum on Women, Law, and Development. 2004. Posting on woman-violence-listserve, December 3 (discussion sponsored by INSTRAW on violence against women).

Ahmadu, Fuambai. 2000. "Rites and Wrongs: An Insider/Outsider Reflects on Power and Excision." In Bettina Shell-Duncan and Ylva Hernlund (eds.), *Female "Circumcision" in Africa: Culture, Controversy, and Change*. Boulder, CO: Lynne Rienner.

Ahmed, Leila. 1992. *Women and Gender in Islam: Roots of a Historical Debate*. New Haven, CT: Yale University Press.

Amnesty International (AI). 2001. *Broken Bodies, Shattered Minds: Torture and Ill-Treatment of Women*. London: Amnesty International.

Amnesty International (AI). 2003. "Mexico: Intolerable Killings: 10 Years of Abductions and Murder in Ciudad Juárez and Chihuahua." AI index: AMR 41/027/2003. <www.amnesty.

org/en/library/asset/AMR41/027/2003/en/dom-AMR410272003en.pdf>, accessed April 24, 2008.

Amnesty International (AI). 2004. "Rwanda: 'Marked for Death,' Rape Survivors Living with HIV/AIDS in Rwanda." <http://web.amnesty.org/library/Index/ENGAFR470072004>

Amnesty International (AI). 2005a. "Israel: Conflict, Occupation and Patriarchy: Women Carry the Burden." Index no. MDE 15/061/2005, published March 31. <www.amnesty. org/en/library/info/MDE15/016/2005>

Amnesty International (AI). 2005b. "Sudan: Continuing Human Rights Violations." Media Briefing. Index no. AFR 54/038/2005. News Service no. 92. April 13. <www.amnesty. org/library/ENGAFR540382005>

Anaya, S. James. 1996. *Indigenous Peoples in International Law*. Oxford: Oxford University Press.

Anderson, K., and D. Umberson. 2001. "Gendered Violence: Masculinity and Power in Men's Accounts of Domestic Violence." *Gender and Society* 15(3): 358–380.

Anon. 1986. "African Women Fight Clitoris Cutting." *Off Our Backs: A Women's News Journal* 26: 18–19.

Anon. 1996. "New Domestic Violence Statistics." *Women's Advocate* 17(3): 18.

Anon. 2004. "Battered Immigrants Face a Hostile Court System." National Immigration Project. October 4, 2004. <www.nationalimmigrationproject.org>

Asch, Michael. 1984. *Home and Native Land: Aboriginal Rights and the Canadian Constitution*. Seattle, WA: University of Washington Press.

Askin, Kelly D. 2003. "Prosecuting Wartime Rape and Other Gender-Related Crimes under International Law: Extraordinary Advances, Enduring Obstacles." *Berkeley Journal of International Law* 21: 288–349.

Association of Widows of the Genocide (AVEGA). 1999. <http://www.avega.org.rw>

Bachman and Saltzman. 1995. Victimization Data, 1992–93. National Crime Victimization Survey. Washington, DC: Bureau of Justice Statistics.

Backhouse, Constance. 1991. *Petticoats and Prejudice: Women and Law in Nineteenth-Century Canada*. Toronto: Women's Press, for Osgoode Society.

Bamberger, Joan. 1974. "The Myth of Matriarchy: Why Men Rule in Primitive Society." In Michelle Zimbalist Rosaldo and Louise Lamphere (eds.), *Woman, Culture, and Society*. Stanford: Stanford University Press. Pp. 263–281.

Baxi, Pratiksha. 2004. "The Social and Juridicial Framework of Rape in India: Case Studies in Gujarat." Ph.D. dissertation, Department of Sociology, Delhi School of Economics, University of Delhi.

Baxi, Pratiksha, Shirin M. Rai, and Shaheen Sardar Ali. 2006. "Legacies of Common Law: 'Crimes of Honour' in India and Pakistan." *Third World Quarterly* 27(7): 1239–1253.

Beechert, Edward D. 1985. *Working in Hawaii: A Labor History*. Honolulu: University of Hawai'i Press.

Bernard, Desiree. 1996. "The Work of the Committee on the Elimination of Discrimination against Women: Its Focus on Nationality, Custom, Culture and the Rights of the Girl-Child." In Andrew Byrnes, Jane Connors, and Lum Bik (eds.), *Advancing the Human Rights of Women: Using International Human Rights Standards in Domestic Litigation*. London: Commonwealth Secretariat. Pp. 72–85.

Bhattacharjee, A. 1997. "The Public/Private Mirage: Mapping Homes and Undomesticating Violence Work in the South Asian Immigrant Community." In C. Mohanty and J. Alexander (eds.), *Feminist Genealogies, Colonial Legacies, Democratic Futures*. New York: Routledge. Pp. 308–329.

Boddy, Janice. 1982. "Womb as Oasis: The Symbolic Context of Pharaonic Circumcision in Rural Northern Sudan." *American Ethnologist* 9: 682–698.

Borrey, Anou. 2000. "Sexual Violence in Perspective: The Case of Papua New Guinea." In Sinclair Dinnen and Allison Ley (eds.), *Reflections on Violence in Melanesia*. Canberra: Hawkins Press and Asia Pacific Press. Pp. 105–119.

Boulding, Elise. 1988. *Building a Global Civic Culture*. Syracuse, NY: Syracuse University Press.

Boyle, Elizabeth Heger. 2002. *Female Genital Cutting: Cultural Conflict in the Global Community*. Baltimore: Johns Hopkins University Press.

Boyle, Elizabeth Heger, and Sharon E. Preves. 2000. "National Politics as International Process: The Case of Anti-Female-Genital-Cutting Laws." *Law and Society Review* 34: 703–737.

Bunch, Charlotte. 1990. "Women's Rights as Human Rights: Toward a Re-Vision of Human Rights." *Human Rights Quarterly* 12: 489–498.

Bunch, Charlotte. 1997. "The Intolerable Status Quo: Violence against Women and Girls." In *The Progress of Nations 1997*. New York: UNICEF. <www.unicef.org/pon97/submenu. htm>

Bunting, Annie, and Sally Engle Merry. 2007. "Global Regulation and Local Political Struggles: Early Marriage in Northern Nigeria." In Sudhir Alladi Venkatesh and Ronald Kassimir (eds.), *Youth, Globalization, and the Law*. Stanford, CA: Stanford University Press. Pp. 321–353.

Bureau of Justice Statistics (BJS). 1994. *Selected Findings: Violence between Intimates* (NCJ-149259), November. Washington, DC: US Department of Justice. <www.ojp.gov/bjs/ pub/pdf/vbi.pdf>

Bush, Diane Mitsch. 1992. "Women's Movements and State Policy Reform aimed at Domestic Violence against Women: A Comparison of the Consequences of Movement Mobilization in the US and India." *Gender and Society* 6: 587–608.

Butalia, Urvashi. 2002. "Confrontation and Negotiation: The Women's Movement Responses to Violence against Women." In Karin Kapadia (ed.), *The Violence of Development: The Politics of Identity, Gender and Social Inequalities in India*. London and New York: Zed Books. Pp. 207–235.

Butler, Judith. 1990. *Gender Trouble: Feminism and the Subversion of Identity*. New York: Routledge.

Cahn, Naomi. 2004. "Beyond Retribution and Impunity: Responding to War Crimes of Sexual Violence." George Washington Law School, Public Law and Legal Theory Working Paper no. 104.

Camacho, Alicia R. 2005. "Ciudadana X: Gender Violence and the Denationalization of Women's Rights in Ciudad Juarez, Mexico." *CR: The New Centennial Review* 5: 255–292.

Center for Human Rights and Global Justice (CHRGJ) and Human Rights Watch. 2007. "Hidden Apartheid: Caste Discrimination against India's 'Untouchables.'" Shadow Report to the UN Committee on the Elimination of Racial Discrimination, February 2007, vol. 19, no. 3.

Chagnon, Napoleon A. 1997. *Yanomamo*, 5th edn. Wadsworth.

Chatterjee, Partha. 1989. "Colonialism, Nationalism, and Colonialized Women: The Contest in India." *American Ethnologist* 16: 622–633.

China Working Group against Domestic Violence (ed.). 2000. *China: Actions Undertaking* [*sic*] *against Domestic Violence*. February 15. Project for Beijing+5. Founded by Hong Kong Oxfam. Booklet in English and Chinese.

Clarke, Kamari Maxine. 2007. "Global Justice, Local Controversies: The International Criminal Court and the Sovereignty of Victims." In Marie-Bénédicte Dembour and Tobias Kelly (eds.), *Paths to International Justice: Social and Legal Perspectives*. Cambridge: Cambridge University Press. Pp. 134–160.

Cohn, Carol. 2003. "Wars, Wimps, and Women: Talking Gender and Thinking War." In Mark Hussey (ed.), *Masculinities: Interdisciplinary Readings*. Upper Saddle River, NJ: Prentice Hall. Pp. 331–344.

Connell, R. W. 1995. "The Science of Masculinities." In *Masculinities*. Berkeley: University of California Press. Pp. 3–44.

Connors, Jane. 1996. "General Human Rights Instruments and Their Relevance to Women." In Andrew Byrnes, Jane Connors, and Lum Bik (eds.), *Advancing the Human Rights of Women: Using International Human Rights Standards in Domestic Litigation*. London: Commonwealth Secretariat. Pp. 27–39.

Cook, Rebecca J. 1993. "Women's International Human Rights Law: The Way Forward." *Human Rights Quarterly* 15: 230–261.

Cook, Rebecca. J. (ed.). 1994a. *Human Rights of Women: National and International Perspectives*. Philadelphia: University of Pennsylvania Press.

Cook, Rebecca J. 1994b. "State Responsibility for Violations of Women's Human Rights." *Harvard Human Rights Journal* 7: 125–175.

Coomaraswamy, Radhika. 1996. "Report of the Special Rapporteur on Violence against Women, its Causes and Consequences, Ms. Radhika Coomaraswamy, submitted in accordance with Commission on Human Rights Resolution 1995/85: Violence in the Family." United Nations Commission on Human Rights. E/CN.4/1996/53. <www2.ohchr.org/english/issues/women/rapporteur/annual.htm>

Coomaraswamy, Radhika. 2002. "Report of the Special Rapporteur on Violence against Women, its Causes and Consequences, Ms. Radhika Coomaraswamy, submitted in accordance with Commission on Human Rights Resolution 2001/49: Cultural Practices in the Family that are Violent towards Women." New York: United Nations Economic and Social Council, E/CN.4/2002/83. <www2.ohchr.org/english/issues/women/rapporteur/annual.htm>

Coomaraswamy, Radhika. 2005. "Preface: Violence against Women and 'Crimes of Honour.'" In Lynn Welchman and Sara Hossain (eds.), *"Honour": Crimes, Paradigms, and Violence against Women*. London: Zed Books. Pp. xi–xiv.

Coomaraswamy, Radhika, and Lisa M. Kois. 1999. "Violence against Women." In Kelly D. Askin and Dorean M. Koenig (eds.), *Women and International Human Rights Law*, vol. 1. Ardsley, NY: Transnational. Pp. 177–217.

Copelon, Rhonda. 1994. "Intimate Terror: Understanding Domestic Violence as Torture." In Rebecca J. Cook (ed.), *Human Rights of Women: National and International Perspectives*. Philadelphia: University of Pennsylvania Press. Pp. 116–152.

Copelon, Rhonda. 1995. "Gendered War Crimes: Reconceptualizing Rape in Time of War." In Julie Peters and Andrea Wolper (eds.), *Women's Rights, Human Rights: International Feminist Perspectives*. New York: Routledge. Pp. 197–215.

Coulter, Robert T. 1994. "Commentary on the UN Draft Declaration on the Rights of Indigenous Peoples." *Cultural Survival Quarterly* 18(2): 37–41.

County of Hawai'i, Department of Research and Development. 1997. *Data Book*. Hilo, Hawai'i.

County of Hawai'i, Police Department. 1947. Annual Report. Hilo, Hawai'i.

Coutin, Susan. 2000. *Legalizing Moves: Salvadoran Immigrants' Struggle for US Residency.* Ann Arbor: University of Michigan Press.

Cowan, Jane K. 2003. "Who's Afraid of Violent Language? Honour, Sovereignty, and Claims-Making in the League of Nations." *Anthropological Theory* 3(3): 271–291.

Crenshaw, Kimberlé Williams. 1994. "Mapping the Margins: Intersectionality, Identity Politics, and Violence against Women of Color." In Martha Albertson Fineman and Roxanne Mykitiuk (eds.), *The Public Nature of Private Violence: The Discovery of Domestic Abuse.* New York: Routledge. Pp. 93–120.

Croll, Elizabeth. 1978. *Feminism and Socialism in China.* London: Routledge and Kegan Paul.

Currah, Paisley, Richard M. Juang, and Shannon Price Minter (eds.). 2006. *Transgender Rights.* Minneapolis: University of Minnesota Press.

Cuthbert, Carrie, Kim Slote, Monica Ghosh Driggers, Cynthia J. Mesh, Lundy Bancroft, and Jay Silverman. 2002. *Battered Mothers Speak Out: A Human Rights Report and Video on Domestic Violence and Child Custody in the Massachusetts Family Courts.* Wellesley, MA: Wellesley Centers for Women. <www.wcwonline.org/title380.html>

Daly, Mary. 1978a. "African Genital Mutilation: The Unspeakable Atrocities." In *Gyn/Ecology: The Metaethics of Radical Feminism.* Boston: Beacon Press.

Daly, Mary. 1978b. *Gyn/Ecology: The Metaethics of Radical Feminism.* Boston: Beacon Press.

Davies, Miranda (ed.). 1994. *Women and Violence: Realities and Responses Worldwide.* London: Zed Books.

Davin, Anna. 1997. "Imperialism and Motherhood." In Frederick Cooper and Ann Laura Stoler (eds.), *Tensions of Empire: Colonial Cultures in a Bourgeois World.* Berkeley: University of California Press. Pp. 87–151.

Davis, Angela. 2000. "The Color of Violence against Women." *ColorLines* 3(3): 4–8.

Davis, Angela. 2001. "Public Imprisonment and Private Violence." In M. R. Waller and J. Rycenga (eds.), *Frontline Feminisms: Women, War and Resistance.* New York: Routledge. Pp. 3–16.

Dembour, Marie-Bénédicte. 2001. "Following the Movement of a Pendulum: Between Universalism and Relativism." In Jane K. Cowan, Marie-Bénédicte Dembour, and Richard A. Wilson (eds.), *Culture and Rights: Anthropological Perspectives.* Cambridge: Cambridge University Press. Pp. 56–80.

Department of the Attorney General of Hawai'i. 1996. *Domestic Violence-Related Homicides in the State of Hawaii 1985–1994.* Cited in Department of the Attorney General, Crime Prevention and Assistance Division, *State of Hawaii Implementation Plan for the S.T.O.P. Violence against Women Grant,* May 1998. Honolulu: State of Hawai'i.

Desai, Manisha. 2002. "Transnational Solidarity: Women's Agency, Structural Adjustment, and Globalization." In Nancy A. Naples and Manisha Desai (eds.), *Women's Activism and Globalization: Linking Local Struggles and Transnational Politics.* New York and London: Routledge. Pp. 15–33.

Des Forges, Alison L. 1999. *"Leave None to Tell the Story": Genocide in Rwanda.* New York: Human Rights Watch; Paris: International Federation of Human Rights. <www.hrw.org/reports/1999/rwanda/>

di Leonardo, Micaela (ed.). 1991a. *Gender at the Crossroads of Knowledge: Feminist Anthropology in the Postmodern Era.* Berkeley: University of California Press.

di Leonardo, Micaela. 1991b. "Gender, Culture, and Political Economy: Feminist Anthropology in Historical Perspective." In *Gender at the Crossroads of Knowledge.* Berkeley: University of California Press. Pp. 1–50.

Dinnen, Sinclair, and Allison Ley (eds.). 2000. *Reflections on Violence in Melanesia.* Annandale, NSW, Australia: Hawkins Press/Asia Pacific Press.

Diop, Aminata. 1993. "Personal Testimony: An African Woman Fleeing the Practice of Excision in Mali." In Leni Marin and Blandina Lansang-De Mesay (eds.), *Women on the Move: Proceedings of the Workshop on Human Rights Abuses against Immigrant and Refugee Women, Vienna, Austria, 18 June 1993.* Workshop co-sponsored by Family Violence Prevention Fund, Coalition for Immigrant and Refugee Rights and Services. San Francisco: Family Violence Prevention Fund. P. 23.

Eaton, Mary. 1994. "Abuse by Any Other Name: Feminism, Difference, and Intralesbian Violence." In Martha Albertson Fineman and Roxanne Mykitiuk (ed.), *The Public Nature of Private Violence: The Discovery of Domestic Abuse.* New York: Routledge. Pp. 195–223.

El-Bushra, Judy. 2000. "Transforming Conflict: Some Thoughts on a Gendered Understanding of Conflict Processes." In Susie Jacobs, Ruth Jacobson, and Jen Marchbank (eds.), *States of Conflict: Gender Violence and Resistance.* London and New York: Zed Books.

Emerson, Robert M. 2004. "Constructing Serious Violence and Its Victims: Processing a Domestic Violence Restraining Order." In Gale Miller and James A. Holstein (eds.), *Perspectives on Social Problems: A Research Annual,* vol. 6. Greenwich, CT: JAI Press. Pp. 3–28.

Enloe, Cynthia. 1990. *Bananas, Beaches, and Bases: Making Feminist Sense of International Politics.* Berkeley: University of California Press.

Enloe, Cynthia. 2000. *Maneuvers: The International Politics of Militarizing Women's Lives.* Berkeley: University of California Press.

Equality Now. 2006. "Mexico: The Abduction and Murder of Women in Ciudad Juarez and Chihuahua City." *Women's Action* 28(1) (August). <www.equalitynow.org/english/actions/action_2801_en.html>

Ericson, Richard V., and Kevin D. Haggerty. 1997. *Policing the Risk Society.* Toronto: University of Toronto Press.

Ericson, Richard V., and Kevin D. Haggerty. 1999. "Governing the Young." In Russell Smandych (ed.), *Governable Places.* Aldershot, UK and Brookfield, VT: Ashgate. Pp. 163–191.

Ewick, Patricia. 1997. "Punishment, Power, and Justice." In Bryant G. Garth and Austin Sarat (eds.), *Justice and Power in Socio-Legal Studies.* Chicago: Northwestern University Press.

Feeley, Malcolm, and Jonathan Simon. 1992. "The New Penology: Notes on the Emerging Strategy of Corrections and Its Implications." *Criminology* 30: 449–474.

Feeley, Malcolm, and Jonathan Simon. 1994. "Actuarial Justice: The Emerging New Criminal Law." In D. Nelken (ed.), *The Futures of Criminology.* London: Sage. Pp. 173–202.

Ferraro, K. 1983. "Negotiating Trouble in a Battered Women's Shelter." *Urban Life* 12(3): 287–306.

Field, Martha H., and Henry F. Field. 1973. "Marital Violence and the Criminal Process: Neither Justice nor Peace." *Social Science Review* 47: 221–240.

Fischer, Karla, and Mary Rose. 1995. "When 'Enough is Enough': Battered Women's Decision-Making around Court Orders of Protection." *Crime and Delinquency* 41(4): 414–429.

Foucault, Michel. 1979. *Discipline and Punish: Birth of the Prison,* trans. A. Sheridan. New York: Vintage.

Foucault, Michel. 1991. "Governmentality." In Graham Burchell, Colin Gordon, and Peter Miller (eds.), *The Foucault Effect: Studies in Governmentality.* Chicago: University of Chicago Press. Pp. 87–105.

Fraser, Nancy. 1989. *Unruly Practices: Power, Discourse, and Gender in Contemporary Social Theory.* Minneapolis: University of Minnesota Press.

Freeman, Marsha A. 1994. "Women, Law and Land at the Local Level: Claiming Women's Human Rights in Domestic Legal Systems." *Human Rights Quarterly* 16: 559–575.

Friedman, Elisabeth. 1995. "Women's Human Rights: The Emergence of a Movement." In Julie Peters and Andrea Wolper (eds.), *Women's Rights, Human Rights.* New York: Routledge. Pp. 18–35.

Friedman, Jonathan. 1996. "The Politics of De-Authentification: Escaping from Identity: A Commentary on 'Beyond Authenticity' by Mark Rogers." *Identities: Global Studies in Culture and Power* 3: 127–137.

Garap, Sarah. 2000. "Struggles of Women and Girls – Simbu Province, Papua New Guinea." In Sinclair Dinnen and Allison Ley (eds.), *Reflections on Violence in Melanesia.* Canberra: Hawkins Press/Asia Pacific Press. Pp. 159–172.

Gardella, Adriana. 2007. "Domestic Violence Case Makes International Claim." <www.womensenews.org/article.cfm/dyn/aid/3083/context/archive>, accessed March 1, 2007.

Garland, David. 2000. *The Culture of Control.* Chicago: University of Chicago Press.

Gender Public Advocacy Coalition (GenderPAC). 2006. "50 under 30: Masculinity and the War on America's Youth." <www.genderpac.org>

Gewertz, Deborah, and Frederick Errington. 1999. *Emerging Class in Papua New Guinea: The Telling of Difference.* Cambridge: Cambridge University Press.

Ginsburg, Faye, and Anna Lowenhaupt Tsing (eds.). 1990. *Uncertain Terms.* Boston: Beacon Press.

Girshick, Lori B. 2001. "Sexual Violence within Lesbian Battering." *Off Our Backs* 31: 31–35.

Girshick, Lori. 2002. *Woman to Woman Violence: Does She Call it Rape?* Boston: Northeastern University Press.

Goldstein, Daniel. 2004. *Spectacular City: Violence and Performance in Urban Bolivia.* Durham, NC: Duke University Press.

Goldstein, Daniel. 2007. "Human Rights as Culprit, Human Rights as Victim: Rights and Security in the State of Exception." In Mark Goodale and Sally Engle Merry (eds.), *The Practice of Human Rights.* Cambridge: Cambridge University Press. Pp. 49–78.

Goldstein, Joshua. 2003. *War and Gender: How Gender Shapes the War System and Vice Versa.* Cambridge: Cambridge University Press.

Gordon, Linda. 2002 [1988]. *Heroes of Their Own Lives: The Politics and History of Family Violence: Boston 1880–1960.* Urbana: University of Illinois Press.

Greenfield et al. 1998. Supplementary Homicide Reports. v, 1. National Crime Victimization Survey. Washington, DC: Bureau of Justice Statistics.

Guo Huimin. 2005. "Obstacles to Legal Treatment of Violence against Women." In *Combating Domestic Violence against Women: China in Action.* Beijing: China Social Sciences Press. Pp. 34–51.

Gutmann, Matthew C. 1997. "The Meanings of Macho: Changing Mexican Male Identities." In Louise Lamphere, Helena Ragone, and Patricia Zavella (eds.), *Situated Lives: Gender and Culture in Everyday Life.* New York: Routledge. Pp. 223–234.

Hagen, John, and Ron Levi. 2005. "Crimes of War and the Force of Law." *Social Forces* 83(4): 1499–1534.

Hanna, Cheryl. 1996. "No Right to Choose: Mandated Victim Participation in Domestic Violence Prosecutions." *Harvard Law Review* 109: 1849–1910.

Hanna, Cheryl. 1998. "The Paradox of Hope: The Crime and Punishment of Domestic Violence." *William and Mary Law Review* 39: 1505–1584.

Harrell-Bond, B. E., and E. Voutira. 1992. "Anthropology and the Study of Refugees." *Anthropology Today* 8(4): 6–10.

Hartog, Hendrik. 2000. *Man and Wife in America: A History.* Cambridge, MA: Harvard University Press.

Harvey, David. 1989. *The Condition of Postmodernity.* Cambridge, MA: Blackwell.

Hautzinger, Sarah. 2007. *Violence in the City of Women: Police and Batterers in Brazil.* Berkeley: University of California Press.

Healey, Kerry, Christine Smith, with Chris O'Sullivan. 1998. *Batterer Intervention: Program Approaches and Criminal Justice Strategies.* Washington, DC: US Department of Justice, Office of Justice Programs, National Institute of Justice.

Hecht, Jonathan. 1998. "Women's Rights, States' Law: The Role of Law in Women's Rights Policy in China." In John D. Montgomery (ed.), *Human Rights: Positive Policies in Asia and the Pacific Rim.* Hollis, NH: Hollis. Pp. 71–96.

Hise, Steev (dir.). 2006. *On the Edge: The Femicide in Ciudad Juárez.* Bloomington, IL: Illegal Art. Documentary film.

hooks, bell. 1997. "Violence in Intimate Relationships: A Feminist Perspective." In Laura L. O'Toole and Jessica R. Schiffman (eds.), *Gender Violence: Interdisciplinary Perspectives.* New York: New York University Press. Pp. 279–284.

Hosken, Fran P. 1981. "Female Genital Mutilation and Human Rights." *Feminist Issues* (summer): 3–23.

Hosken, Fran P. 1982. *The Hosken Report: Genital and Sexual Mutilation of Females,* 3rd rev. edn. Lexington, MA: Women's International Network News.

Huang Lie and Rong Weiyi (eds.). 2005. *Combating Domestic Violence against Women: China in Action.* Beijing: China Social Sciences Press.

Human Rights in China. 1995. *Caught between Tradition and the State: Violations of the Human Rights of Chinese Women.* New York: HRIC. <www.hrichina.org/public/contents/article?revision%5fid=2602&item%5fid=2601>

Human Rights in China, Asia Monitor Resource Centre, China Labour Bulletin, and Hong Kong Christian Industrial Committee. 1998. *Report on Implementation of CEDAW in the People's Republic of China: A Report with Recommendations and Questions for the Chinese Government Representatives.* December. New York: 350 Fifth Ave., Room 3309.

Human Rights Watch. 1996. "No Guarantees: Sex Discrimination in Mexico's Maquiladora Sector." <www.hrw.org/reports/1996/Mexi0896.htm>

Human Rights Watch. 1998. "Rwanda Tribunal to Rule on Akayesu Case." Human Rights News, September 1. <http://hrw.org/english/docs/1998/09/01/rwanda1312.htm>

Human Rights Watch, Africa. 1996. *Shattered Lives: Sexual Violence during the Rwandan Genocide and Its Aftermath.* New York, Washington, London, and Brussels: Human Rights Watch.

Human Rights Watch, Women's Rights Project. 1996. *All Too Familiar: Sexual Abuse of Women in U.S. State Prisons.* New York: Human Rights Watch.

Hunt, Alan. 1999. *Governing Morals: A Social History of Moral Regulation.* Cambridge: Cambridge University Press.

Hunt, Nancy Rose. 1997. "'Le bebe en brouse': European Women, African Birth Spacing, and Colonial Intervention in Breast Feeding in the Belgian Congo." In Frederick Cooper and Ann Laura Stoler (eds.), *Tensions of Empire: Colonial Cultures in a Bourgeois World.* Berkeley: University of California Press. Pp. 287–321.

Hyndman, Jennifer. 2000. *Managing Displacement: Refugees and the Politics of Humanitarianism.* Minneapolis: University of Minnesota Press.

Incite! Women of Color against Violence. 2006. *The Color of Violence: The Incite! Anthology*, eds. Andrea Smith, Beth E. Richie, and Julia Sudbury. Boston: South End Press.

Incite! Women of Color against Violence. 2007. *The Revolution Will Not be Funded: Beyond the Non-Profit/Industrial Complex*. Boston: South End Press.

Inter-American Court of Human Rights (IACHR). 2003. "The Situation of the Rights of Women in Ciudad Juárez, Mexico: The Right to be Free from Violence and Discrimination." <http://www.cidh.org/annualrep/2002eng/chap.vi.juarez.htm>, accessed April 30, 2008.

International Initiative for Justice in Gujarat (IIJ). 2003. *Threatened Existence: A Feminist Analysis of the Genocide in Gujarat*. Bombay: Forum against Oppression of Women.

International Institute for Population Sciences. 2000. *National Family Health Survey (NFHS-2) India*. Mumbai, India: International Institute for Population Sciences; Calverton, MD: ORC Macro.

Jackson, Jean. 1995. "Culture, Genuine and Spurious: The Politics of Indianness in the Vaupes, Columbia." *American Ethnologist* 22: 3–28.

Jethmalani, Rani (ed.). 2001. "Bride Burning and Dowry." Special issue. *Kali's Yug: Women and Law Journal* (March). New Delhi, India: WARLAW.

Johnson, Kay Ann. 1983. *Women, the Family, and Peasant Revolution in China*. Chicago: University of Chicago Press.

Jolly, Margaret. 1996. "Woman Ikat Raet Long Human Raet O No? Women's Rights, Human Rights, and Domestic Violence in Vanuatu." *Feminist Review* 52: 169–190.

Kapadia, Karin (ed.). 2002. *The Violence of Development: The Politics of Identity, Gender and Social Inequalities in India*. New Delhi: Kali for Women/London: Zed Books.

Karlekar, Malavika. 1999. "Breaking the Silence and Choosing to Hear: Perceptions of Violence against Women." In Fanny M. Cheung et al. (eds.), *Breaking the Silence: Violence against Women in Asia*. Hong Kong: Equal Opportunities Commission. Pp. 59–81.

Keck, Margaret E., and Kathryn Sikkink. 1998. *Activists beyond Borders: Advocacy Networks in International Politics*. Ithaca, NY: Cornell University Press.

Kelly, Liz. 2000. "Wars against Women: Sexual Violence, Sexual Politics and the Militarised State." In Susie Jacobs, Ruth Jacobson, and Jen Marchbank (eds.), *States of Conflict: Gender Violence and Resistance*. London and New York: Zed Books.

Kenyatta, Jomo. 1962. *Facing Mount Kenya*. New York: Vintage Books.

Kerr, Joanna (ed.). 1993. *Ours by Right: Women's Rights as Human Rights*. London: Zed Books.

Kesic, Vesna. 2000. "From Reverence to Rape." In Marguerite Waller and Jennifer Rycenga (eds.), *Frontline Feminisms*. New York: Garland.

Kim, Samuel S. 1991. "The United Nations, Lawmaking, and World Order." In Richard A. Falk, Samuel S. Kim, and Saul H. Mendlovitz (eds.), *The United Nations and a Just World Order*. Boulder, CO: Westview Press. Pp. 109–125.

Kulick, Donald. 1999. "The Gender of Brazilian Transgendered Prostitutes." *American Anthropologist* 99(3): 547–585.

Kumar, Radha. 1993. *A History of Doing: An Illustrated Account of Movements for Women's Rights and Feminism in India, 1800–1990*. New Delhi: Zubaan, for Kali for Women.

Kumar, Radha. 1999 [1995] "From Chipko to Sati: The Contemporary Indian Women's Movement." In Amrita Basu (ed.), *The Challenge of Local Feminisms: Women's Movements in Global Perspective*. Delhi: Kali for Women. Pp. 58–87.

Lamphere, Louise, Helen Ragone, and Patricia Zavella (eds.). 1997. *Situated Lives: Gender and Culture in Everyday Life*. New York: Routledge.

Lancaster, Roger. 1992. *Life is Hard*. Berkeley: University of California Press.

Lawyers' Collective. 1992. *Legal Aid Handbook 1: Domestic Violence*. Del, India: Kali for Women.

Lazarus-Black, Mindie. 2007. *Everyday Harm: Domestic Violence, Court Rites, and Cultures of Reconciliation*. Urbana and Chicago: University of Illinois Press.

Lentin, Ronit (ed.). 1997. *Gender and Catastrophe*. London and New York: Zed Books.

Lewin, Ellen (ed.). 1996. *Inventing Lesbian Cultures in America*. Boston: Beacon Press.

Lewin, Ellen, and William L. Leap (eds.). 2002. *Out in Theory: The Emergence of Lesbian and Gay Anthropology*. Urbana: University of Illinois Press.

Li Hongxiang. 2000. "Definition of Domestic Violence in Law Theory." In China Law Society et al. (ed.), *Research on Prevention and Control of Domestic Violence*. Beijing: Qunzhong. Pp. 75–82.

Liu Donghua. 2001. "Domestic Violence in China: Research, Intervention and Prevention." Newsletter, no. 3.

Liu Meng. 2001. "Domestic Violence in China: Research, Intervention and Prevention." Newsletter, no. 3.

Liu Meng and Cecelia Chan. 1999. "Enduring Violence and Staying in Marriage: Stories of Battered Women in Rural China." *Violence against Women* 5(12): 1469–1492.

Liu Meng and Cecelia Chan. 2000. "Family Violence in China: Past and Present." *New Global Development* 16: 74–87.

Liu Meng and Zhang Li-Xi. 2002. "Current Situation, Attitude, and Prevention Survey Report on Domestic Violence in China." National Survey subproject DVRIP. Trans. Wei-Ying Lin. On file with author.

Lutz, Catherine. 2002. "Making War at Home in the United States: Militarization and the Current Crisis." *American Anthropologist* 104: 723–735.

Macklin, Audrey. 2004. "Like Oil and Water, with a Match: Militarized Commerce, Armed Conflict, and Human Security in Sudan." In Wenona Giles and Jennifer Hyndman (eds.), *Sites of Violence: Gender and Conflict Zones*. Berkeley: University of California Press.

Mama, Amina. 1997. "Sheroes and Villains: Conceptualizing Colonial and Contemporary Violence against Women in Africa." In C. Mohanty and J. Alexander (eds.), *Feminist Genealogies, Colonial Legacies, Democratic Futures*. New York: Routledge. Pp. 46–62.

Mamdani, Mahmood. 2002. *When Victims Become Killers: Colonialism, Nativism, and the Genocide in Rwanda*. Princeton: Princeton University Press.

Mani, Lata. 1990. "Contentious Traditions: The Debate on Sati in Colonial India." In Kumkum Sangari and Sudesh Vaid (eds.), *Recasting Women: Essays in Indian Colonial History*. New Brunswick, NJ: Rutgers University Press. Pp. 88–126.

Mani, Lata. 1998. *Contentious Traditions: The Debate on Sati in Colonial India*. Berkeley: University of California Press.

Mason, Merrin. 2000. "Domestic Violence in Vanuatu." In Sinclair Dinnen and Allison Ley (eds.), *Reflections on Violence in Melanesia*. Canberra: Hawkins Press/Asia Pacific Press. Pp. 119–139.

Mathur, Kanchan. 2004. *Countering Gender Violence: Initiatives towards Collective Action in Rajasthan*. New Delhi: Sage.

Mayaram, Shail. 2002. "New Modes of Violence: The Backlash against Women." In Karin Kapadia (ed.), *The Violence of Development: The Politics of Identity, Gender and Social Inequalities in India*. London: Zed Books. Pp. 393–424.

McGillivray, Anne, and Brenda Comaskey. 1999. *Black Eyes All of the Time: Intimate Violence, Aboriginal Women, and the Justice System*. Toronto: University of Toronto Press.

Meintjes, Sheila, Anu Pillay, and Meredith Turshen (eds.). 2001. *The Aftermath: Women in Post-Conflict Transformation*. New York: Zed Books.

Mendelson, Margot. 2004. "The Legal Production of Identities: A Narrative Analysis of Conversations with Battered Undocumented Women." *Berkeley Women's Law Journal* 19(1): 138–216.

Merry, Sally Engle. 1990. *Getting Justice and Getting Even: Legal Consciousness among Working Class Americans*. Chicago: University of Chicago Press.

Merry, Sally Engle. 1994. "Courts as Performances: Domestic Violence Hearings in a Hawai'i Family Court." In Susan Hirsch and Minde Lazarus-Black (eds.), *Contested States: Law, Hegemony, and Resistance*. New York: Routledge. Pp. 35–59.

Merry, Sally Engle. 1995a. "Gender Violence and Legally Engendered Selves." *Identities: Global Studies in Culture and Power* 2: 49–73.

Merry, Sally Engle. 1995b. "Wife Battering and the Ambiguities of Rights." In Austin Sarat and Thomas Kearns (eds.), *Identities, Politics, and Rights*. Amherst Series in Law, Jurisprudence, and Social Thought. Ann Arbor: University of Michigan Press. Pp. 271–307.

Merry, Sally Engle. 1997. "Legal Pluralism and Transnational Culture: The Ka Ho'okolokolonui Kanaka Maoli Tribunal, Hawai'i 1993." In Richard A. Wilson (ed.), *Human Rights, Culture and Context: Anthropological Perspectives*. London: Pluto Press.

Merry, Sally Engle. 1998. "Global Human Rights and Local Social Movements in a Legally Plural World." *Canadian Journal of Law and Society* 12: 247–271.

Merry, Sally Engle. 2000. *Colonizing Hawai'i: The Cultural Power of Law*. Princeton: Princeton University Press.

Merry, Sally Engle. 2001a. "Spatial Governmentality and the New Urban Social Order: Controlling Gender Violence through Law." *American Anthropologist* 103: 16–30.

Merry, Sally Engle. 2001b. "Women, Violence, and the Human Rights System." In Marjorie Agosin (ed.), *Women, Gender, and Human Rights*. New Brunswick, NJ: Rutgers University Press. Pp. 83–98.

Merry, Sally Engle. 2002. "Governmentality and Gender Violence in Hawai'i in Historical Perspective." *Social and Legal Studies* 11(1): 81–110.

Merry, Sally Engle. 2006. *Human Rights and Gender Violence: Translating International Law into Local Justice*. Chicago: University of Chicago Press.

Messer, Ellen. 1993. "Anthropology and Human Rights." *Annual Review of Anthropology* 22: 221–249.

Messer, Ellen. 1997. "Pluralist Approaches to Human Rights." *Journal of Anthropological Research* 53: 293–317.

Metzl, Jamie Frederic. 1997. "Rwandan Genocide and the International Law of Radio Jamming." *American Journal of International Law* 91(4): 628–651.

Miller, Peter, and Nikolas Rose. 1990. "Governing Economic Life." *Economy and Society* 19: 1–27.

Monzini, Paola. 2005. *Sex Traffic: Prostitution, Crime and Exploitation*, trans. Patrick Camiller. London: Zed Books.

Morgan, Robin, and Gloria Steinem. 1983. "The International Crime of Genital Mutilation." In Gloria Steinem (ed.), *Outrageous Acts and Everyday Rebellions*. New York: Holt, Rinehart and Winston. Pp. 292–300.

Morrow, Betty Hearn. 1994. "A Grass-Roots Feminist Response to Intimate Violence in the Caribbean." *Women's Studies International Forum* 17: 579–592.

Murthy, Sheela. 2004. "Impact of September 11, 2001 on U.S. Immigration." *Maryland Bar Journal* 37(2): 5–6.

Namaste, Vivianne K. 2006. "Genderbashing: Sexuality, Gender, and the Regulation of Public Space." In Susan Stryker and Stephen Whittle (eds.), *The Transgender Studies Reader*. New York: Routledge. Pp. 584–601.

Naples, Nancy A. 2002. "Changing the Terms: Community Activism, Globalization, and the Dilemmas of Transnational Feminist Praxis." In Nancy A. Naples and Manisha Desai (eds.), *Women's Activism and Globalization: Linking Local Struggles and Transnational Politics*. New York and London: Routledge. Pp. 3–15.

Narayanan, Revathi. 2002. "Grassroots, Gender and Governance: Panchayati Raj Experiences from Mahila Samakhya Karnataka." In Karin Kapadia (ed.), *The Violence of Development: The Politics of Identity, Gender and Social Inequalities in India*. London: Zed Books. Pp. 295–351.

Nathan, Debbie. 2003. "The Juárez Murders." Amnesty International Magazine. <www.amnestyusa.org/magazine/spring_2003/juarez/>

Obermeyer, Carla Makhlouf. 1999. "Female Genital Surgeries: The Known, the Unknown, and the Unknowable." *Medical Anthropology Quarterly* 13(1): 79–105.

Ofei-Aboagye, Rosemary Ofeibea. 1994. "Altering the Strands of the Fabric: A Preliminary Look at Domestic Violence in Ghana." *Signs: Journal of Women in Culture and Society* 19: 924–938.

Oller, Lucrecia. 1994. "Domestic Violence: Breaking the Cycle in Argentina." In Miranda Davies (ed.), *Women and Violence*. London: Zed Books. Pp. 229–234.

O'Malley, Pat. 1992. "Risk, Power and Crime Prevention." *Economy and Society* 21: 252–275.

O'Malley, Pat. 1993. "Containing Our Excitement: Commodity Culture and the Crisis of Discipline." *Research in Law, Politics, and Society* 13: 151–172.

O'Malley, Pat. 1996. "Indigenous Governance." *Economy and Society* 25: 310–326.

O'Malley, Pat. 1999. "Consuming Risks: Harm Minimization and the Government of 'Drug-Users.'" In *Governable Places: Readings on Governmentality and Crime Control*. Aldershot, UK: Dartmouth. Pp. 191–215.

O'Malley, Pat. 1999. "Governmentality and the Risk Society." *Economy and Society* 28: 138–148.

O'Malley, Pat, and Darren Palmer. 1996. "Post Keynesian Policing." *Economy and Society* 25: 137–155.

Ortner, Sherry B. 1974. "Is Female to Male as Nature is to Culture?" In Michelle Zimbalist Rosaldo and Louise Lamphere (eds.), *Woman, Culture, and Society*. Stanford: Stanford University Press. Pp. 67–87.

Pancho. 2005. "Vietnam in the Andes." In Orin Starn, Carlos Ivan Degregori, and Robin Kirk (eds.), *The Peru Reader: History, Culture, and Power*, 2nd edn. Durham and London: Duke University Press. Pp. 357–363.

Parker, Seymour, and Hilda Parker. 1979. "The Myth of Male Superiority: Rise and Demise." *American Anthropologist* 81(2): 289–309.

Paterson, Kent. 2006. "Femicide on the Rise in Latin America." International Relations Center (March 8) <http://americas.irc-online.org/am/3142>

Peach, Lucinda Joy. 2008. "Female Sex Slavery or Just Women's Work? Moral Conflicts over Prostitution and Female Subjectivity within Anti-Trafficking Discourses." In Kathy E. Ferguson and Monique Mironesco (eds.), *Gender and Globalization in Asia and the Pacific*. Honolulu: University of Hawai'i Press.

Pederson, Susan. 1991. "National Bodies, Unspeakable Acts: The Sexual Politics of Colonial Policymaking." *Journal of Modern History* 63(4): 647–680.

Pence, Ellen, and Michael Paymar. 1993. *Education Groups for Men who Batter: The Duluth Model*. New York: Springer.

Peters, Julie, and Andrea Wolper (eds.). 1995. *Women's Rights, Human Rights*. New York: Routledge.

Peterson, Dale, and Richard Wrangham. 1997. *Demonic Males: Apes and the Origins of Human Violence*. Boston: Houghton Mifflin.

Pleck, Elizabeth Hafkin. 1987. *Domestic Tyranny: The Making of Social Policy against Family Violence from Colonial Times to the Present*. New York: Oxford University Press.

Polgreen, Lydia, and Marlise Simons. 2007. "Hague Court Inquiry Focuses on Rapes." *New York Times* (May 23): A6.

Poonacha, Veena, and Divya Pandey. 1999. *Responses to Domestic Violence in the States of Karnataka and Gujarat*. Mumbai, India: Research Centre for Women's Studies, SNDT Women's University.

Povinelli, Elizabeth. 1998. "The Sense of Shame: Australian Multiculturalism and the Crisis of Indigenous Citizenship." *Critical Inquiry* 24: 575–611.

Povinelli, Elizabeth. 2002. *The Cunning of Recognition: Indigenous Alterities and the Making of Australian Multiculturalism*. Durham, NC and London: Duke University Press.

Power, Samantha. 2002. *A Problem from Hell: America and the Age of Genocide*. New York: Harper Perennial.

Ptacek, James. 1988. "Why do Men Batter Their Wives?" In Kersti Yllö and Michele Bograd (eds.), *Feminist Perspectives on Wife Abuse*. Newbury Park, CA: Sage. Pp. 133–158.

Ptacek, James. 1999. *Battered Women in the Courtroom: The Power of Judicial Responses*. Boston: Northeastern University Press.

Qi Huaying. 2003. "Report and Summary: Subproject regarding Legal Assistance to Battered Women from Domestic Violence." In *Domestic Violence and Legal Assistance*. Domestic Violence Research and Intervention Project. Published in Chinese and English. Beijing. Pp. 157–218.

Rahman, Anika, and Nahid Toubia (eds.). 2000. *Female Genital Mutilation: A Guide to Laws and Policies Worldwide*. New York: St. Martin's Press.

Rajagopal, Balakrishnan. 2003. *International Law from Below: Development, Social Movements, and Third World Resistance*. Cambridge: Cambridge University Press.

Razack, Sherene H. 2004. *Dark Threats and White Knights: The Somalia Affair, Peacekeeping, and the New Imperialism*. Toronto: University of Toronto Press.

Razack, Sherene H. 2000a. Gendered Racial Violence and Spatialized Justice: The Murder of Pamela George. *Canadian Journal of Law and Society* 15(2): 91–130.

Razack, Sherene H. 2000b. "From the 'Clean Snows of Petawawa': The Violence of Canadian Peacekeepers in Somalia." *Current Anthropology* 15(1): 127–163.

Riles, Annelise. 1999. "Infinity within the Brackets." *American Ethnologist* 25: 1–21.

Ristock, Janice. 2002. *No More Secrets: Violence in Lesbian Relationships*. New York: Routledge.

Roberts, Hanna. "The Human Rights of Women in the United Nations: Developments 1993–1994." <www.amnesty.se/women/23ae.htm>

Rodriguez, Noelle Maria. 1988. "A Successful Feminist Shelter: A Case Study of the Family Crisis Shelter in Hawaii." *Journal of Applied Behavioral Science* 24: 235–250.

Rogers, Mark. 1996. "Beyond Authenticity: Conservation, Tourism, and the Politics of Representation in the Ecuadorian Amazon." *Identities: Global Studies in Culture and Power* 3: 73–127.

Romany, Celia. 1994. "State Responsibility Goes Private 2002: A Feminist Critique of the Public/Private Distinction in International Human Rights Law." In Rebecca J. Cook (ed.), *Human Rights of Women: National and International Perspectives*. Philadelphia: University of Pennsylvania Press. Pp. 85–115.

Rong, Weiyi. 2002. "The Interaction between the Police and the Community." DVRIP Conference 2002, trans. Wei-Ying Lin.

Rosaldo, Michelle. 1974. "Woman, Culture, and Society: A Theoretical Overview." In Michelle Zimbalist Rosaldo and Louise Lamphere (eds.), *Woman, Culture, and Society*. Stanford: Stanford University Press. Pp. 17–43.

Rosaldo, Michelle, and Louise Lamphere. 1974a. "Introduction." In Michelle Zimbalist Rosaldo and Louise Lamphere (eds.), *Woman, Culture, and Society*. Stanford: Stanford University Press. Pp. 1–17.

Rosaldo, Michelle Zimbalist, and Louise Lamphere (eds.). 1974b. *Woman, Culture, and Society*. Stanford: Stanford University Press.

Rose, Nikolas. 1989. *Governing the Soul: The Shaping of the Private Self*. London: Routledge.

Rose, Nikolas. 1996. "The Death of the Social? Re-figuring the Territory of Government." *Economy and Society* 25: 327–356.

Rose, Nikolas. 1999. *Predicaments of Freedom*. Cambridge: Cambridge University Press.

Rose, Nikolas, and Peter Miller. 1992. "Political Power beyond the State: Problematics of Government." *British Journal of Sociology* 43: 173–205.

Rose, Nikolas, and Mariana Valverde. 1998. "Governed by Law?" *Social and Legal Studies* 7: 541–551.

Rosenbaum, Michael D. 1998. "To Break the Shell without Scrambling the Egg: An Empirical Analysis of the Impact of Intervention into Violent Families." *Stanford Law and Policy Review* 9: 409–427.

Rubin, Gayle. 1975. "The Traffic of Women: Notes on the Political Economy of Sex." In Rayna R. Reiter (ed.), *Toward an Anthropology of Women*. New York: Monthly Review Press. Pp. 157–210.

Salcido, Olivia, and Madelaine Adelman. 2004. "'He Has Me Tied with the Blessed and Damned Papers': Undocumented-Immigrant Battered Women in Phoenix, Arizona." *Human Organization* 63(2): 162–172.

Sanday, Peggy Reeves. 1981. *Female Power and Male Dominance: On the Origins of Sexual Inequality*. Cambridge: Cambridge University Press.

Santos, Boaventura de Sousa. 1995. *Toward a New Common Sense: Law, Science, and Politics in the Paradigmatic Transition*. New York: Routledge.

Sarkar, Tanika. 2001. *Hindu Wife, Hindu Nation: Community, Religion, and Cultural Nationalism*. London: Hurst.

Schechter, Susan. 1982. *Women and Male Violence: The Visions and Struggles of the Battered Women's Movement*. Boston: South End Press.

Scheper-Hughes, Nancy, and Philippe Bourgois. 2004. "Introduction: Making Sense of Violence." In Nancy Scheper-Hughes and Philippe Bourgois (eds.), *Violence in War and Peace*. Malden, MA and Oxford: Blackwell. Pp. 1–33.

Schneider, Elizabeth. 1994. "The Violence of Privacy." In *The Public Nature of Private Violence: The Discovery of Domestic Abuse*. London: Routledge.

Schneider, Elizabeth M. 2000. *Battered Women and Feminist Lawmaking*. New Haven, CT: Yale University Press.

Schneider, Elizabeth M. 2004. "Transnational Law as a Domestic Resource: Thoughts on the Case of Women's Rights." *New England Law Review* 38(3): 689–724.

Schuler, Margaret (ed.). 1992. *Freedom from Violence: Women's Strategies from around the World*. New York: UNIFEM.

Segura, Denise A. 1997. "Chicanas in White-Collar Jobs: 'You Have to Prove Yourself More.'" In Louise Lamphere, Helena Ragone, and Patricia Zavella (eds.), *Situated Lives: Gender and Culture in Everyday Life*. New York: Routledge. Pp. 292–310.

Sengupta, Somini. 2004. "Relentless Attacks on Women in Western Sudan Draw an Outcry." *New York Times* (October 26): A1, A9.

Shalhoub-Kevorkian, Nadera. 2002a. "Femicide and the Palestinian Criminal Justice System: Seeds of Change in the Context of State Building?" *Law and Society Review* 36: 577–603.

Shalhoub-Kevorkian, Nadera. 2002b. "Reexamining Femicide: Breaking the Silence and Crossing 'Scientific' Borders." *Signs* 28(2): 581–608.

Shalhoub-Kevorkian, Nadera. 2004. "Racism, Militarisation and Policing." *Social Identities* 10(2) (November): 171–193.

Sharma, Aradhana. 2008. *Logics of Empowerment: Gender, Governance, and Development in Neoliberal India*. Minneapolis, MN: University of Minnesota Press.

Shell-Duncan, B. 2001. "The Medicalization of Female 'Circumcision': Harm Reduction or Promotion of a Dangerous Practice?" *Social Science and Medicine* 52: 1013–1028.

Sherman, Lawrence W., and Richard A. Berk. 1984. "The Specific Deterrent Effects of Arrest for Domestic Assault." *American Sociological Review* (April): 261–272.

Shostak, Marjorie. 1981. *Nisa: Life and Words of a !Kung Woman*. Cambridge, MA: Harvard University Press.

Sierra, Maria Teresa. 1995. "Indian Rights and Customary Law in Mexico: A Study of the Nahuas in the Sierra de Puebla." *Law and Society Review* 29: 227–255.

Silard, Kathy. 1994. "Helping Women to Help Themselves: Counselling against Domestic Violence in Australia." In Miranda Davies (ed.), *Women and Violence*. London: Zed Books. Pp. 239–246.

Simon, Jonathan. 1993a. "From Confinement to Waste Management: The Postmodernization of Social Control." *Focus on Law Studies* 8: 4–7.

Simon, Jonathan. 1993b. *Poor Discipline: Parole and the Social Control of the Underclass, 1890–1990*. Chicago: University of Chicago Press.

Smith, Andrea. 2005. *Conquest: Sexual Violence and American Indian Genocide*. Cambridge, MA: South End Press.

Snow, David A. 2004. "Framing Processes, Ideology, and Discursive Fields." In David A. Snow, Sarah A. Soule, and Hanspeter Kriesi (eds.), *The Blackwell Companion to Social Movements*. Malden, MA: Blackwell. Pp. 380–412.

Spindel, Cheywa, Elisa Levy, and Melissa Conner. 2000. *With an End in Sight: Strategies from the UNIFEM Trust Fund to Eliminate Violence against Women*. New York: United Nations Development Fund for Women.

Srivastava, Nisha. 2002. "Multiple Dimensions of Violence against Rural Women in Uttar Pradesh: Macro and Micro Realities." In Karin Kapadia (ed.), *The Violence of Development: The Politics of Identity, Gender and Social Inequalities in India*. London: Zed Books. Pp. 235–295.

St. Joan, Jacqueline. 1997. "Sex, Sense, and Sensibility: Trespassing into the Culture of Domestic Abuse." *Harvard Women's Law Journal* 20: 263–308.

Steinberg, Allen. 1989. *The Transformation of Criminal Justice Philadelphia: 1800–1880*. Chapel Hill: University of North Carolina Press.

Stephenson, Carolyn M. 1995. "Women's International Nongovernmental Organizations at the United Nations." In *Women, Politics, and the United Nations*. Westport, CT: Greenwood Press. Pp. 135–155.

Stoler, Ann. 1991. "Carnal Knowledge and Imperial Power: Gender, Race, and Morality in Colonial Asia." In Micaela di Leonardo (ed.), *Gender at the Crossroads of Knowledge: Feminism in Anthropology in the Postmodern Era*. Berkeley: University of California Press. Pp. 55–101.

Stoler, Ann L. 1997a. "Making Empire Respectable: The Politics of Race and Sexual Morality in Twentieth-Century Colonial Cultures." In Louise Lamphere, Helena Ragone, and Patricia Zavella (eds.), *Situated Lives: Gender and Culture in Everyday Life*. New York: Routledge. Pp. 373–399.

Stoler, Ann Laura. 1997b. "Sexual Affronts and Racial Frontiers: European Identities and the Cultural Politics of Exclusion in Colonial Southeast Asia." In Frederick Cooper and Ann Laura Stoler (eds.), *Tensions of Empire: Colonial Cultures in a Bourgeois World*. Berkeley, CA: University of California Press. Pp. 198–237.

Strathern, Marilyn. 2004. "Losing (Out on) Intellectual Resources." In *Law, Anthropology, and the Constitution of the Social: Making Persons and Things*. Cambridge: Cambridge University Press. Pp. 201–233.

Takaki, Ronald. 1983. *Pau Hana: Plantation Life and Labor in Hawai'i, 1835–1920*. Honolulu: University of Hawai'i Press.

Tang, Catherine So-Kum, Day Wong, Fanny M. C. Cheung, and Antoinette Lee. 2000. "Exploring How Chinese Define Violence against Women: A Focus Group Study in Hong Kong." *Women's Studies International Forum* 23: 197–209.

Taussig, Michael. 1984. "Culture of Terror – Space of Death: Roger Casement's Putumayo Report and the Explanation of Torture." *Comparative Studies in Society and History* 26(1): 467–497.

Tengan, Ty P. Kawika. 2008. *Native Men Remade: Gender and Nation in Contemporary Hawai'i*. Durham, NC: Duke University Press.

Tennant, Chris. 1994. "Indigenous Peoples, International Institutions, and the International Legal Literature from 1945–1993." *Human Rights Quarterly* 16: 1–57.

Thomas, Cheryl. 1999. "Domestic Violence." In Kelly D. Askin and Dorean M. Koenig (eds.), *Women and International Human Rights Law*, vol. 1. Ardsley, NY: Transnational. Pp. 219–256.

Thomas, D., and M. Beasley. 1993. "Domestic Violence as a Human Rights Issue." *Human Rights Quarterly* 15(1): 36–62.

Thomas, Dorothy Q. 1994. "In Search of Solutions: Women's Police Stations in Brazil." In Miranda Davies (ed.), *Women and Violence*. London: Zed Books. Pp. 32–43.

Thomas, Dorothy Q. 2000. "We are Not the World: U.S. Activism and Human Rights in the Twenty-First Century." *Signs* 25: 1121–1124.

Thompson, Karen Brown. 2002. "Women's Rights are Human Rights." In Sanjeev Khagram, James V. Riker, and Kathryn Sikkink (eds.), *Restructuring World Politics: Transnational Social Movements, Networks, and Norms*. Minneapolis: University of Minnesota Press. Pp. 96–123.

Toubia, Nahid. 1988. "Women and Health in Sudan." In Nahid Toubia (ed.),*Women of the Arab World: The Coming Challenge: Papers of the Arab Women's Solidarity Conference (AWSA)*. Atlantic Highlands, NJ: Zed Books. Pp. 99–109.

Toubia, Nahid. 1994a. "Female Circumcision as a Public Health Issue." *New England Journal of Medicine* 33(11): 712–716.

Touibia, Nahid. 1994b. "Female Genital Mutilation." In Julie Peters and Andrea Wolper (eds.), *Women's Rights, Human Rights: International Feminist Perspectives*. New York: Routledge. Pp. 224–237.

Toubia, Nahid. 1999. *Caring for Women with Circumcision: A Technical Manual for Health Care Providers*. New York: RAINQ.

Trask, Haunani-Kay. 1993. *From a Native Daughter: Colonialism and Sovereignty in Hawai'i*. Monroe, ME: Common Courage Press.

Tuhus-Dubrow, Rebecca. 2007. "Rites and Wrongs: Is Outlawing Female Genital Mutilation Enough to Stop it from Happening Here?" *Boston Globe* (February 11), 3rd edn., Ideas section: E1.

Turner, Terence. 1997. "Human Rights, Human Difference: Anthropology's Contribution to an Emancipatory Cultural Politics." *Journal of Anthropological Research* 53: 273–291.

Ulrich, Jennifer L. 2000. "Confronting Gender-Based Violence with International Instruments: Is a Solution to the Pandemic within Reach?" *Indiana Journal of Global Legal Studies* 7: 629–654.

United Nations. 1995a. "Beijing Declaration and Platform for Action: Platform 3." *The IV World Conference on Women, 1995–Beijing, China: Official Documents*. New York: United Nations.

United Nations. 1995b. *From Nairobi to Beijing: Second Review and Appraisal of the Implementation of the Nairobi Forward-Looking Strategies for the Advancement of Women*. New York: United Nations.

United Nations 1997. "The Progress of Nations 1997." <www.unicef.org/pon97/>

United Nations 2000. "Protocol to Prevent, Suppress and Punish Trafficking in Persons, especially Women and Children, supplementing the United Nations Convention against Transnational Organized Crime." New York, November 15. <http://untreaty.un.org/English/TreatyEvent2002/CTOC_Prot1_9.htm>

US Committee for Refugees and Immigrants. 2004. "World Refugee Survey." <www.refugees.org/article.aspx?id=1156>

Valentine, David. 2003. "'The Calculus of Pain': Violence, Anthropological Ethics, and the Category Transgender." *Ethnos* 68(1): 27–48.

Valverde, Marianna. 1998. *Diseases of the Will: Alcohol and the Dilemmas of Freedom*. Cambridge: Cambridge University Press.

Valverde, Mariana, Ron Levi, Clifford Shearing, Mary Condon, and Pat O'Malley. 1999. "Democracy in Governance: A Socio-Legal Framework." A Report for the Law Commission of Canada on Law and Governance Relationships, Toronto.

Van Bueren, Geraldine. 1995. "The International Protection of Family Members' Rights as the 21st Century Approaches." *Human Rights Quarterly* 17: 732–765.

Wali, Sima. 1995. "Human Rights for Refugee and Displaced Women." In Julie Peters and Andrea Wolper (eds.), *Women's Rights, Human Rights: International Feminist Perspectives*. New York: Routledge. Pp. 335–344.

Walley, Christine J. 1997. "Searching for 'Voices': Feminism, Anthropology, and the Global Debate over Female Genital Operations." *Cultural Anthropology* 12(3): 405–438.

Wang Kairong. 2001. Domestic Violence in China: Research, Intervention and Prevention. Newsletter, no. 3.

Wang Xingjuan. 1999. "Domestic Violence in China." In Fanny M. Cheung et al. (eds.), *Breaking the Silence: Violence against Women in Asia*. Hong Kong: Equal Opportunities Commission. Pp. 13–37.

Warren, Kay. 2007. "The 2000 UN Human Trafficking Protocol: Rights, Enforcement, Vulnerabilities." In Mark Goodale and Sally Engle Merry (eds.), *The Practice of Human Rights: Tracking Law between the Global and the Local*. Cambridge: Cambridge University Press. Pp. 242–270.

Warsame, Aamina, Sadiya Ahmed, and Aud Talle. 1985. "Social and Cultural Aspects of Female Circumcision and Infibulation: A Preliminary Report." Somali Academy of Sciences and Arts and Swedish Agency for Research Cooperation with Developing Countries. Typescript.

Washington Office on Latin America (WOLA). 2004. "WOLA Memo on the Case of Victor García Uribe." <www.wola.org/index.php?option=com_content&task=viewp&id=126& Itemid=2>, accessed January 7, 2007.

Washington Office on Latin America (WOLA). 2005. "Crying Out for Justice: Murders of Women in Cuidad Juárez, Mexico." <www.wola.org/index.php?option=com_content& task=viewp&id=282&Itemid=2>, accessed January 7, 2007.

Washington Office on Latin America (WOLA). 2006a. "Still Waiting for Justice: Shortcomings in Mexico's Efforts to End Impunity for Murders of Girls and Women in Ciudad Juárez and Chihuahua." <www.wola.org/index.php?option=com_content&task=viewp&id= 128&Itemid=2>, accessed January 7, 2007.

Washington Office on Latin America (WOLA). 2006b. "Violence against Women in Ciudad Juárez." <www.wola.org/Mexico/hr/ciudad_juarez/juarez_updated_05.htm>, accessed January 7, 2007.

Wassef, Nadia. 2001. "Male Involvement in Perpetuating and Challenging the Practice of Female Genital Mutilation in Egypt." In Caroline Sweetman (ed.), *Men's Involvement in Gender and Development Policy and Practice: Beyond Rhetoric*. Oxford: Oxfam. Pp. 44–51.

Weil-Curiel, Linda. 1993. "Human Rights and Women: The Case of Aminata Diop." In Leni Marin and Blandina Lansang-De Mesay (eds.), *Women on the Move: Proceedings of the Workshop on Human Rights Abuses against Immigrant and Refugee Women, Vienna, Austria, 18 June 1993*. Workshop co-sponsored by Family Violence Prevention Fund, Coalition for Immigrant and Refugee Rights and Services. San Francisco: Family Violence Prevention Fund. Pp. 25–26.

Welchman, Lynn, and Sara Hossain. 2005. "Introduction: 'Honour', Rights and Wrongs." In Lynn Welchman and Sara Hossain (eds.), *"Honour": Crimes, Paradigms, and Violence against Women*. London: Zed Books. Pp. 1–22.

Weston, Kath. 1992. "Production as Means, Production as Metaphor: Women's Struggle to Enter the Trades." In Faye Ginsburg and Anna Lowenhaupt Tsing (eds.), *Uncertain Terms*. Boston: Beacon Press. Pp. 137–151.

Wilmsen, Edwin (ed.). 1989. *We are Here: Politics of Aboriginal Land Tenure*. Berkeley: University of California Press.

Wilson, Richard A. 1996. "Introduction: Human Rights, Culture and Context." In Richard A. Wilson (ed.), *Human Rights, Culture and Context: Anthropological Perspectives*. London: Pluto Press.

Wing, Adrien Katherine. 2000. "A Critical Race Feminist Conceptualization of Violence: South African and Palestinian Women." In A. K. Wing (ed.), *Global Critical Race Feminism: An International Reader*. New York: New York University Press. Pp. 332–346.

Wittner, J. 1997. "Reconceptualizing Agency in Domestic Violence Court." In N. Naples (ed.), *Community Activism and Feminism Politics*. New York: Routledge. Pp. 81–103.

Wood, Sarah. 2004. "VAWA's Unfinished Business: The Immigrant Women who Fall through the Cracks." *Duke Journal of Gender Law and Policy* 2: 141.

World Health Organization (WHO). 2005. *WHO Multi-Country Study on Women's Health and Domestic Violence against Women: Summary Report of Initial Results on Prevalence, Health Outcomes and Women's Responses*. Geneva: World Health Organization.

World Health Organization (WHO). 2008. "Eliminating Female Genital Mutilation: An Interagency Statement: OCHCR, UNAIDS, UNDP, UNECA, UNESCO, UNFPA, UNHCR, UNICEF, WHO." NLM classification WP 660. Geneva, Switzerland: World Health Organization. <www.who.int/reproductive-health/publications/fgm/fgm_statement_2008.pdf>

Wright, Melissa W. 2001. "Feminine Villains, Masculine Heroes, and the Reproduction of Ciudad Juárez." *Social Text* 69: 93–113.

Yllö, Kersti, and Michele Bograd. 1988. *Feminist Perspectives on Wife Abuse.* Newbury Park, CA: Sage.

Yngvesson, B. 1988. "Making Law at the Doorway: The Clerk, the Court, and the Construction of Community in a New England Town." *Law and Society Review* 22: 409–448.

Yngvesson, Barbara. 1993. *Virtuous Citizens, Disruptive Subjects: Order and Complaint in a New England Court.* New York: Routledge.

Zechenter, Elizabeth M. 1997. "In the Name of Culture: Cultural Relativism and the Abuse of the Individual." *Journal of Anthropological Research* 53: 319–347.

Zhang Naihua, with Wu Xu. 1995. "Discovering the Positive within the Negative: The Women's Movement in a Changing China." In Amrita Basu (ed.), with C. Elizabeth McGrory, *Women's Movements in Global Perspective.* Boulder, CO: Westview Press. Pp. 25–58.

# Index